HUMANITY ON TRIAL

HUMANITY ON TRIAL

A Brief for the Defense

By HORACE J. BRIDGES

WITH AN INTRODUCTION BY
PROF. HANS KOHN

Essay Index Reprint Series

 BOOKS FOR LIBRARIES PRESS
FREEPORT, NEW YORK

First Published 1941
Reprinted 1971

INTERNATIONAL STANDARD BOOK NUMBER:
0-8369-2039-2

LIBRARY OF CONGRESS CATALOG CARD NUMBER:
74-142609

PRINTED IN THE UNITED STATES OF AMERICA

INTRODUCTION

T HE PRESENT world crisis is a universal crisis, not only in the geographic sense but also because it involves simultaneously all aspects of human existence, political, economic, cultural and spiritual. Its deeper reasons can be found in the intellectual and moral bewilderment into which the growing complexity of life and the fantastic tempo of changes and innovations have thrown mankind since the end of the eighteenth century. The disintegration of our moral world in the twentieth century has led on the one hand to an irresponsible cynicism and the loss of all faith in absolute values; on the other hand to a search for a restatement of the foundations of a renewed confidence in human nature, in the existence of right and truth. In such a situation, when we all are confronted with the necessity of thinking about the meaning of life and history, every sincere contribution will be most welcome to the serious seeker for truth, the more so when it comes from a man who for forty years has experienced the problematic situations of our time, both as a religious leader and as a thinker and writer on the questions of ethics and human relations. He has been for many years, first in Great Britain and then in the Middle West, a leader of the Society for Ethical Culture, one of the few organized religious movements which have felt the whole seriousness of the situation of man in modern society and have tried to find a solution which affirms the existence of a spiritual universe and at the same time recognizes the impossibility of any dogmatic knowledge of that spiritual realm. The book by Dr. Bridges will be read and gratefully appreciated by all those who in the present confusion seek a path to that reality out of which man lives.

HANS KOHN

Smith College, March, 1941

PREFACE

TENNYSON, in his poem in memory of the Duke of Wellington, said that that great soldier's language was "rife with rugged maxims *hewn from life.*"

The sole justification I can offer for publishing the thoughts linked together in this volume is that they have been honestly come by through the same sort of labor that yielded the Iron Duke's "rugged maxims." They have been "hewn from life," in the course of over forty years' struggle to understand myself and my fellow-men, the world we live in and our relation to it, and the reasons why our race, which has done such marvelous things in art, science and industry, and has thought out such high and radiant ideas in philosophy and religion, has yet failed so utterly and abjectly in adjusting the relations of man to man and nation to nation, and in distributing the material goods which its science has enabled it to multiply in such lavish profusion.

If any spur could more poignantly urge a man onward in such a quest than the need to find a tenable standing-ground for his own feet amid the shifting sands and ensnaring morasses of our chaotic age, I have found such a spur in the stabbing and torturing responsibility of guiding others who looked to me for leadership over the almost pathless and fog-environed terrain which I was myself exploring. More than twenty-eight years ago the Chicago Ethical Society honored me by asking such guidance from me. I have often marveled since, and marvel still, at the youthful audacity (pardonable only to inexperience) which overrode my consciousness of inadequacy and emboldened me to accept their trust.

But even to my naïve pre-1914 rashness there were limits; and the one condition that made the venture possible for me was the complete freedom to think and explore for myself which was explicitly accorded. For my associates (whom I was to lead in this one department, whilst in many another I conciously needed and gladly accepted guidance from them) had already lived deeply enough to know that the conditions of our age had made all dogmatic systems whatsoever—theological, economic, political, sociological, and even ethical—completely untrustworthy and undependable. To one conviction only they collectively held: namely, that there is a conscience in us—however we may have come by it—which forbids us to acquiesce in teachings (then already widespread and popular) the logical and practical outcome of which must be the reduction of human life to the level of the slave-pen and the stud-farm and the jungle.

I had already seen clearly, and through the years came to see more clearly still, from my reading of Nietzsche, Ernst Haeckel, Mark Twain, Bertrand Russell, H. L. Mencken, and a whole legion of scribblers who parroted them, that this must be the consequence of their doctrines if ever those doctrines came to be fully believed and fearlessly acted upon. I can even claim such credit as may be due (not that I think much *is* due) for having plainly said so, a full seven years before anybody in America had heard so much as the name of Adolf Hitler. This I did in a book called *Taking the Name of Science in Vain,* which was based upon the Jayne Memorial Lectures delivered by me at Philadelphia in 1926.

But what at that time it needed critical study and analysis to foresee has now been demonstrated before all men's eyes, with the brutal conclusiveness of experience. Hitler, Mussolini, and their subordinate gangsters have simply practiced what a whole host of sophisticated thinkers in Germany, England and America had long preached,—and had been admired and rewarded, and made the oracles of colleges, magazines, women's clubs, and select social coteries, for preaching. The horrified recoil of all free men from these developments must surely bestir them to seek some effective and rationally tenable refutation of the doctrines which entail such results.

Here then I offer, to my own sons (of draft age) and to all other sons and parents equally concerned, my own attempt both to destroy the dragons' teeth which produce such crops as the world is now reaping, and to show how, with good intellectual conscience, with no self-deception or blinking of ugly facts, it is still possible to believe honestly in a divine element in man, and therefore in a better future for human society. Con-

vinced as I am (and millions of other men also are) that
the dogmatic doctrinal systems of Romanism, Protestantism and Judaism, which failed to prevent this
world-calamity, must equally fail to cure it, I see no recourse but for every man who has the needed courage
to think out anew the entire problem of the nature of
human reason, human conscience, and human aesthetic
power, and of their place in the world of time and space.
Only sound thinking can overthrow what false thinking has built up. The final victory of democracy and
civilized morality over totalitarian slavery and dehu-
manization cannot be won on battlefields,—indispensable as victory there most certainly is. It must—and it
will—be won by destroying the ideas and the dogmas
of which dictatorship is the inevitable product.

—H. J. B.

Chicago,
   March, 1941

CONTENTS

xiii

HUMANITY ON TRIAL

CHAPTER I

THE REVOLT AGAINST REASON AND CONSCIENCE

To MANY observers of the strange and discouraging developments of the past quarter-century, the most startling phenomenon they reveal, when they are viewed against the background of historical precedent, is not the cruelties and barbarisms which have been practiced in so many parts of the earth. For these, after all, only repeat an old and familiar story with which history is unhappily crowded. Some men have always been ready to be "wolves to man" to the full extent of their power. This strange appetite for fratricide and the infliction of savage torture has been equipped with new instruments of power, and therefore is able to glut and gratify itself on an unprecedented scale. But the appetite itself is as old as the oldest Stone Age. What does really startle the student in the present situation is the deliberate repudiation of objective truth, the denial of the real world postulated by science, and the rejection of that Reason in man which has found in science its most convincing expression and most impressive product.

Those who have taken the trouble through the years to familiarize themselves with the outspoken and oft-repeated utterances of Mussolini, Rosenberg, Hitler, and the whole supporting chorus of their colleagues and sycophants, know that this repudiation of reason is a fact which, far from making any attempt to conceal it, they proclaim in the most blatant and extravagant fashion. The volume by Rauschning, entitled "The Voice of Destruction," abounds in statements which prove this. Some of these we shall later consider. Far more thorough in its exposition of this side of the Nazi movement is the splendid work by Aurel Kolnai, "The War against the West." This is the best and most systematic survey I have found of the doctrines of these crusaders against civilization. It possesses the special merit of presenting these doctrines always in the exact words of their propounders.

The purpose of these repudiations of the common reason of mankind is to justify the blind will-to-power of the dictators and their cliques, and to furnish them with such plausible pretenses as are possible for their procedure in hypnotizing their enslaved populations. This has been done by ramming down their throats what are frankly called myths, and making these myths the basis of those processes of mental perversion which (in Germany especially) have been substituted for education. One specimen of these myths is the doctrine of "blood and soil." It is the sole basis offered by the Nazis for their claim to dominate the world in virtue of the alleged natural superiority of Germans to all other men (plus, of course, the natural superiority of the ruling clique to all other Germans). Closely connected with it is the kindred doctrine of race, which, as

expounded with pure arbitrariness by the literary re-
tainers of this cult, warrants the ascription to all other
peoples of descending grades of inferiority. It thereby
justifies that persecution of Jews which by the end of
1940 had been carried to the pitch of complete impoverishment and final enslavement. The same doctrine
furnished the pretext for the similar persecution and
exploitation of Austrians, Czechs, Slovaks, and Poles,
culminating in the enslavement of all of these. An in-
vestigator who had enjoyed unusual opportunities of
ascertaining the facts, declared that by the spring of
1940 only fifty thousand Jews were left in Vienna, as
compared with the quarter million who were there prior
to its annexation by Hitler. He added specifically that
these fifty thousand were already reduced to beggary,
and he prophesied with complete confidence that before
the end of 1940 none at all would remain, since expul-
sion or extermination would by then have disposed of
this remnant.

The propounders of these doctrines of blood, soil,
race, and systematic anti-rationalism, make no pretense
—at least when talking among themselves—that they
are objectively true. Hitler, with complete insouciance,
admitted to Rauschning his full awareness that "Sci-
entifically speaking there is no such thing as race."

This confession from him may be discounted, or regarded as exceptional; since he long ago proved to all
the world that he cares nothing whatsoever for truth
or consistency in any relation. Other minds, however,
which for various reasons of choice or necessity have

prostituted themselves to the service of his tyranny, have sought to make the official impostures more respectable by denying that there is any such thing as objective truth or universally valid science. The idea of a body of truth which is identical for all rational minds whatsoever is, they say, a mere figment of imagination. All so-called "truths" are merely means to ends and are justified if and in so far as they "work"; *i.e.*, if they attain the ends desired by those who affirm them. The human intellect is like the lobster's claws or the pelican's beak; it is merely a tool, evolved in the struggle for existence for the strictly utilitarian purpose of finding means whereby to fulfill the cravings of the will.

According to this fiat of what Pope called the "uncreating Word," * morality shares the fate of scientific

---

* The reader may appreciate being reminded of the closing lines of "The Dunciad," which, although written in fun, constitute a realistic prophecy of what has now actually occurred:

> Signs following signs lead on the mighty year;
> See! The dull stars roll round and re-appear.
> She comes!—The cloud-compelling power behold!
> With Night primaeval, and with Chaos old.
> Lo, the great Anarch's ancient reign restored;
> Light dies before her uncreating word.

> .   .   .   .   .

> Thus at her felt approach, and secret might,
> Art after art goes out, and all is night.
> See skulking Truth in her old cavern lie,
> Secured by mountains of heaped casuistry:
> Philosophy, that touched the heavens before,
> Shrinks to her hidden cause, and is no more:
> See Physic beg the Stagirite's defence!
> See Metaphysic call for aid on sense!

truth. The dictators and their academic toadies agree completely with Bertrand Russell's assertion that "outside human desires there is no moral standard." What is more, they have proceeded to act upon this dictum, with a ruthless consistency which must have horrified its pacifistic propounder. But also—and again with a measure of consistency far greater than Lord Russell's —they maintain that outside human desires there is no *rational* standard. Will, they say, is the one fundamental reality in man; and power of every description is its object.

Accordingly, the one criterion which can determine who is to be master of a nation, and finally of the world, is strength of arm and purpose: that is, physical force and cunning, accompanied by the completely unscrupulous exploitation of all means to power. That alone is right which furthers the ends of the most powerful; for there is no right apart from might. It is worth recalling that when Hitler made his speech after the capture of Warsaw in 1939, he referred, in his usual ill-tempered manner, to the fact that the means he had used to obtain possession of Austria, Czecho-Slovakia, and Poland, had been criticized on the score that they had involved successive insincerities and breaches of

> See mystery to Mathematics fly!
> In vain! They gaze, turn giddy, rave and die!
> Thy hand, great Dulness, lets the curtain fall,
> And universal darkness buries all.

Pope published these lines in 1742. Nobody would have been more horrified than he, if he could have foreseen their fulfillment across the gulf of two centuries.

plighted faith. The fact that other men had detected his
systematic lying and treachery had pierced even his
tough hide, far enough to make him feel that an answer
must be made. But it never occurred to him that any
other answer could be necessary than the one he gave:
which consisted solely in pointing out that the means
he had used were justified *by their success*. The fact
that those means had included every possible variety of
bad faith, assassination, and massacre, was entirely ir-
relevant. So long as the game was won, it mattered not
by what means.

With such a conception of the nature and function
of truth, needless to say, any myth that may be found
useful will be as good as any other. For, according to
the doctrine, the only choice men have is between different myths, there being no such thing as objective
truth. Why not then embrace and exalt the myth that
shall serve your own ends? And why not attack all rival
doctrines—as the Nazis have invariably done—not with
reasoned criticism to expose their falsity, but with
sneering denunciations of them as unmanly or old-
womanish, and as the contemptible means devised by
"inferior natures" to protect themselves against the one
true aristocracy of strength?

For this, remember, is the beginning and end of the
Nazis' case against Christianity, Judaism, democracy,
political liberalism, and every doctrine or fact of science which stands in their way. One cannot fail to admit
a certain insane consistency in their utter refusal to
adopt the standpoint and apply the criteria of their

opponents. Those opponents say, "Our doctrines are true and yours are false. We can prove this by factual and historical evidence." The Nazi master-minds reply, "There is no truth. What men call so is only a flattering name for what they choose to believe, or profess to believe, because it serves their ends. With regard to our own doctrines, we admit this frankly. You deny it in the case of yours. Which of us is the wiser will be decided by the outcome of the struggle we intend to make. For this will show which of us is the stronger; and *that* is the sole criterion which nature permits and recognizes."

Only upon this basis can we understand the disgusting devices whereby the "purgation" of the German universities was effected. Typical of them all was the case of Professor Lips, the famous Cologne anthropologist. When he was told that he could keep his place if he would consent to teach as scientific truth the Nazi doctrines of blood and soil, and that form of the race-myth which exalts the Germans and depreciates everybody else, he replied that this official doctrine was a pack of lies that only fools could believe, and that no anthropologist in the world would disgrace himself by affirming such nonsense. The answer he received amounted to this: "Clear out, then. We will replace you with a man willing to teach all this, and we will make the Germans believe that *he* is an authority on anthropology."

In full accord with this, Rauschning reports Hitler as having uttered the following dicta, all of which could be many times multiplied from the writings and official pronouncements of Nazi henchmen: —

"We are now at the end of the Age of Reason. The intellect has grown autocratic, and has become a disease of life."

"There is no such thing as truth, either in the moral or in the scientific sense ... The idea of free, unfettered science, unfettered by hypotheses, could only occur in the age of Liberalism. It is absurd."

"The slogan of objective science has been coined by the Professorate, simply in order to escape from the very necessary supervision by the power of the State."

"We must distrust the intelligence and the conscience, and must place our trust in our instincts. We have to regain a new simplicity."

"People set us down as enemies of the intelligence. We are. But in a much deeper sense than these conceited dolts of bourgeois scientists ever dreamed of."

I draw particular attention to the last but one of the foregoing quotations. The statement that "We must distrust the intelligence and the conscience, and must place our trust in our instincts," means, precisely and obviously, that we are to distrust everything in us which is distinctively human, and fall back on that in us which is merely animal.

Presented thus nakedly, without disguise or embroidery, this position will strike any ordinary educated man as downright madness. For such a man has been taught all his life to believe with Bishop Butler, that "Things are what they are, and their consequences will be what they will be." In other words, he believes that

statements are either true or false, according as they
do or do not correctly indicate unchangeable facts or
relations which exist in the nature of things; and that
the bearing of any statement upon the particular wants
or interests of any man has nothing whatsoever to do
with its truth or falsehood. He believes that there really
is an "objective world,"—meaning by this a world
which is the same for all sane minds. He is certain that
that world existed before his individual consciousness
came into being on earth, and will remain after he is
dead.

A man of ordinary education likewise believes that
reason in us is a power whereby we gradually discover
the nature of this objective world, and the laws its phenomena exemplify. Though it be true that this reason
has developed in us through the exigencies of a struggle
for existence, nevertheless it has proved useful even for
that purpose only in so far as it has disclosed to us those
objective environmental conditions which are what they
are once for all and unchangeably; and to which, accordingly, we must adapt ourselves, since otherwise we
should perish.

Now to anybody brought up on these beliefs, the
statement that there are different types or brands of
science, and that the differences between these have
nothing to do with the great given reality which they
purport to unveil, but depend solely upon the "blood"
and the willed ends of different kinds of men, will sound
like raving lunacy.

That this attitude is indeed essentially insane, and

that its full logical development would involve universal madness—or rather the relapse of man into the animal —I should be the last to deny. I not merely admit, but contend that this is the case. Nevertheless, there are two points about it which forbid us to dismiss it with this judgment. The first of these considerations is that its exploitation in the interests of the dictatorship of Hitler and his gangsters, and to a less extreme degree by Mussolini, was prompted not by madness in the ordinary sense, but by diabolical wickedness and cunning, for a severely practical purpose: that of dominating the world.

The second reason why we cannot be contented merely to call it mad and let it go at that, is that whereas we now see in Germany and Italy its extreme, undisguised expression and application, nevertheless this anti-rational doctrine is no novelty of the dictators' invention. Rather, it is the outcome—long ago discerned and predicted—of tendencies of thought which go far back in time, and have had, and still have, their exponents in many nations, including our own.

If I may venture to introduce a purely personal note, I would explain that the reason why, throughout my mature life, and especially in my earlier years as leader of the Chicago Ethical Society, I have concerned myself with the subtle problems of philosophy and metaphysics, is simply that my study of these types of thinking had made plain to me what was coming. I therefore felt desperately concerned to equip myself, and those whom I could teach, with mental weapons to meet this menace whenever it should develop.

Erroneous ideas, we must never forget, are potent forces. For the practical effectiveness of any idea depends not upon its truth, but upon the energy with which it is believed and acted upon. Many false ideas, the practical outcome of which would be ruin and disaster, have been entertained and expounded by men who not only meant well to their fellows, but secured acceptance for their teachings by the earnestness of their own convictions, by powerful presentation, and by all the charm of literary genius. Such men it was who innocently originated the anti-rational and anti-ethical doctrines which in our time have borne their poisonous and blighting fruit.

It is often difficult to determine when and where a particular idea started. For practical purposes, however, we may date this aberration from reason, in its modern Western form, from that extraordinary genius, Arthur Schopenhauer. I say "in its modern Western form," because I do not forget the fact that Schopenhauer had imbibed it from ancient Eastern sources: specifically, from the profoundly pessimistic thought of Buddhist and pre-Buddhist India. But to trace its earlier history in that ancient land would be superfluous for our present purpose.

It is also needless to say that Schopenhauer was as far as possible from being anything like a modern Nazi. We are merely pointing out that, all unawares, he sowed some of those dragons' teeth from which the mod-

ern Nazis have grown. Schopenhauer, indeed, was a
man of abnormally sensitive and sympathetic nature. It
was his hypersensitiveness to suffering which made him
a pessimist; exactly as with our own Mark Twain. He
conceived of humanity as driven by a blind will-to-live,
which was the source of all sorrow and suffering. Happiness and pleasure were merely illusions; the baits of
nature by which the race was fooled into perpetuating
itself. Accordingly (like Buddha, who had traveled the
same road of thought and placed the same interpretation upon experience), Schopenhauer advocated the
renunciation of the will-to-live, as the sole possible way
to that final escape from the torment of life which the
Buddhists call Nirvana, but which he would have called
extinction.

This doctrine is set forth with extraordinary intellectual power and literary charm in that remarkable production of Schopenhauer's youth called "The World as
Will and Idea" ("Die Welt als Wille und Vorstel-
lung"). To be sure, when we analyze it, we find it
as self-contradictory as all efforts to discredit reason
by reason must finally be. For if I place before you a
series of arguments to show that reason cannot be
trusted, and you accept this conclusion, you will clearly
be doing so upon the strength of your faith in the trustworthiness of *my* reason. It is really extraordinary how
often men are beguiled into accepting conclusions which
presuppose and depend upon the very truth they are
intended to overthrow. In all its forms, this widespread

modern undertaking to discredit reason turns out inevitably to be an instance of this fallacy.

The Schopenhauerian doctrine, moreover, involves
the contradictory notion of an absolutely blind will
—a mere striving of insatiable desires, both anterior
and inferior to intellect—which yet nevertheless knew
so well what it was after that it was capable of evolving
the intellect as its instrument for reaching its ends. The
chief of those ends, however, is the maintenance of life;
and this, according to the argument, can involve only
suffering. Renounce, therefore, the will to live; will,
instead, to die; will the extinction of the human race!—
Such was the conclusion of Schopenhauer.

Now the work in which these views were set forth,
though almost entirely neglected at the time of its publication, became widely famous thirty or forty years
later. And this, its fundamental doctrine, was seized
upon by Nietzsche and violently wrenched into what he
called an "optimistic" interpretation. To considerate
readers, however, the hectic and falsetto "optimism" of
Nietzsche proclaimed itself as in truth more tragically
repellent than the candid pessimism of Schopenhauer.
It was, indeed, the optimism of defiant despair; and the
frantic effort to maintain it ended in the insanity of its
proclaimer. From Nietzsche, however, it has percolated
down, in this delirious form, to multitudes of followers,
most of whom are wholly unaware of its origin.

An interesting case in point is Bernard Shaw, who
in play after play avowed himself not only a believer in
but a worshipper of the "Life-Force," and struggled

desperately and incongruously to reconcile his Nietz-
scheism and belief in the Superman with his earlier
commitment to democracy. The logical impossibility of
this attitude exhibits itself in the form of a perpetual
seesaw of contradictions throughout Shaw's plays, and
especially throughout his Prefaces.

Our own William James was far indeed from being,
like Shaw, the mere retailer of a borrowed doctrine, the
history of which he did not know, and the meaning of
which he never rightly understood. Unhappily, however, the kind of Pragmatism or Radical Empiricism
to which James committed himself, although reached
by him quite independently of the Schopenhauer-
Nietzsche doctrine of will, was yet tainted with the
same infection of anti-rationalism and anti-intellectualism. For this, too, degraded and denatured the intellect
into a mere instrument to ends essentially sub-intellec-
tual, and reduced "truth" to the level of a designation
for such beliefs—*i.e.*, any beliefs whatsoever—as actually served to attain those ends. "Truth is what works,"
said the Jamesian Pragmatism, in its earlier and bolder
form. And it is hardly too much to say that the remain-
der of James's philosophic life was one protracted endeavor to water this down, and escape from its more
preposterous implications, without completely disavow-
ing it.

Now this type of thought, so brilliantly expounded
by James, has since become dominant in American
philosophy, thanks to its development in modified form
by Professor John Dewey. Some of my readers may be

aware of a fact which seems to be generally forgotten: namely, that Felix Adler, the founder of the Ethical Movement, saw in Dr. Dewey's system the extreme antithesis of his own; and that, notwithstanding all his high regard for Dewey's personality and sincerity, and the incidental value of many portions of his teaching, Adler regarded this system as fundamentally false, and as a most dangerous snare, especially for young students. This is one of the points on which I am bound to confess that I find myself increasingly in agreement with Adler.

And yet there can be no doubt that the popular suffrage of our nation has been won by James and Dewey. Several of Dr. Dewey's books, notwithstanding their obscurity of style and great difficulty for the reader, are reprinted in cheap form in the Modern Library; which can only mean that they have an immense circulation. James's books, though all more than thirty years old, have not been reduced in price by a single penny; and yet they are still widely bought and read.* And the other side of the great philosophical argument—the side represented by men like Josiah Royce and Adler—nowadays scarcely gets a hearing at all.

But at this point I must expect to be asked, "What on earth has all this to do with the man in the street? He knows nothing of the difficult and tortuous dialectics of metaphysics. He wouldn't understand even the

*The Varieties of Religious Experience. Philosophy of William James (Both titles are now in the Modern Library).

simplest of James's books, if he tried to read it. How, then, can you pretend that these works are exercising a dangerous influence in America,—an influence which leads in the same direction, and might conceivably emerge at the same point, as the anti-rational madness of Germany?"

The question is apposite. But the answer to it is plain enough. The first part of the reply is this: Even the most original of philosophers must deal with his problems as they are affected by and reflected in the particular exigencies of his own time. His problems may indeed be timeless; but the form they take for him will depend on the scientific knowledge and theories, the political and economic circumstances, the social and moral conditions, of his own age. And the second (and more immediately important) portion of the answer is this: The philosopher's ideas will filter down to the man in the street through countless mediums—novelists, dramatists, journalists, and the myriad college students who imbibe them directly from him. Thus it comes about that the man in the street absorbs them, at third or fourth hand, without the least awareness of their source, or any notion of the dialectical battles out of which they emerged.

This relation between the innovations of solitary thinkers and the beliefs of the masses can be tested in many ways. One way is by considering the jargon which has now become fashionable; for this cannot fail to betray the situation to an attentive student. When we hear people talking, as we always do nowadays, of "re-

actions," "behavior-patterns," and "complexes," or
bandying similar *clichés*, we may know at once that
they are parroting, possibly at tenth hand, what in
those who coined these words were real, meaningful,
energetic ideas.

For this is the language of determinism and materialism, interspersed and varied with that of the fashionable game of guesswork called psycho-analysis. If we
attempt to translate it into sane English, we find that
the word "reaction," as currently used, is invariably
the haziest of vaguenesses; for it may mean either *feeling, opinion,* or *judgment,*—and would certainly mean
one of the three, if only its user knew which he meant.
But when we speak of "*feeling, opinion,* and *judgment,*" we are using the language of free intellect and
self-determining personality; whereas the word "reaction" belongs to the vocabulary of chemistry and
physics, which are necessarily built upon the determinis-
tic hypothesis.

So, too, with that other lovely counter, constantly
flung upon the conversational table by those with whom
words are substitutes for thoughts: the term "behavior-
pattern." Somehow it always makes me think of floor-
cloth. The important point, however, is that there is
no such thing as a "behavior-pattern" *except in nature
below the personal level.* This expression may accurately describe the actions of "plants and animals under
domestication," to use Darwin's phrase; because these,
we are told, can be accurately predicted by trained observers familiar with all the stimuli applied to them. In

reference to men, however (except when their minds are asleep and they act automatically, as if from hypnotic suggestion) the term is ludicrously inapplicable. Nevertheless it was quite definitely meant by its inventors to deny that man is a self-determining person, and to assimilate him with the mechanism of the inorganic, or with the merely instinctive response of animals to stimulus. A "pattern" is a pre-determined configuration indefinitely and inevitably repeated. In other words, it does not mean the ways in which men *choose* to behave; it means the ways in which they *cannot help* behaving.

In venturing to call psycho-analysis a fashionable game of guesswork, I do not of course deny that a large part of our psychic life is subconscious or extraconscious. This is simply a fact; and one, moreover, which was every whit as well known of old to Socrates, to the Psalmist who said that "The heart of man is deceitful above all things, and desperately wicked," and to Francis Bacon and Henry More in the seventeenth century, as it is to anybody now living. The term "guesswork," however, is properly applicable to the huge and contradictory systems of theory, interpretation, and psychic treatment erected on the basis of this fact by Freud, Adler, Jung, and others. Their radical mutual incompatibilities prove that these systems have no claim to any other name than guesswork;—unless, indeed, politeness should prompt us to call them this in Greek instead of English, by using the terms "hypothesis" and "hypothetical."

By such subtle and indirect influences, gradually fil-
tering down from the originating thinkers at the top,
has the common man in Europe and America been
cheated out of his common sense. And thus is public
opinion cunningly perverted, and disarmed beforehand
against the subsequent onslaught of those who mean business by exploiting this situation in the interests of the
will-to-power. Such are some of the stages which clear
the way toward dictatorship, by sapping and mining
at the *only* beliefs which can justify faith in liberty,
democracy, and the inalienable rights of man. For to
talk of the "inalienable rights" of an animal or a
mechanism is to talk manifest nonsense. Reduce man to
either the one or the other, and you cannot fail to find
that in the process his rights will have evaporated.

Only by the seeping into common life of this rampant
anti-intellectualism is it possible to explain many of
the other phenomena of the present age. The collapse
of moral standards, and the current rebellious impatience with the very idea of duty, are manifestly due to
it. Less directly, but I am convinced not less certainly,
must we ascribe to it the omnipresent insanities in what
is called "art," such as those developments in painting
and sculpture which flout all tradition and all reason
by *not* being "the likeness of anything in the heavens
above, or in the earth beneath, or in the waters under
the earth"; those novelties in music which substitute the
ugliest of noises and discords for the ancient beauties of
harmony and melody; those books (by Gertrude Stein
and others) which are mere collections of sounds without

meaning, words that do not make sentences, subjects
without predicates and predicates without subjects;
and those vagaries of "free verse" which have effectively
freed it alike from rhyme, rhythm, beauty, grammar,
and meaning.

When the world recovers from this systematic cult of
insanity (as I believe it will), the connection here indicated between end-results and originative causes will be
clearly traced out by historians of thought and practice.

But if the fact be as I have stated it, how is the situation to be met? I would answer, Only by means of a
campaign as thoroughly thought-out, and as ready for
effective action at all points of the line, as the defense
of a nation against foreign invasion would require.
Readers of my books will know me too well to imagine
that I intend by this to set bounds to any man's freedom of thought. Far, indeed, from it. What I mean is
that every thought contributory to the triumph of ir-
rationalism should be compelled to face its opposite in
fair fight. Nobody should be allowed to grow to maturity without knowing the history of this aberration, and
the full strength of the case against it. For just as we
have learned by bitter experience that there is a way of
using political liberty to destroy political liberty, so is
it now demonstrated that there is a way to use freedom
of thought to destroy not only freedom of thought, but
the very belief in its possibility. In the insane denials of
behaviorism this last stage of self-stultifying absurdity
has been reached.

Why, moreover, may we not ask, has it come about that this one single fashion of philosophy—or pseudo-philosophy, as I venture to call it—has attained so vast an ascendancy in our universities and colleges that most of those graduated from them during the past ten or fifteen years are completely steeped in it? They automatically use its jargon, and seem to know no other. They seem unaware, too, that there are alternative systems, which, all down the ages, have won the support of far profounder minds than those who established and uphold the current fashion. Why were these other systems of philosophy either passed over wholly in the education of our recent graduates, or referred to only with such sneers and subtle disparagements that the students came to feel about them much as people feel about outmoded styles of dress,—*i.e.*, not only that they are now ridiculous, but that they always were so?

As we have noted, too, we constantly encounter in present-day books, newspapers, and conversation, what is provably the jargon of materialistic and mechanistic determinism, or of one or other of those polar opposites, the "behavioristic" and the Freud-Adler-Jung brand of "analytic" psychology. How came this fresh issue of the currency of conversation, with the accompanying subtle suppression of the language of common sense and liberty, to prevail so exclusively that people seem incapable either of using any alternative vocabulary, or of perceiving the muddle-headed vagueness and ambiguity that their words invariably betray?

The failure responsible for this tremendous declen-

sion is part of that deep-seated and widespread failure
of all education which many of our leading educators
are now (somewhat belatedly) confessing and bemoan-
ing. From grade-school to university, we seem to have
forgotten, these thirty years and more, that there is
such a thing as an art of thinking; and that the overriding purpose of all the manifold "subjects" taught in
schools and colleges is nothing else than to equip men
and women for practicing this art, thoroughly and independently, in relation to the real world, and to all
ideas and problems whatsoever.

Forty years ago, one of the ablest of modern German
philosophers, Friedrich Paulsen, wrote a devastating
and annihilating criticism of the materialistic dogmatism blatantly proclaimed in Ernst Haeckel's then
newly published and enormously popular book, "The
Riddle of the Universe." Paulsen ended his review with
words which I translate as follows:

I have read this book with burning shame—with shame
for the level of general culture and of philosophic culture
among our people. That such a book was possible—that it
could have been written, printed, bought, read, admired,
and believed by the nation that possesses a Kant, a Goethe,
a Schopenhauer: this is painful.

But there are countless books in high reputation
among us today which deserve, yet unhappily do not
receive, the same systematic exposure and outspoken
denunciation which Paulsen gave to Haeckel. They do
not get this, partly because of the sheepish way in

which we mistake popularity for authority, and confound publicity and salability with importance.

Some attempt at the revindication of reason has been made in recent years by the new school of Liberal Catholic writers who are endeavoring to popularize once again the philosophy of St. Thomas Aquinas. The attempt is welcome, since anything which causes people to doubt the current dogmatism cannot but do good service. Nevertheless, this philosophy is simply Aristotle rehashed. It is pre-Baconian, and in that sense pre-scientific. Moreover, it was devised to buttress a system of dogmas within the sphere of which the free use of reason has always been prohibited. It would thus exclude from critical discussion many of those problems of morals and theology in which the freest and most thorough use of reason is most imperatively necessary.

I cannot but consider it a disgrace, therefore, to the thinking class of America—and specifically to the faculties of Philosophy and the Humanities in our myriad centers of higher learning—that the personality-destroying doctrines of anti-intellectualism and anti-moralism should so long have enjoyed their glamorous near-monopoly; and that the only movement against them noteworthy enough to have caught any measure of public attention should be an upsurge of Roman Catholic Neo-Thomism.

That this state of things should speedily be changed is not only necessary and desirable, but so obviously indispensable that all who can lend a hand to the task, in however small a way, should feel the obligation to do so. For, as I have endeavored to show, what the man in the street thinks today is what the philosopher or the scientist was thinking forty years ago. And what this class is thinking today is what the man in the street will be believing and acting upon forty years hence.

If, then, the current revolt against reason and conscience is permitted to run its course among us, with no more effectual challenge or check than it received in Germany, we may in due course assuredly expect to see happen here what has happened there. For what has happened there is nothing but the logical, natural, and foreseeable application by a ruthless cabal of those soul-destroying views of man which the masses are thus unconsciously imbibing.

CHAPTER II

THE ANATOMY OF FOLLY

IT IS an old and trite observation that if some intelligent being from another region of space—say from the planet Mars, or from Sirius—could visit the Earth, he would soon be convinced, by the contradictions confronting him, that he had landed in the insane asylum of the Solar System. For here he would see a family of rational creatures, notable for intellectual development, who had reached no mean degree of scientific knowledge and practical mastery over the resources of nature. So great, indeed, has been their progress that they have solved the problem of production to a stage at which it is physically possible for abundance of all the necessities and many of the luxuries of life to be provided for every one of them. Yet the visitor would see that the parallel problem of distribution remains wholly unsolved; so that millions of the Earth's inhabitants are destitute, and plunged into the deepest ignorance and squalor; while other millions of the most advanced of them devote all their energies to destroying one another, and ruining their own wealth-producing capacity.

Our visitant would see frantic wars, the cost of which in loss and misery even to the victors must be immensely

greater than any material advantages they could hope
to derive from them. Within each nation he would see a
swirling strife of parties, classes and sects, each thwarting its own well-being in the very measure in which it
succeeds in thwarting that of others. Even within the
narrow circles of private homes, he would see in myriads of cases what should be the happiest of relations
turned to gall and bitterness by mutual petulance, jealous egoism, and insensate quarrelsomeness.

Since the fact would be perfectly clear to such a visitant that all the children of earth do in truth constitute
a single family, he would assuredly be driven to conclude his survey with the words of Puck: "Lord, what
fools these mortals be!" And he would find the irony of
the situation not a little intensified by the sharp-eyed
readiness of almost every man to perceive and condemn
the folly of other people, while serenely preserving a
complete and indulgent blindness to his own.

At the head of any comment on this situation, or any
attempt to explain it, we might well place, by way of
text, some words written over four hundred and thirty
years ago by the great Erasmus of Rotterdam, in his
delightful monologue, "The Praise of Folly":

"That Creator who out of clay first tempered and
made us up, put into the composition of our humanity
more than a pound of passions to an ounce of reason;
and reason he confined within the narrow cells of the
brain, whereas he left passions the whole body to
range in."

Many years ago, I chanced upon this remark by the

late G. K. Chesterton: "You will find all the new ideas
in the old books." This, to be sure, was one of "G. K.'s"
characteristic exaggerations. If anybody had taken it
seriously enough to challenge it, Chesterton would have
been sorely troubled when asked to duplicate in "the
old books" such a list of "new ideas" as the challenger
could easily have prepared. Nevertheless, the paradoxical statement contains far more truth than is generally
recognized. For example, the words just cited from
Erasmus contain the pith of many a recent treatise on
the psychology of the subconscious, the authors and
readers of which, because they use a new jargon, and
because they have never read or have forgotten the "old
books," believe their ideas to be new. This quotation,
moreover, could be supplemented by many a phrase
from books far older even than Erasmus,—e.g., from
the Bible and from Plato—to prove the antiquity of
many insights which nowadays are often presented as
novelties.

Erasmus in his "In Praise of Folly" was writing as a
satirist. The book consists of humorous but pungent
pictures of a series of follies and crimes which in his
other works are treated, sometimes humorously indeed,
but more often sadly. The only real difference between
him and the modern writers who elaborate through hundreds of pages what he puts in a sentence, is that he
lumps together under the single word "passions" what
they divide up into distinct groups of subconscious
promptings, emotional impulses, psychic propensions,
and instinctive desires. However accurate such lists may

be, or however much they may need to be extended and further discriminated by future psychologists, it will remain true that for all the purposes of common sense Erasmus was precise enough in his indication of the source of follies. Nor shall we depart seriously from his line of thought if we define as follies *all those actions of human beings which are neither prompted by reason, nor can be approved by it.*

Let us carefully guard ourselves against being supposed to characterize as folly everything which is not prompted by reason. There is a vast range of intuitions and inspirations, of the origin of which we can give no account whatsoever, except to say negatively that they do *not* spring from conscious thinking or discursive reasoning. Among these are to be found the creative causes of the greatest art, and of much that is finest in ethics and religion. Of these beneficent inspirations we can but say, in the words of Thomas à Kempis, "Left to ourselves we sink and perish; visited, we rise up and live." * I suppose that every man who has written much has sometimes had the feeling that he was writing, as it were, from dictation, like an amanuensis. Often, too, it is the very best of his literary production which seems to have been thus given to him, and not originated by himself.

In these cases, however, the conscious reason completely approves what it does not originate. In view of the frequency of such experiences, we might do well to recognize that some part of our mental and spiritual

* "Relicti mergimur et perimus; visitati vero erigimur et vivimus."

life could be pictorially described rather as super-conscious than as conscious or sub-conscious, in the customary sense of these terms. I say "pictorially," because *all* the terminology of that new department of psychology which began with F. W. H. Myers and Freud, and has since been so widely extended and modified by Freud's followers and critics, is necessarily pictorial and analogical. Human personality is imaged by this school under the figure of a series of strata in a rock formation, or under that of cellars and upper stories in a house. The necessity for some such picturing cannot be disputed; nor is it likely to do any great harm, so long as the theorists and their readers remain aware of what they are about. The difficulty, of course, is that personality and consciousness are not spatial; whereas the only language we possess has been evolved through the exigencies of our action upon matter in space. Accordingly, the different phases of personality cannot be described at all except by analogies borrowed from space, and therefore necessarily misleading when they are mistaken for facts instead of figures of speech. But there is reason to fear that this mistake is all too often made.

Yet it may be well to suggest to workers in this field that, in the terms of their usual imagery, there is at least as much room and as good warrant for a hypothesis of super-consciousness as for one of sub-consciousness. Since both terms are metaphorical, the one is as legitimate as the other, and would seem to offer more promise of light upon the highest human achievements than does a theory which fetches these achievements from some region "below the threshold of consciousness." If the nether limit of consciousness is not where men formerly supposed, why should the common idea as to its upper limit be correct?

With this possible higher sphere of human motivation, however, we are not at present concerned. Our theme is "The Anatomy of Folly." We set out, accordingly, with a provisional definition: the term "folly" may be taken to cover all human actions, and all the motivations leading to them, which reason neither supplies nor can approve. This clearly means that folly is not limited to the persons classed as insane, mentally deficient, or sub-normal. Every normal person, including the most sagacious and prudent of human beings, is capable of it, and sometimes guilty of it. There is no distinct class of fools; nor can we create one by talking Greek instead of English, and calling them "morons." When a person is called a fool, this generally means only that somebody is angry with him. Alternatively, it may mean that he does foolish things more frequently than his accuser thinks *he* does, or than the average person is assumed to do them.

But if we ask (as our visitor from Mars would certainly do) why it is that beings endowed with reason should constantly do things which all reason, including their own, must condemn, we shall find the first part of the answer in the fact stated by Erasmus; namely, that "passion" in us is in the proportion of sixteen parts to one of reason. Nowadays, however, we hold it necessary to account for this fact a little differently than Erasmus did. We are less ready to attribute it to the deliberate irony of a Creator; instead, we ascribe it to the evolutionary emergence of reason in and through the still-surviving animal nature of man's psycho-physical organism.

In this connection, however, it behooves us to remember a fact which is generally forgotten. The evolutionary account, while certainly more in accord with our present knowledge of nature and human nature than the creation hypothesis, still does not throw the faintest glimmer of light upon the actual source of the new human endowment, or upon the causes which produced it. The development of a single line of animals into men, when described in terms of the theory of evolution, remains as utterly unfathomable a mystery as it was when accounted for by the direct action of an all-wise Creator. The most we can really affirm with certainty is that this wholly inexplicable development *must* have happened; because geologists and paleontologists, when deciphering the record of the Earth's crust, suddenly come upon evidence of operations which clearly attest the exercise of human powers; whereas before they have evidence only of the presence and activity of animals. For those of us who have neither time nor skill to interrogate the terrestrial crust in the manner of the geologist, a little introspection will compel the same affirmation. We are ourselves walking proofs that this transformation has occurred; for we ourselves are most certainly animals, yet metamorphosed in the manner stated.

The animal part of us, linked as it is by heredity with all prior animal life through unimaginable millions of years, is incomparably older than the human part, which is relatively a thing of yesterday. Tennyson, in his poem "By an Evolutionist," put it that "The Lord let the house of a brute to the soul of a man." The point I here stress is that the "house" which the new tenant was obliged to occupy was an incredibly old one. And herein must lie the explanation (not the justification, —there is no justification) for our frequent lapses from the standards prescribed by our reason.

(For present purposes the word "reason" is used as a generic term to cover *everything* which distinguishes man from the animal. Under it are included conscience and the power of discriminating and creating beauty, as well as the logical and scientific part of our make-up.)

"Folly" we use as the generic name for all activities, not of rational origination, which entail harm, unhappiness, or injury upon the doer of them. Activities which produce similar ill effects upon others, though they be equally non-rational in origin, may be approved by the reason of their perpetrator; for it is unfortunately true that reason can be perverted into a tool for malevolent purposes, or distorted to trump up justifications for evil deeds. When it is thus perverted, the beautifully precise terminology now in vogue calls the resulting impostures "rationalizations." For "rationalizing" is the exact modern scientific term for being deliberately, and on principle, irrational.

In such cases, however, we call the acts injurious to others, which give rise to these sham justifications, *crimes* or *sins* as distinguished from follies. They may, to be sure, be follies as well as crimes. If they prove to be so, this is because reason shows that in the long run they injure their perpetrator as well as his victims; and this is commonly, if not always, the case. Nay, I believe (with Socrates) that in reality it is always the case; that, in a most profound sense, any evil deliberately inflicted upon another entails a yet greater evil upon its perpetrator. This conviction, however, is one of those intuitions of faith, or moral postulates, which cannot always be experimentally proved true.

Now the purpose of education is not solely to impart information and develop the power by which knowledge is acquired and increased. Its further and more important scope is to strengthen the very imperfect sway of reason over the non-rational promptings of our psychophysical organization. Education should aim at installing rational prudence as the controller and director of all our self-regarding activities, and humane conscientiousness as the controller and director of all our acts which affect other people.

It is astonishing and discouraging, however, to note how constantly we sin against the light of rational prudence in matters affecting ourselves. The number and variety of human follies is so vast that no catalogue could exhaust them. They have afforded scope for the wit of satirists in all ages. But, alas! the satirists themselves, when their careers are brought under the searchlight, turn out to have been as far to seek in prudence and goodness as were those whom they pilloried.

Some years ago Mr. Walter Pitkin wrote an enormous book which he called "A Short Introduction to the History of Human Stupidity." Somewhere in the course of its hundreds of huge pages, he explained that it was but a preface to a larger work (in forty or fifty volumes) which ought to follow upon it. Far, therefore, from claiming that he had enumerated all the varieties of his subject-matter, he professed only to have indicated the types of stupidity which are most specially and frequently characteristic of different nationalities and varieties of mankind. Being human, of course, in doing this he perpetrated not a few stupidities of his own; some of which, however, he had the good grace to acknowledge when they were pointed out to him.

Now, what Mr. Pitkin could not do in a huge volume obviously cannot be done here within the limits of a single chapter. To bring our theme within manageable compass, therefore, I must perforce limit it to the consideration of one or two specimen follies which are conspicuously current among ourselves, and to an inquiry as to the prospects (if any) of finding remedies for these. To keep the argument clear in the reader's mind, let me repeat that I use the term "follies" to characterize all actions injurious to health or otherwise harmful to themselves, which people commit without consulting their own reason, or in defiance of its dictates.

In order, moreover, to avert so far as possible any imputation of arrogance or censoriousness, the writer is bound to confess plainly that, in common with all other men, he has always had and still has his own full share of such aberrations; insomuch that (although he prefers not to do it) he could easily write a book as large as Mr. Pitkin's, to be entitled, "A Short Introduction to the Follies of Horace J. Bridges."

The first instance I select of a folly common among all nations, but exceptionally widespread among ourselves, is gambling. With its graver moral aspects— at the stage at which it becomes a vice or crime—I shall not now deal, but shall limit our consideration to the folly which is the mother of these extremes, though it fortunately happens that many gamblers never become guilty of them. The vicious stage of gambling is that at which people risk money which they cannot afford to spare, and the loss of which not only injures themselves, but also inflicts great evils upon others for whom they are responsible.

The magnitude of this evil was first brought home to me when I discovered its wide prevalence among the men who were my fellow-workers in youth. From 1897 to 1905 I was in intimate daily association with several hundreds of men, at least one-half of whom were inveterate gamblers. My observation of this convinced me that the evils which these men brought upon their wives and children were greater even than those produced by excessive drinking. And it is matter of well-estab-

lished fact that many suicides are caused by the ruin
and loss of social status entailed by this vicious practice.

But there is a measure of gambling which is only a
folly and not a crime. The losses it entails are not ruin-
ous; they only involve a shortage of dispensable luxuries and a deprivation of current spending-money. One
great reason, apart from its costliness, for calling this
a folly is the preposterous way in which many of its
addicts waste their time on the study of the supposed
prospects of the horses, dogs, or teams of players upon
which they wager. The number, and the wide circulation, of books and papers devoted to this subject is the
proof of this charge. Countless people in this way dissipate time which would have greatly improved their
education or culture if they had used it wisely. The
foolish class of gamblers also frequently manifest a
ludicrous confidence in the counsels of "tipsters" who
obviously would not need to sell their "tips" for paltry
prices if they were dependable; since in that case they
could easily enrich themselves by "backing" them.

Some friends of mine in England are (or were) engaged in the business of buying and selling race-horses.
These men could not conduct their business successfully
unless they were themselves experts in veterinary science, and equipped with the fullest knowledge procur-
able regarding the pedigree of every horse on the turf.
I have seen in their offices books which have kept this
information up to date ever since the eighteenth century. If any group of men could be considered masters
of the kinds of knowledge which make possible the suc-

cessful prediction of the results of horse-races, these were they. But precisely because their knowledge was so complete, not one of them ever wagered a single dollar on the outcome of any race; and this not so much from moral principle as from the constant experience which showed them how perennially the clearest prob-abilities based on biological knowledge were frustrated by incalculable factors. As one of them said to me, "I can tell you which horse *ought* to win a race. When the race is over, I can tell you why it won or why it lost. Nevertheless, my own guesses as to the outcome of races are wrong at least seven times out of ten."

Gambling persists among us not only in spite of the considerations just mentioned, but also despite repeated exposures of the dishonesty of its promoters and ex-ploiters. The Chicago "Daily News" recently did a useful service by printing a series of illustrated articles which exposed the fraudulent character of the devices (such as slot-machines, roulette-wheels, dice, and the like) which are manufactured for use in gambling-houses. No reader of these articles could ever again enter such a place without the certain knowledge that he was about to be swindled. Nor can anybody be sure of "a square deal" even as regards the outcome of horse or dog-races; for these also are far from being above suspicion of manipulation. Mr. Lincoln Steffens in his Autobiography positively asserts that to his per-sonal knowledge the horse-races with which he was familiar in California in his youth were all "fixed." The insiders who arranged which horses were to win were therefore betting on certainties. In other words, they stole the money that they seemed to win. And what Mr. Steffens witnessed seventy years ago would seem to be still not quite obsolete; for I found in Los Angeles, in November, 1940, that the Courts were engaged in trying numerous persons accused of the same fraudulent practices.

Many men who know and admit these facts yet say that they "like to take a chance." They have a superstitious faith in a mythical agency called "luck," which, like most superstitions, is proof against any amount of disillusioning experience. For all such persons, in the long run, lose far more than they gain. If they kept records of their successes and failures, they could not fail to know this. One suspects that the very reason why most of them do not keep such records is because they are not willing to bring to clear knowledge what, nevertheless, they must vaguely know. They actually prefer not to learn how much their folly costs them.

Now it is neither good sense nor good morals to place all manifestations of a given propensity, no matter how unequal their degrees, on the same level of folly or guilt. With the strongest possible detestation of drunkenness, I, for one, have never felt that the evils caused by this constitute any argument against the moderate use of alcoholic beverages; any more than the gluttony of a few people is a reason why others should abstain from the rational use of the foods which the glutton abuses. On the same principle, I flatly refuse to class as "gambling," even of the kind censurable as folly, the playing

at games of cards for microscopic stakes, where none
of the players can possibly lose more than he would
readily spend for any other kind of an evening's fun.

The line between fun and folly is no more difficult
to draw than the line between moderation and excess
in respect to any other indulgence. The admission that
there is an area within which playing for stakes does
not deserve even the censure of folly, in no wise detracts
from one's recognition of the area of folly adjacent
to it, and of the sphere beyond folly in which the gam-
bler deprives his family of necessary things, and so
becomes guilty of something far worse.

As a second instance of a widespread folly by which
our theme may well be illustrated, I select credulity and
its consequences.

I define credulity as the habit of believing without
evidence, or against evidence, at the behest of some
unexamined and unjustifiable personal predilection.
Like all our other tendencies to error or vice, this is
"natural" in beings of animal origin whose distinctive
endowments of reason and conscience are as yet but
imperfectly developed. In the savage and in the child
credulity is inevitable, and therefore innocent. But in
adults ostensibly educated it may become the sin of sins
against reason; and even at best it is a costly folly.

Let me guard against the assumption that I am
merely repeating the current uncritical objection to
"wishful thinking." All thinking whatsoever—whether
savage or civilized, whether that of a child, or the great-

est master of science, or the most dispassionate and disinterested philosopher—is prompted by *some* hope or
fear or wish. Since, then, there is no thinking which is
not "wishful," this adjective is pleonastic; and its use,
nine times in ten, is merely a substitution of abuse for
argument. The true case against credulity rests upon
the position that we are responsible to ourselves and
to others for the *kinds* of wishes that we allow to prompt
our thinking. We ought to wish (in the phrase Matthew
Arnold was fond of quoting from Bishop Wilson) "to
make Reason and the Will of God prevail"; that is, all
our thinking should be directed towards ascertaining
and establishing truth and right. The credulity which
is to be censured as a folly springs from wishes that we
should know to be madly selfish or absurd if we applied
our reason to them disinterestedly.

Perhaps the most conspicuous of the many evidences
of excessive credulity among ourselves is the immense
vogue in America of what are nowadays called "religious rackets." Though this term is comparatively new,
the phenomena it describes are a very old story. We
have been in modern times the most prolific producers
of "fancy religions." We are the inventors and pat-
entees of Mormonism and Christian Science. It was
among us, over eighty years ago, that the revival took
place of the materialistic superstition ironically called
Spiritualism. Theosophy is not indeed an American
invention, but we have furnished the biggest market for
its wares. And, in our own day, a host of fantastic cults
flourish gaily in California and elsewhere.

But why does one stigmatize all these as evidences of credulity? Common fairness demands the admission that in the three systems I have named there are large elements of good; and also that among their adherents are numbers of worthy people who in the ordinary relations of life prove themselves capable of soundly critical and uncredulous judgment. Nevertheless, it remains true that each of these systems professes to be based on certain fundamental *facts;* and these facts every man, as a matter of intellectual honor, ought to insist upon verifying before he accepts it. There was, for example, the original "revelation" underlying Mormonism: the famous engraved plates—which nobody has seen; and now there is the Book of Mormon, which betrays the quality of its inspiration by an amazing ignorance even of familiar facts in the history of the American Continent.

Theosophy affirms, as one of its underlying tenets, the existence of Mahatmas, or "supernormal Masters of Wisdom," by the study of whose disclosures important truths, inaccessible to ordinary human intelligence, can be learned. These living oracles were conveniently located by Madame Blavatsky in Tibet,—that being the only country on the globe sufficiently unknown for the purpose. The simple truth, however, is that these egregious persons do not exist and never did. They are as plain a product of fictional imagination as the midgets and giants of "Gulliver's Travels." Therefore all the alleged "ancient wisdom" ascribed to them must be equally a fabrication.

Whatever may be the case with Christian Science nowadays, it originally rested, as expounded by the late Mrs. Eddy herself, on two alleged facts. The first of these was the curative power, *at a distance*, of mind upon mind—and therefore inclusively upon the body, since in this system the body was only an idea, thought-form, or illusion in the mind. The second fact, equally prominent in the thought of the founder, was what she called "malicious animal magnetism," or the power of mind, without any material means, to inflict injury at a distance upon other minds, and upon the bodies organic to them. Now if either of these beliefs were a fact, it could be verified under experimental test conditions in any hospital or psychological laboratory. But neither of them has been or can be thus verified; therefore neither can be regarded as a fact.

But with the disappearance of the factual bases alleged to underlie these systems, their whole superstructure logically collapses. What remains of good or truth in any of them is no product or exclusive property of its own, but a part of the general treasure of human wisdom which has been selectively gathered up around the nucleus of its distinctive affirmations. Accordingly, it is no unfair criticism of these systems to brand as credulity the profession of any one of them by persons who have not troubled to verify the alleged basic truth underlying it; still more, perhaps, after the said "truth" has been tacitly abandoned or overtly rejected.

On a much lower level than any of those mentioned are certain of the cults now rampant, especially in that

happy hunting-ground of psychological and thaumaturgic charlatans, the Pacific Coast.

I made my first acquaintance with one of these in
Los Angeles in 1939: the cult of the "I Am." This is
an imposture which, as I was later told, originated in
Chicago. I learned at Los Angeles, however, that its
exploiters had begun business there some five or six years
earlier; being then, to all appearances, impecunious.
In 1939 they occupied an entire floor at the most ex-
pensive hotel in the city, traveled in the most exotic of
automobiles, and displayed every visible evidence of
unlimited prosperity. This cult had invented a machinery of "Ascended Masters" and "Cosmic Beings," with
whom it placed its devotees in contact, so that they became charged with "electronic force" and enabled to
exercise their will and attain all their desires by means
of "thought-projection." A mere reading of its pro-
spectus was enough to show any moderately-educated
person that the enterprise was a transparent fraud.
Incidentally, one of its three originators has since died,
—to the embarrassment of the two survivors, who had
confidently affirmed his immortality.

Now it is not difficult to understand the appeal of
such impostures to frustrated persons who are fundamentally uneducated. But the boundless success of many
such systems in extracting riches from their deceived
adherents is a saddening proof that, after all our vast
expenditure and unlimited labor to promote sound education, the numbers in America who must still be called
fundamentally uneducated are to be counted by millions.

It imports us, however, to recognize this fact, unpleasant as it may be, in order that, freed from self-delusion, we may devote ourselves to the indispensable task of remedying what is so clearly amiss in our educational system.

We must abandon the error of confounding mere literacy with education, and supposing that the capacity to decipher printed symbols and utter them in parrot fashion is identical with mastery of the profoundly difficult art of reading. What is needed to expose and defeat these fraudulent freak religions is a constant fire of outspoken and fearless criticism. For legal action against them (except in cases where disillusioned followers can prove financial fraud) is unfortunately impossible.

Herbert Spencer long ago arrived at gloomy conclusions about the question how far it is possible for the law to protect foolish people from the consequences of their folly. He was, to be sure, excessively pessimistic. Experience since his day has shown that in this matter law can do much more than he thought. It can make impossibly hard the way of the confidence-trickster. It can put a stop to the ravages of the "blue-sky" stock swindler, and impose effective penalties upon the fraudulent misrepresenter of commodities offered for sale. And it can, as we have recently seen, compel the furnishers of such public utilities as telephone and telegraph service to refuse their facilities to the racketeers of gambling, and thereby terminate their discreditable partnership with them.

I believe that the law could do yet more. It could, and it should, make impossible the activities of palmists, astrologers, and other humbugs who extort money for "fortune-telling" and the casting of horoscopes. This it could do upon the ground that such persons obtain money by false pretenses. What is more, the law can, and it increasingly does, protect the public from downright lies by vendors of adulterated packaged foods, patent medicines, soaps, cosmetics, and the like. There was a time when dangerously habit-forming drugs and heavily-charged alcoholic "tonics" and "specifics" were freely vended, to the ruin of the bodily and moral health of many innocent persons. Thanks solely to the enforcement of an intelligent Food and Drugs Act, that day is over. And the recent reinforcement of our legislation in this department is effecting further reforms not less salutary.

Still we have to face the hard fact that merely protecting the foolish does not cure them of their folly. Every time the law puts a stop to an imposture that it *can* reach, it leaves the foolish multitudes all the safer and more profitable prey for the subtler racketeers whom it cannot touch. Such are the vendors of those freak religions of which we have been speaking, who give people access to "electronic force," "supernormal Masters of Wisdom," and "Cosmic Beings," without specified charge,—but in return for voluntary "love-gifts" which the Internal Revenue Department apparently finds insuperable difficulty in tracing.

Such, too, are the organizers and exploiters of

utopian economic movements, like the Townsend Plan,
or the imposture (defeated by California in 1939 at
the expense of a general election, but still propagandiz-
ing as vigorously as ever) called the "Ham-and-Eggs"
scheme for paying "thirty dollars every Thursday" to
everybody over fifty years of age. These utopian fallacies are as prolific, and seemingly as prosperous, in the
Far West as are the thaumaturgic frauds already mentioned. It is surprising to see in California, Oregon,
and Washington, the vast and costly scale on which the
advertising and propaganda of these devices are organized. But above all is it shocking to see the kindly,
honest old people who have been deceived into believing
these impossibilities and contributing money to their
advocates.

These are the sort of exploitations of credulity for
which the only remedies are free criticism and better
education. For it must be recognized that no government could be powerful enough to suppress such evils
without being also powerful enough to suppress freedom of speech and publication, organization and criticism, and every liberty upon which democracy depends.
Such power is too great and too dangerous to be entrusted to any administration composed of human beings.

What is more, even if people could be protected in
this fashion, they would still remain at the mental level
of children. Their folly would continue whole and entire. The only trustworthy recourse, accordingly, is to
an education which will furnish them with inward re-

sources for self-protection. This is the one really effective defense against the exploitations of the vultures
who menace them. But let no man hope for a speedy
reformation in this matter. History shows that the
frauds now flourishing are only modified forms of those
which prospered in ancient Rome and ancient Egypt.

The required education, let us remember, is ethical
as well as intellectual. It will consist in an understanding of the wrongness of "seeking something for nothing," whether by means of gambling or of magic. It
will impart a heightened sense of the ethics of the intellect, and teach the duty to our neighbors and society
of ordering our own thought and utterance upon the
high level of factual accuracy demanded by science.
Such an education would help to make the pretenses
of impostors more transparent, by impelling its recip-
ients to insist upon verification of their claims. Above
all, such education would contribute hugely to moral
progress by filling people with a stronger realization
of the long-range consequences, to themselves and
others, which their conduct will entail.

I remember reading in my youth a statement to the
effect that "the greatest defect of man is the lack of
motives strong and clear enough to induce him always
to do right." Among these motives is foresight of the
certain long-range consequences of present action. So
powerful is this incentive to right where it does exist
that no less a person than Socrates was convinced that
no other was necessary. He held that all sin was igno-

rance: a false conclusion from the thoroughly sound premise that "evil as evil cannot be desired."

Unhappily, we know from self-experience, as well as from observation of others, that it is perfectly possible —nay, is a thing of daily occurrence—for people to purchase some trifling present good, usually in the form of sense-satisfaction, at the cost of distant but certain and enormous evil. Knowledge alone, therefore, although indispensable, is not all-sufficient. Other motives to right conduct must be equally inculcated and cultivated. But sounder knowledge will help us by making us realize vividly what we foolishly forget: namely, the certainty and the magnitude of the remote penalties upon the follies and self-indulgences to which we are prone.

In the three ensuing chapters we shall examine some of the present-day hindrances to character and common sense, which account for the readiness of rogues to exploit their fellow-men, and perhaps explain the ease with which their victims succumb to their blandishments.

Chapter III

THE RARENESS OF "COMMON" HONESTY

EVERYBODY COMPLAINS of dishonesty, particularly in public life. That there is also plenty of crooked and unfair dealing in business is undoubtedly true, despite all the efforts made through "codes of ethics" by business to reform itself, and by legislation to protect the public against it. In recent years, the complaints in the press, and in common conversation, have seemed to imply that in this matter the world is growing worse. My own conviction is that the truth is the very contrary of this. Rather it would seem that the multiplication of such criticism points in the opposite direction, at least to the extent of evidencing a growth of sensitiveness in the public conscience regarding what has always been an all-too-common fault.

A cross-section of the present state of the world in almost any regard, unless it be checked by comparison with the past, is always likely to provoke pessimism. It is true that the world only grows better very slowly; and that even such small measure of progress as is made is never automatic, but always the result of determined and persistent efforts. Yet to refute the impression that in this matter of honesty there has been deterioration, it might suffice to quote the words placed by Shakespeare on the lips of Hamlet: "To be honest, as this world goes, is to be one man picked out of ten thousand"; to which Polonius replies, "That is very true, my Lord." And somewhat later in the same scene, when Hamlet asks Rosencrantz, "What is the news?," Rosencrantz replies, "None, my Lord, but that the world's grown honest." Upon this Hamlet retorts, "Then is doomsday near! But your news is not true."

These citations may fairly be taken to show that, as regards the prevalence of dishonesty in their time, sensitive men in the sixteenth century felt much as our own critics feel today. We may, however, derive some comfort from remembering the obvious fact that if Hamlet's remark, about only one man in ten thousand being honest, had been true, society must have dissolved completely. Among the few social generalizations which can be quite certainly held as true, is this: that the economic continuance of any community would be impossible unless the majority of people acted honestly in the majority of their dealings. All forms of crime which involve dishonesty are a parasitism upon the industry and resources of the honest. It cannot be otherwise. If then, the parasites vastly outnumbered their hosts, is it not obvious that the latter would starve to death?

In regard to the valuation placed upon it by the common conscience of mankind, honesty ranks somewhat low in the scale of virtues. It is one of those qualities the absence of which is always blamed, but the presence of which is rarely praised. Robert Louis

Stevenson expressed the general feeling about it when
he said that "Trying to be kind and honest seems an
enterprise too simple and too inconsequential for gentlemen of our heroic mould." Nevertheless, honesty is
one of those qualities of character which constitute the
cement of human society. It is an everyday necessity;
whereas the high and heroic virtues, by comparison with
which the more commonplace ones are depreciated, are
only needed upon rare occasions, as in time of war or
natural disaster.

No doubt, as the common complaints testify, the
prevalence of dishonesty in our public life is one of the
great disgraces of America. But far worse than this is
the acquiescence of the public in this condition, as
though it were inevitable and incurable. Conviction of
malfeasance in the handling of public funds does not
involve the political death of the offender, as it clearly
ought to do. Again and again the voters have returned
to office parties which have been convicted of great
corruption, though they have given no sign of repentance.

I believe there are sound reasons for thinking that, in
spite of this lamentable fact, the average level of honesty among us is as high as among any other people.
I attribute the dishonesty in our public life to certain
manifest defects of our political system, which almost
invite the corruptionist to a lucrative political career.
But I can find no reason for believing that the average
standard in industry and private life is lower in this
country than elsewhere. How could the immense use of

credit in business transactions continue if this were the case? And how could so many bargains, concluded by word of mouth, be fulfilled every whit as punctiliously as though they had been confirmed by written agreements?

The honesty of private life, however, is threatened in our time by two dangers. The first of these is the seepage into private life of the villainous practices that are common in public life. It is established beyond question that in many of our cities there is a definite alliance between crime and politics; and it is impossible that the corrupt politician and his ally, the racketeer, should fail to undermine the character of those whom they use for their sinister purposes.

In a recent Illinois case, for example, it was demonstrated that members of juries impaneled for the trial of vote-fraud cases had accepted bribes; with the result that parties clearly guilty were acquitted in the face of conclusive evidence. There could be no more fatal stab at the very heart of democratic society than this debasement of the integrity of the jury system; and no punishment for such offenders could be too severe. Together with the falsification of electoral verdicts by tampering with the ballots, it is the most fatal kind of "boring from within," and the quickest means of substituting (even though only locally) dictatorship for democracy. All loyal citizens should enlist for a campaign of sleepless activity until both these infamies are rooted out of our life.

The other danger which threatens the honesty of

private life is the corrupting influence (traced in Chapter I) of the philosophy of moral nihilism. The effect of this is to confuse plain people by the poisonous suggestion that all morality whatsoever is only a matter of convention, and that the prevalent convention has no better credential than that it was established for the maintenance of the vested interests of the class dominant at the period when it began. For many years this opinion has been insidiously spreading, thanks to its adoption by many popular writers. Its leading exponent today is Bertrand Russell, who seems to endorse (as doubtless Nietzsche would have endorsed) the words of Shakespeare's Richard III:

> "Conscience is but a word that cowards use,
> Devised at first to keep the strong in awe."

I, at all events, can see no other meaning in Lord Russell's statements that "Outside human desires there is no moral standard," that there is nothing objective about right, and that the rule for each should be to do what he himself really wants to do; not what he "ought" to do, since that means simply what other people would like him to do.

To illustrate the manner in which such sophistications as these have affected the moral thinking of young people for many years past, we can hardly do better than cite the testimony of the late Mr. Lincoln Steffens. He tells us how he was disturbed in his college days by the discovery that "all knowledge rests on assumptions." While he seems to recognize that this applies to the en-

tire range of the physical sciences, he was especially
troubled by the fact that it applies particularly to
ethics. "There is," he says, "no scientific reason for
saying, for example, that stealing is wrong." If this is
true, then by parity of reasoning it follows that there
is no "scientific" reason for saying that murder, arson,
lying, libel, or many another crime, is wrong.

Mr. Steffens tells us how he discovered, when a student in Germany, that there is no more satisfactory
philosophical than there is scientific basis for ethics.
These are his words:

"I had gone through Hegel with Kuno Fischer, hoping
to find a basis for an ethics; and the professor thought he
had one. I had been reading in the original the other
philosophers whom I had read also in Berkeley, and they,
too, thought they had it all settled. They did not have
anything settled. Like the disputing professors at Berkeley, they could not agree upon what was knowledge, nor
upon what was good and what evil, nor why. The philosophers were all prophets, their philosophies beliefs, their
logic a justification of their—religions. And as for their
ethics, it was without foundation. The only reasons they
had to give for not lying or stealing were not so reasonable as the stupidest English gentleman's 'It isn't done.'"

Mr. Steffens, however, seems not to have realized
the full force of his own admission that *all* knowledge
—including the physical sciences—rests upon assumptions. If so, it clearly follows that ethics is no worse off
than physics or astronomy. And to look for a "scientific
reason" why dishonesty is wrong would be but to seek
a road from one quicksand to another,—*if* the fact that

knowledge is based upon assumptions is to be held fatal to it.

The confusion in Mr. Steffens's mind is manifested by his further distress upon finding that he could not extract from experimental psychology any ground for a "science" of ethics. He thought that this might be possible some day,—when psychology itself shall have become "scientific." But this statement seems a trifle naïve. The basis of science, of course, is *fact*; but the basis of ethics is *ought*. From what *is* to what *ought to be* there can be no road, unless we are rationally warranted in giving full credit and ascribing commanding authority to the value-creating conscience of mankind. And this means that ethics must stand squarely upon its own ground, in as full independence of the facts of physical science as of the dogmas of theology.

We need feel no difficulty in admitting that to some extent Mr. Steffens was right in his discovery. All knowledge (and consequently all belief) does rest upon assumptions; the cardinal one being the great act of faith that we necessarily make in the validity of the deliverances of our own consciousness. Where the assumptions are easy, because they fall in with our wants and habits (in which cases most people never even realize that they *are* assumptions), the knowledge or belief resting upon them is held with unperturbed certitude.

An instance in illustration of this position is the universally applied and trusted belief of science in the universality and necessity of the "law" of cause and effect. In practice, nobody doubts it. Yet, according to the famous skeptical analysis of David Hume, there is never anything in an antecedent phenomenon to compel the consequent. The belief itself, Hume says, is only a strong psychological habit of ours, the expression of what he calls our "tendency to feign." Merely because we have seen things happen in a certain order many times, we think they *must* so happen; and we objectify this bias of our own minds into an external natural law.

I cannot find that this skeptical conclusion of Hume's regarding the *nexus* between phenomena has ever been successfully refuted. The attempt to refute it by analyzing the cause of any given phenomenon into "the sum of the conditions" amid which it appears, seems to be only a well-meant self-deception. For if in any one of these "conditions" there is no compulsive or coercive element, how can there be in all of them taken together? It would be an odd kind of arithmetic which should profess to arrive at a positive quantity by multiplying zeros. Nor does it seem a very hopeful enterprise to smuggle that causality which our minds demand past the skeptical scrutiny of Hume by substituting the phrase "invariable antecedent" for the word cause; since the commonest experience shows us multitudes of "invariable antecedents" that clearly have nothing to do with producing or compelling their invariable consequents. Day and night, for example, are each the invariable antecedent of the other, as each season is of its successor; yet nobody supposes them to be connected as causes and effects of each other.

So much for the alleged *necessity* of "the law of cause

and effect." What about its universality? Thomas Henry Huxley confessed, with a candor rare among the physical scientists of his day, that this universality could never be proved "by any amount of experience." Despite this, of course, he unhesitatingly believed in it, and used it as the indispensable working hypothesis of his scientific thinking. Does not this mean, however, that the very basis of science, like that of religion and morals, is, and can only be, a certain kind of faith? And are we not entitled to insist that all arguments which attribute to "science" a kind and degree of certainty denied to ethics, are either self-deceptions or impostures?

Consider, too, that even if we could arrive at demonstrative certainty regarding the bases of science, as verified for the entire past and down to the present moment, we should still have no power of extending this certainty to their continued validity in the future. Whenever our astronomers predict the recurrence of a comet, or the simplest peasant affirms that the sun will rise tomorrow, the prediction, if fully drawn out, would have to take this form: "*If* the order of the universe continues to be what it has hitherto been, the sun will rise tomorrow, and Halley's comet will turn up again in July, 1986." Obviously, it all depends upon the "*if*"; and we are entirely without means of eliminating that troublesome little word, or the state of mind it betrays.

To plain people, of course, assumptions in this field carry no difficulty. Either they are unconscious of them, or they disregard them if brought to their attention. But where an assumption is more readily perceived to be such, and especially where the acceptance of it entails consequences disagreeable to our natural self-love or our spontaneous desires, there is far greater reluctance to accept it.

Now it seems to me impossible to doubt that the moral chaos prevalent in the world today—and not any other factor—is the cause of the world-depression of the past ten years, and of the existing war. But the ethical nihilists, who are so largely responsible for creating this chaos, are extremely arbitrary and inconsistent in the subjects of their skepticism. Because they find ethics to be based upon assumptions, they therefore reject the assumptions and the superstructure with them. This fact, which is quite clear in the writings of Lord Russell, could be endlessly illustrated from the chorus of writers who echo him. But the same men wholly ignore the similar weakness of physical science, the findings of which they accept with blind faith. Indeed, they offer what they call "facts of science" as reasons for rejecting ethical standards; for all the world as though one indemonstrable premise could logically invalidate another.

Some part of this modern moral nihilism must be admitted to be due to arbitrary dogmatism in the past. The sets of assumptions upon which morals have been popularly based have often been not merely unverifiable, but destitute of any real authority. This is a great misfortune to mankind. The thinkers of Greece made a magnificent start towards establishing a system of ethics

on the true foundations of experience, as interpreted
and evaluated by the human conscience. The destruction of Greek civilization, and the turning of the Western World to a system based not upon reason and experience but upon revelation, put a stop to this development. Every honest student of history must admit the
ethical and spiritual contribution of Christianity to
have been immense. Nevertheless, it remains a misfortune that from very early days the theologians of the
Church bound up its moral teachings with the unverifiable dogmas which they elaborated into their creeds.
Whoever builds upon such foundations is storing up
trouble for the time when their real nature shall have
become perceptible to men's awakening intelligence.

Matthew Arnold long ago insisted with truth that if
religion is based upon unverifiable grounds, its devotees
will sooner or later have to pay for this. We are living
in the time when this long-accrued debt in regard to
morals has had to be paid. In remote antiquity, and
among savage peoples, the accepted ethical codes were
grounded upon magical beliefs. Western civilization for
the past two thousand years has grounded them upon
supernaturalistic dogmas. And since these dogmas are
now undergoing the fate of the earlier magical beliefs,
the result inevitably is an ever more widespread moral
skepticism.

This point seems to have been overlooked by so
learned and ingenious a writer as Sir James Frazer.
In his volume entitled "Psyche's Task," he defended
the superstitions of primeval times, on the plausible

ground that it was better for men to believe in the sanctity of life, government, marriage, and property, for fantastic and mythological reasons than not to believe in them at all. The true reasons for attributing sanctity to these foundations of society they could not understand; therefore, since the foundations are indispensable, false reasons they had to have. But what was sure to happen when men came to realize the baselessness of their taboos and mythological stories, Sir James Frazer failed to consider.

The ethical beliefs of Western civilization have similarly been based upon doctrines that were unverifiable. To be sure, like the earlier magic and myths, these doctrines served well enough as incentives and sanctions to the conduct necessary for society's preservation so long as this peculiarity in them was not detected. For many people, undoubtedly, they still suffice. But the number of those of whom this is true is decreasing; whereas, for ever-increasing multitudes, these ancient sanctions fail. Today it is but a burden and a complication to present morality as the expressed will of a personal God, to regard the Bible as the revelation of that will, and (as one great section of Christendom holds) to proclaim the Church as the infallible interpreter of the revelation.

None of these beliefs can be verified in the sense in which we speak of "verification" regarding matters of fact and scientific beliefs. Not, of course, that the existence of man or his relation to the universe has been rendered any less mysterious than of yore by the progress of natural knowledge. It is as true as ever that "We are men, and we know not how." We know that we are not self-created. We know that we depend upon a universal system which we can only think of as infinite and eternal. But that the inmost nature of this reality is a self-conscious Personality,—*this* we neither know nor can know. Even if we assume it to be so, still the idea that right and wrong could be constituted by the fiat of *any* person, even an infinite one, will not really stand analysis. When we honestly face the problem, we find it downright impossible to conceive of any personality, even an infinite one, to whom the standards of truth and right would not be as external, objective, and commanding as they are to us; or, in other words, by whom these standards could have been *made* and not *found*.

As with this great initial belief, so with the deductions from it. With our present knowledge of history and literature, the Bible can no longer sustain its traditional character of an infallible revelation. Still less can any Church sustain the character of an infallible authority upon faith or morals, or anything else.

Most unfortunately, too, all the Churches, in their dealings with the laity, have stressed to excess their dogmatic and sacramental teaching, and have laid all too little emphasis upon the ethical part of Christianity. A Chicago newspaper, commenting recently upon the prevalent indifference of the public to proved dishonesty, asked whether the Church, the school, and the family have not neglected their plain duty of teaching honesty. Unhappily, there seems too good reason to believe that this is the case. This same newspaper once reprinted from a Catholic periodical a very noble article (written, if I remember rightly, by a Jesuit priest) which denounced the dishonorable and thievish conduct of certain Catholic public officials, and pointed out the very grave reflection upon the Church's character and influence which these derelictions of duty must constitute in the eyes of the general public. I had hoped that this article would be the opening gun of a continuous campaign. Unhappily it seems to have been a solitary exceptional utterance which has had no sequel.

For any valid foundation of morals, then, we must turn to our experience of ourselves and of the world; and all experience, as we have seen, involves assumptions. But not all assumptions are of the same rank. Some are merely arbitrary; others are simply inevitable; and these are so fruitful of results satisfactory alike to reason and conscience that we accord to them the rank and authority of postulates. (By this term we denote the inescapable first principles of thought; that is, beliefs which cannot be verified for the simple reason that they are inevitably presupposed in all arguments, even arguments intended to prove or disprove them.)

It is an ancient criticism upon ethical philosophers, that much as they seem to disagree in theory, their agreement regarding practice is suspiciously complete. With few exceptions they call the same things right and wrong; but they differ as to *why* they are right and wrong. Is this a sound reason for satirizing the various schools of ethical thinkers? I cannot believe so.

For one thing, we sometimes find among physical scientists a parallel agreement about facts coupled with corresponding disagreement about the explanation of them; that is, about their real nature and causes. A few years ago, for example, there was considerable difference as to the origin of "cosmic rays" between Messrs. Millikan and Compton, our two greatest experts regarding them. But at no time were these experts in any disagreement about the fact that the rays in question really exist and operate.

In the field of morals we discover a certain set of modes of conduct which everybody really agrees to consider wrong. I say "really agrees," because even the ethical nihilists of the school of Lord Russell, whose theory involves (among other consequences) the view that stealing is not wrong, would yet emphatically think it wrong for their own personal property to be stolen from them. In the early days of the great depression, when unemployment was at its worst, and there was a particularly severe winter, the Chicago Urban League, with which I was then actively associated, was compelled to provide shelter for certain unemployed negroes by installing cots in the corridors of a local jail. It happened one morning that a prisoner who was in that jail for theft complained, in wailful tones of virtuous indignation, that one of the negroes had stolen his (the thief's) shoes.

With a like lordly scorn for consistency, many of

those who profess to think, *e.g.*, that marriage is an exploded superstition, would yet object to the practice of free love by their own wives or daughters, or to the efforts of others to enter into free-love relationships with members of their families. Even Professor Pitkin, who flatly denies that anything is sacred, or that there are any inherent and inviolable human rights, might possibly feel driven to make an exception if his own life were threatened.

Now even a thinker of the nihilistic school, if (unlike the Nazi leaders) he still professes to be rational, can scarcely say that a given thing done to others is not wrong, yet that the same thing done to himself would be wrong. He can hardly say that *he* has a right to anything in the way of treatment from others which other men have no right to expect from him. Let us, then, accept the fact that when foolish sophistications are set aside, there is now in mankind a developed conscience which finds certain things unconditionally wrong. Among these are violations of the rights to life, liberty, property, bodily integrity, personal reputation, and so forth. It is also the fact that this conscience has the same authority for conduct as reason has for scientific beliefs.

But the agreement on this fact is accompanied by what looks like deep disagreement about the reasons for it. And this is where so many of the younger generation are unnecessarily yet dangerously confused and bewildered. They seem to think that the uncertainty as to the reasons extends to and involves the fact. But this is by no means true.

Consider a parallel case. There are different speculations among physicians as to the causes of cancer. This being so, it inevitably follows that there are differences also as to its treatment. But nowhere is there any doubt that cancer does exist and is a fatal disease. So, too, there is no doubt that murder and stealing are wrong, although there are differences as to the exact reasons why they are so. And there is some uncertainty, in exceptional cases, as to whether particular acts of killing or appropriation of goods should be called murder or stealing.

This entire debate illustrates the ludicrous arrogance of rejecting the garnered wisdom and experience of the past; an attitude, or pose, insanely encouraged today by many who profess to speak with the authority of science. Every day for the past quarter-century expressions of contempt for "Victorianism" have been written or uttered by persons who owe all that they know, all they have, and all they are, to Victorian parents and teachers, and who manifestly know very little indeed of the great history and achievements of the period they affect to despise. So is it, too, in regard to morals. But lines of practice which have the universal backing of civilized mankind, and are unwittingly endorsed even by those whose theory discredits them, should be recognized as wiser than any or all of the reasons currently assignable for them.

Let us take a passing glance at some of the chief of

these reasons in relation to honesty and dishonesty. The
Utilitarian theorist will tell us that stealing is wrong
because it detracts from the greatest happiness of the
greatest number. This is demonstrably true. If stealing in any one case is permitted or condoned, no man's
possessions will be safe. What is more, every man will
be doomed to a constant anxiety which would be worse
and more burdensome even than an occasional loss.
Credit is the foundation of business; and its prime
meaning is belief and trust in the honesty of other men.
The maintenance and reinforcement of this confidence
is clearly indispensable to "the greatest good of the
greatest number."

But this argument will fail with the man who insists that he does not care about "the greatest good
of the greatest number." This is the logical crux of
Utilitarianism. It bars itself out from appealing to anything intuitive, anything inwardly authoritative and
self-evident prior to experience. When we say that a
man *ought* to care for the general welfare, we introduce a word from a different school of ethical doctrine.
We may, indeed, call a self-confessed egocentric an un-
grateful hound for *not* caring for the common good,
since he plainly owes to society all that he is and has.
But if, as a fact, he is anti-socially selfish, I do not
see how a strict Utilitarian can meet him by argument.
You cannot show by utilitarian arguments that men
ought to obey the utilitarian criterion.

The Intuitive school of moralists will say, of course,
that the selfish man's assertion falsifies the testimony of

his own conscience, and merely pretends that it does not command him to respect the property rights of others. Whatever the merits or demerits of this argument, at least it is clear that if the egotist does not find this commandment within himself, he cannot complain of being robbed by other men who choose to assert that their consciences no more announce it than his own does.

Another historically famous principle advanced as a criterion of right action is the celebrated maxim of Immanuel Kant: "So act that the principle of your action shall be fit to become a universal law." This is what he called the Categorical Imperative. If everybody acted as the thief does, society would be impossible. We should revert to the jungle condition of universal war. It was the conviction of Kant that this maxim actually is the deliverance of every sane human consciousness. If so, we clearly ought not to violate it, and cannot excuse ourselves if we do so. But the sort of moral lunatic who would scoff at the utilitarian argument would find this one equally contemptible.

Another standard is the famous "Golden Rule," which, with various differences of phrasing, has been propounded by moral teachers before and since the time of Jesus. But this valuable rule also *assumes* that the interest of our neighbor not only ought to be, but actually is, as dear to us as our own. And this again is the very thing that the Nietzschean and the disciple of Bertrand Russell will scornfully deny.

The most recent addition to this series of criteria of

right action is the famous rule propounded by Felix Adler: "So act as to elicit the best in others, and thereby in thyself." If ever the philosophy underlying this maxim comes to be generally understood, I believe it will prove the most powerfully effective of all the ethical axioms at which we have glanced. For one thing, it eliminates the difficult opposition between egoism and altruism. It justifies, and buttresses by powerful arguments, the penetrating remark of Bishop Wilson: "It is not so much my neighbor's interest as my own that I love him." Unless or until they become the victims of some deep-reaching perversion, human beings naturally do desire to make the possible best of themselves, to actualize their latent potentialities, to become in fact what they are in possibility. So long as this natural ambition remains unperverted, any course which would effectually thwart it will be recognized as an act of spiritual suicide or self-maiming.

According to Adler's argument (which experience verifies), it is only by touching other spirits to their finest possible issues that our own best possibilities can be realized. From this point of view, dishonesty and theft are self-injuries so horrible that no gain of possession can compensate for them. Not only are they the death of self-respect, but they render impossible those relations with others through which alone we can pursue the activities necessary to elicit and mature our own best powers.

My main reason, however, for enumerating these various standards of right conduct has been to show that the differences between ethical philosophers are not self-contradictory and mutually exclusive, but mutually supplementary. A man who holds, for example, Kant's or Adler's view, can also, without any logical difficulty, admit fully the force of the utilitarian principle. The only difference is that such a man would call the utilitarian rule a prudential rather than a strictly ethical one. But no Intuitive moralist has ever denied the validity of the prudential canon, that we should anticipate and weigh the consequences of our actions. Such a theorist will say, with James Martineau, that "ethics is concerned with the springs of action within us, and prudence with the effects of actions upon us." That "honesty is the best policy," on the whole and in the long run, for society, is undeniable. It may not be so for particular individuals in particular circumstances. But do we not spontaneously scorn a person who for this reason departs from honesty in his own practice?

Our reflections come, then, to this: Stealing, as a fact, is wrong. We know this in the same way as we know any other fact. No individual can rationally deny it without thereby giving the world at large *carte blanche* to steal from him. And there are many reasons why stealing is wrong. Different ones are stressed by different thinkers; but the stressing of one does not discredit the others.

We began by admitting that dishonesty is hideously prevalent today regarding matters of public property; and we have seen that there are special causes at work

which threaten to undermine the present standards of
honesty in business and private life. In many quarters
today there seems to exist a fear of calling things by
their right names. It is seldom that the convicted grafter
is without circumlocution called a thief, as he should be.
Part of the reason why there have been Pendergast
machines in Kansas City, Huey Long looting gangs in
Louisiana, and unsavory and unatoned exploitations of
the public by one "gang" after another in Illinois, is the
tolerance of the public for the system which renders
these depredators possible, and the failure to visit upon
them, in unmistakable terms, the loathing, indignation
and ostracism which their conduct should evoke.

It is sometimes argued, by way of apology for violations of the traditional standards of honesty, that the
existing distribution of property is unjust. As with
every human institution, there is undoubtedly some
truth in this charge. But for an individual on this pretense to appropriate to himself what another legally
possesses can only be to worsen whatever injustice may
exist. Two blacks, as we say, cannot make a white. To
go about to cure the injustices of our present civilization by reverting to the law of the jungle, which uni-
versalizes injustice, would clearly be insane.

One of the great needs of our American public opinion today is the development of a keener conscience
with relation to this problem. We ought to expect and
demand a higher standard in public life. But a part
of the necessary preparation of public opinion for this,
must be such a re-examination of the problem as we

have here attempted; the acceptance of a higher standard in private life; and clearer convictions concerning
the moral values and disvalues involved. Progress can
only consist in extending and deepening our notion of
what constitutes theft, not in breaking down the hard-
won, but still insufficiently enlightened conscience that
humanity has already attained. The old proverb says,
"It is a sin to steal a pin." This is true because the
very smallest theft opens a breach in the wall of honor
and social defense which mankind has erected for the
protection of the individual, the family, and society.
He who steals a pin has *begun* to repudiate that sense
of the sacredness of personality upon which the sanctity
of property, like all other human rights, depends.

Progress towards the twofold ideal of perfected individuals in a perfected society demands the further
refinement of conscience, as much as it demands the improvement of practice. This extension of ethical knowledge and deepening of insight should be the steady
purpose of all genuine religion. And this is why we
should sturdily discountenance the demoralizing sophis-
try concerning commonplace, everyday duties that is
now so disastrously prevalent.

Chapter IV

IS EXTREME TRUTHFULNESS DANGEROUS?

ONE OF the finest ethical philosophers of the nineteenth century was Thomas Hill Green. He wrote a treatise entitled "Prolegomena to Ethics," which alike for its metaphysical power and its psychological wisdom is one of the classics of the subject. After completing this, he planned a further work which was to have been devoted to what he called "the detail of goodness"; that is, the study of separate "virtues," or desirable elements of character, and the precise valuation and grading due to each. His early death, most unfortunately, deprived the world of this and other possible productions of an extraordinarily profound and luminous intellect.

More than half a century has since elapsed; yet no other writer (to my knowledge) has adequately met the need which Green had planned to supply, although in the greatest work on the subject which modern Germany has given to the world—the "Ethics" of Nicolai Hartmann *—some parts of the ground are excellently covered. Our consideration of Honesty and the current menaces to it, and the present discussion of Truthfulness, may serve, I hope, as the beginnings of a tentative

* English translation by Stanton Coit.

effort toward a contribution in this department. For some fresh thinking upon these issues is so desperately needed that the attempt can hardly seem unjustified, whatever may be the inadequacies of any given writer.

The first duty of such a contributor—unless I am strangely mistaken—will be to get rid of a general and appallingly misleading error. This error is the idea that people already know, as it were by the light of nature, all that needs to be known concerning right and wrong. This delusion is certainly of the widest prevalence. To myself it is utterly astonishing how in any thoughtful person's mind it can survive a single day's experience of the unescapable and often insoluble problems of conduct.

Let me at this point anticipate an obvious criticism. "Do you not believe," I may be asked, "that human beings are endowed with conscience, and that it is our guide in matters of right and wrong?" Most certainly I do, as the preceding chapters have already shown. But I do not believe that this conscience is infallible, or that it is any less in need of education than all our other human powers. We are likewise endowed with reason, to be our guide in matters of truth and falsehood. But even the wisest of us has to spend his entire life in educating his reason; and no matter how intensely even the most gifted of men may do this, it never becomes either omniscient or infallible. So is it also, to my thinking, with our conscience.

The common error regarding this theme was expressed in classical form by no less a man than Matthew

Arnold, a writer to whom the educated world owes an immense debt, and to whom I feel in a special degree personally indebted. Yet on this subject Arnold could write the following—to me—amazing statement:

"Surely, if there be anything with which metaphysics have nothing to do, and where a plain man, without skill to walk in the arduous paths of abstruse reasoning, may yet find himself at home, it is religion. For the object of religion is conduct; and conduct is really, however men may overlay it with philosophical disquisitions, *the simplest thing in the world*. That is to say, *it is the simplest thing in the world as far as understanding is concerned;* as regards doing, it is the hardest thing in the world. Here is the difficulty,—to do *what we very well know ought to be done*." *

The impression these words make upon my own mind is one of sheer bewilderment. The forty years which have passed since I approached the stage of relative maturity have been devoted to this study above all others. All my excursions into science, philosophy, history, and analogous themes, have been in quest of light upon this, my central mental responsibility. Yet, after this experience, I find myself in doubt at almost every turn regarding what it is right for me to do, and still more perplexed concerning the counsel I am often called upon to give to others faced with conflicts of duty.

Nor can I believe that my own experience in this matter is in any wise exceptional. Does not every day's experience show to the business man, the lawyer, the physician, the trade-union leader, the statesman or leg-

___
* "Literature and Dogma." (Italics mine.)

islator, the consul or diplomatist, the teacher or parent, that in almost every task or situation confronting him there exist elements of doubt and uncertainty? Does not each constantly find himself confronted with alternative courses between which he has to choose? Is not the choice often so difficult as to seem incapable of rational determination? Is not every man often driven to his decision by the mere compulsion to act *somehow*, though he remains in grave doubt whether the action on which he plunges is the wisest or best possible?

When, therefore, I encounter a statement like the foregoing, made by a man of Arnold's vast knowledge and true genius; and when, moreover, I find that statement endorsed, openly or impliedly, by a whole army of preachers and by the common tone of public opinion; I am sometimes tempted almost to doubt my own sanity. How is it possible (I ask myself) that such multitudes of people, some of them older and many of them far wiser than I, can feel so sure and safe about what to me is the greatest, the most constant, the most perplexing of difficulties?

For a man, however, whose duties are those of a public teacher and personal counselor, it would be the gravest dereliction of professional responsibility simply to submit to the authority of what seems to be a majority, and conclude that he must himself be in the wrong. Moreover, I return with reinforced courage to the conviction I hold, when I remember that there exists a whole vast literature devoted to the very doubts and perplexities which trouble me; a library of works which illustrate those difficulties by the contradictory decisions on the selfsame problems laid down by writers of equal ability and sincerity.

This great literature (about which most lay people know nothing—not even that it exists) deals with what is called Moral Theology, or Casuistry. In the previous chapter I have ventured the criticism that the Christian Churches have lamentably over-emphasized doctrine and sacrament, and under-emphasized ethical teaching, in their instructions to the laity. In saying this, however, I did not forget the enormous literature just mentioned. These books were written not for the laity, but for the guidance of priests and confessors; and they deal in minute detail with ethical problems and the psychological conditions underlying them. They deal with motives, intentions, dispositions of will, and overt acts. In their pages these are to be found exhaustively analyzed, for the purpose of determining the moral and religious standing of the lay people in whom such various states of soul, or grades of merit and demerit, were found.

By far the greater number of these works on Casuistry were produced within the Roman Church. In the minds of the majority of Protestants (scholars as well as lay people) they have acquired a very bad name. This ill repute is in part deserved, because of the great laxity of some of the casuistical writers; but it is still more due to the misunderstanding of their purpose by many of their critics.

The situation may be illustrated by citing two classical cases of such misunderstanding. One of these is that remarkable classic, the "Provincial Letters" of Blaise Pascal, written in the seventeenth century. No finer monument of the French prose of the period exists. It displays a humor and a polished irony astonishing to readers of Pascal's other works. Competent critics have declared that it contains more wit than the finest of Voltaire's comedies.—The other instance alluded to is the attack by Charles Kingsley upon John Henry Newman in the nineteenth century, which provoked Newman into writing that equally wonderful book, the "Apologia."

Pascal denounced the moral theologians of his own Church, apparently under the misapprehension that they were presenting norms and standards of conduct; whereas, in fact, they were endeavoring to define the very *minimum level* upon which confessors could regard their penitents as Christians at all, and allow them to remain within the Church. This is not to say, however, that Pascal's indictment was entirely without justification; for the teachings of some of the casuists he exposed were infamously lax, and in these cases his denunciations were deserved. But this was by no means always the case.

Kingsley, to judge by his pamphlet entitled, "What then Does Father Newman Mean?", not only shared Pascal's error, but unluckily happened to be chiefly familiar with one of the very worst writers of the casuistical school, St. Alfonso da Liguori. This author does indeed seem to sanction what any plain man would call downright lying, and equivocations of the meanest and basest description. Unfortunately for himself, too, Kingsley brought the charge of endorsing such teaching not only against the Catholic casuists generally, but by implication against the Roman clergy as a class, and against Newman personally. This gave Newman the opportunity, for which he had yearned for twenty years, to put himself right with his fellow-countrymen. The result, accordingly, was a tremendous flare-up, and the enrichment of our literature with the most poignant, personal, and valuable of all Newman's books. The vindication of Newman's veracity in the eyes of his compatriots was complete; but, incidentally, the true original issue—namely, whether "truth for its own sake" was regarded as a virtue by the Roman Church generally—was completely side-tracked and forgotten.

This, however, is by the way. The question it concerns us to raise is this: Why should these endless volumes of subtle analysis and close discrimination ever have been needed, or have been written, if conduct were the ridiculously simple matter "as regards knowing" that Arnold called it? I have recently spent some time in re-reading, in the greatest work of Casuistry ever produced by an Anglican divine in our own language, many huge pages devoted to the subject of truthfulness and lying. The work to which I refer is the "Ductor Dubitantium" ("Guide for the Perplexed") of Jeremy Taylor. I have before me the first edition of this ponderous treatise, published in 1650. It consists of two folio volumes, containing over eleven hundred closely printed pages.

Whoever will give himself the pleasure of conning the sections of this work devoted to truthfulness and lying, will find the subtlety and thoroughness of Taylor's examination of the problem not only endlessly stimulating, but a valuable contribution to the development of his own powers of moral judgment. He may also find himself put upon the track of the explanation as to how the common error proclaimed by Matthew Arnold arose.

The explanation is this: that the *general principles* of right conduct, in regard to almost all the moral virtues or recognized duties of life, are indeed so plain and simple that a child can understand them. But when it comes to *applying* these principles, amid all the endlessly varying characters and circumstances of mankind, the case becomes profoundly different. Not only the right method of applying a clear principle, but even the decision as to which of many principles needs to be applied in a given situation, becomes a difficult puzzle, and one sometimes impossible to solve confidently without the chance of error.

In regard to truthfulness, for example, the general rule can indeed be understood by a child of seven; for it is simply that we should always tell what we believe to be the truth. The reason for this, as Taylor truly said, is that "there is in mankind a universal contract implied in all their intercourses." It is simply the natural fact, independent of any theological or philosophical explanation of it, that we are bound together as

members of one family. We are children all of us, in
body, mind, and spirit, of collective mankind. Accordingly, therefore, we are responsible to each other and
to our posterity for preserving and enhancing the great
gift of civilization which we have inherited; which can
only be done by strengthening and buttressing its
ethical foundations.

This is one of the elementary truths which by many
people to-day are scornfully denied in theory and
ignored in practice. But the plain results of this denial
are war between nations, war between classes, the corruption of public service, the impairment of private
relations, the flaunted imbecility of racial and national
self-deification, and ruin generally. Accordingly, every
man whose highest task in life is the promotion of
ethical knowledge and practice may in all quiet confidence hold that the elementary truth just stated is vin-
dicated as decisively by the consequences of its violation as it could be by the blessed results of general conformity to it.

The same natural justice which commands respect
for every man's right to "life, liberty, and the pursuit
of happiness," prescribes the rule of truthfulness as
one of those rights in each man which constitute a duty
for all men. It is noteworthy, too, that men in all states
of society have alike perceived and proclaimed this.
Pagans, Jews, and Christians have unanimously insisted, with equal rigor, on this duty. Aristotle, Plato,
and Plutarch are in no more doubt about the matter
than are the Hebrew Prophets and Christian Apostles,

from whose teaching on the subject their own is indistinguishable. But Pagan philosophers, Hebrew Prophets, and Christian Apostles also recognized that the *discharge* of this duty admits of qualifications, complications, and sometimes of complete exceptions.

It was, for instance, a Christian Archbishop who told the story of the downright lie for the telling of which a martyr in the Near East was annually honored. A certain renegade Saracen in an Eastern town (as Jeremy Taylor narrates the story) had committed the sin of defiling a mosque. The local authorities naturally charged the small resident Christian community with the offense, with the result that all of them were condemned to death. One of their number, a young man, as the only possible way out of this situation, quite falsely took upon himself the guilt of the crime, and confessed to it, in order to secure the salvation of his brethren. He did this with full knowledge of the certain sequel, which was that he was tortured and executed. His deliberate breach of the rule of truthfulness was justly held to have earned for him the reverence due to a martyr.

At first blush this might be regarded as a wildly extreme case. Nevertheless, it is the sort of episode which might occur any day in territory occupied by an invading army, or under such conditions of persecution as now prevail in Germany and the lands it has violated. The point, however, is this: What becomes of the alleged simplicity of the rule of truth-telling, when its *direct violation* under certain circumstances may be regarded not only as permissible, but as an exercise of the most heroic virtue? Who can deny the need for a thoroughly thought-out Casuistry to guide men in such cases?

The great error of Puritanism was that it ignored the whole subject of these problems. With pedantic rigidity it insisted upon inflexible and unvarying standards. It dealt in dead blacks and whites, refused to admit conditions and degrees in the applicability of moral rules, and regarded the slightest departure from the letter of an authoritative principle, irrespective of circumstances, as equally sinful with the most flagrant violation of its spirit.

Mr. W. E. Collier, of the Philadelphia Ethical Society, dealt with this subject in the December, 1939, issue of "The Standard." His admirable article represents a sincere effort to make due allowance for some of the circumstances under which departure from the strict letter of the law of veracity may be either compulsory, or at least permissible. With the general spirit of his essay I am in full sympathy, though I venture to doubt whether he has in every case chosen his instances wisely. I quite agree, for example, with his contention that the so-called "Oxford Group," which proclaims "absolute truthfulness" as one of its four rules of life, and simply ignores the problem of the inevitable qualifications and variations which wisdom requires in the application of this standard, thereby shows itself to be absurdly naïve.

Mr. Collier's other instance, however, which plainly

reflects the perplexities of a personal experience, is one that seems to me beside the point. It is that of a man of his own profession, when he is called upon to address members of another religious body, and so finds himself confronted with the problem as to how far he is to expose before them the differences between his own theological views and theirs. I can but say for myself that, having often stood in that position, I never experienced any difficulty with it. For one thing, those who invite one to make such addresses know what one's views are, even though the rank and file of their congregations may not. My published works have been before the world for many years; some of them for a quarter of a century; and however limited their general circulation, they are known at least to the leaders of most denominations. For another thing, it is always understood that on the subject on which he has been asked to speak, any man in such a position shall be free to express his full thought. If, as the result of this, some of his hearers are offended, either their complaint is unjust, or their real grievance lies not against the speaker but against those responsible for his appearance.

Not seldom it happens that what is mistaken for extreme truthfulness is only extreme tactlessness. Neither in social intercourse, nor in a man's work as a public speaker, does the rule of truthfulness require one perpetually to harp upon the differences between one's own religious or political beliefs and those of one's hearers. A man, as I hold, is bound by the rule of truthfulness never to say anything inconsistent with his real beliefs. But if on every possible occasion he drags in by the scruff of the neck every conviction of his own which differs from those of his hearers, especially in cases where these differences are such as must be painful to them, his conduct should be described not as extreme truthfulness, but as crass bigotry.

There is a well-known principle, recognized ever since the days of the Greeks, called Economy in the imparting of truth. By this is meant that one is to tell truth not as though truth-telling were the only moral duty in the world, but with proper regard to the whole circle of duties, and with special consideration for the effect of one's words upon the person or persons addressed, and upon other persons whom one's statements may affect for good or for ill; and particularly with regard to the capacity of one's hearers for understanding what one has to say.

The use of this principle within Christianity is founded upon the words of Jesus, "Cast not your pearls before swine," and upon his use of parables which were frankly devised to convey only so much of his meaning as his hearers were capable of receiving: "He that hath ears to hear, let him hear." "The early Christians," says Newman, "did their best to conceal their creed on account of the misconceptions of the heathen about it. Were the question asked of them, 'Do you worship a Trinity?' and did they answer 'We worship one God and none else,' the inquirer might or would infer that they did not acknowledge the Trinity of Divine Persons."

Here we have a clear case (and, what is more, a somewhat unfavorable one) of the use of the so-called Economy. The answer Newman quotes is almost, if not quite, an equivocation. For though it is completely true—a properly instructed Christian Trinitarian being every whit as rigid a monotheist as any Jew or Mohammedan —yet it concealed a part of the truth, and passed over in silence the very point upon which an answer was demanded.

In judging whether such an Economy is justified, this point must be clearly remembered: that most of the writers who have attempted to define the conditions under which any departure from the rigid rule of truth-telling is permissible, have stringently insisted that such departure is never permissible at all *without just cause*. This condition clearly throws upon the conscience of the individual concerned the responsibility of determining the justice of the cause: which is the very sort of responsibility that all moral action whatsoever must involve.*

Let us glance for a moment at the above-cited equivocation used by Christians when interrogated by heathens. An answer that told the *whole* truth might have entailed persecution, not only of the person questioned, but of his brethren. It would certainly have been misunderstood as meaning that Christians worshiped three gods, and therefore were guilty of lying when they declared that they worshiped only one. The answer cited,

* A fuller development of this argument will be found in Chapter VII below.

therefore, was a partial suppression of truth; but it did not involve even the suggestion of falsity, and it had regard at once to the integrity of the Creed, to the safety of the company of believers, and also to the understanding of the heathen questioners.

For my own part, I should further urge that in such cases one has likewise the right to consider whether the person asking the question is *entitled* to the information he demands. This is a phase of the matter which in everyday life men have to judge most carefully; as when they are questioned, say, by enemies; by actual or potential rivals in business; or by people whose objects and interests conflict not merely with their personal ones, but with large public causes for which they are responsible.

To take an example which recent events have made conspicuous: Every diplomatic or consular representative, of our own or any country, is most solemnly bound not to disclose facts the knowledge of which by aliens would, or even might, produce effects injurious to the country he represents. Yet such a man is constantly solicited to betray these secrets; sometimes with a subtlety which it requires extreme watchfulness to circumvent. Or again, in the press conferences of the President of the United States, he is every day asked questions which it would be positively wrong for him to answer with detailed truthfulness.

Under such circumstances, one has a full right to remember that the questions themselves are unwarranted. The President either refuses to answer them, or forbids his answer to be quoted. In his high office, he can safely count upon his injunctions being observed. But a consul or ambassador is generally in a less commanding and secure position. His duty to his government is for him the dominant consideration. He has a full right to recognize that the questioner is not exercising a proper claim to the "natural justice" represented by truth-telling, but is prying for information to which he is not entitled. He is deliberately seeking to place his victim in a false position, and entrap him into a violation of duty.

I may be allowed to recall an early experience of my own which brought home vividly to my mind the sometimes complex nature of this problem. In my seventeenth year, I was anxious to secure a position on one of the morning or evening newspapers of London, where the wages, for the sort of work I was already doing elsewhere, were about double what I was receiving. The rule prevailed, however (whether by law or custom I am not sure), that only boys over eighteen years of age were allowed to do this work on newspapers. I applied for such a position, and satisfied the head printer of a certain journal as to my capacity. He then asked me the direct question, "How old are you?" I answered him truthfully; whereupon he expressed real regret that he could not engage me. This was a great disappointment to me. A short time later, however, another opening was thrown in my way by a friend; and this time I was questioned only as to my capacity and not as to my age. I answered all the questions asked of me, but volunteered no statement about a question which had not been put. I still feel, as I did at the time, that this measure of Economy was justified.

These almost random instances show that there is an indefinitely large class of cases in which so-called extreme or absolute truthfulness would be not only dangerous but sometimes foolish and sometimes criminal. In the cases of statesmen, ambassadors, and the like, if mere refusal to answer is not accepted, or if silence would be (as in some cases it easily might be) itself a kind of disclosure of what should be concealed, some measure of evasion, by changing the subject, by equivocating, or in extreme cases by falsehood, is clearly permissible. For this is only so far a violation of the rule of truthfulness as is indispensable to the fulfillment of other principles of duty that are equally binding, and of superior importance in the given circumstances.

Consider, again, the large class of cases indicated by the ancient jocular saying, "*Mentiris ut medicus*"— "You lie like a doctor." Now the Hippocratic Oath, as is well known, imposes upon the medical profession an uncommonly high ethical standard. But it has never been held a part of the doctor's duty to blurt out "the truth, the whole truth, and nothing but the truth" to every patient under every possible set of circumstances, or to the wife, husband, parent, or child of every patient. A doctor's business is to use his best judgment not only as to what treatment, but as to what statement by him regarding his patient's condition and prospects, will be most conducive to the overriding duty of effecting a cure. Or, if he knows a cure to be impossible, then he is to see that his patient's last days or hours shall be attended only with the unavoidable minimum of suffering, both of mind and body.

This statement of medical duty, however, does not mean that physicians enjoy a plenary dispensation to ignore the rule of veracity at all times. That duty is every whit as binding upon them as it is upon other men. Like other men, however, they have to reconcile it with other duties that are equally imperative; and in their case it happens that the occasions when the one duty conflicts with others are more frequent than with most men, and require more alert and delicate discrimination.

Again, every teacher knows that to try to impart the whole truth at once regarding the subject-matter of any study would merely make the attainment of his goal impossible. It would simply perplex and discourage his pupil, to such an extent as to paralyze those mental energies which, properly encouraged and disciplined, would be capable of a complete, albeit gradual, mastery of the given subject. This is another case where the Economy of truth is simply necessary. St. Paul was merely observing a condition of wise pedagogy, not violating a rule of truthfulness, when he spoke of administering doctrinal "milk to babes" and meat to strong men.

Boswell records the answer made by that sturdy moralist Dr. Johnson, when asked what he would do if an intending murderer questioned him as to the direc-

tion which his destined victim had taken. Johnson
bluntly declared that under such circumstances he
would lie. Newman, commenting on this, evades the
issue by saying that, from all we know of old Samuel,
his first act would have been to knock the inquirer
down, and his next to call in the police. Undoubtedly,
this is what Johnson would have done if possible; but
he was supposing a case in which it would not be so.
Most men, I apprehend, will agree with him in thinking
that in such an exigency the "lie" would be right.

Cases arise in the experience of most of us which
force us to recognize that silence, too, may sometimes
be a crime. The commandment, "Thou shalt not bear
false witness against thy neighbor," is based on a principle which also involves the converse,—"Thou *shalt*
bear *true* witness on behalf of thy neighbor,"—in any
case in which he is falsely accused or maligned, whether
in a court of law or otherwise. Again, where the disclosure of facts would injure another "in mind, body, or
estate," he who knows the relevant facts has to decide
whether in the given instance the publication of them
would be a crime or a duty. For this, too, depends upon
circumstances; and cases are easily conceivable in which
the decision would be very difficult.

Suppose one discovers, for example, that a neighbor,
who is to all appearances living honestly and doing
useful work, is actually an escaped prisoner from another region. Is the truth to be disclosed, despite the
fact that the man's livelihood, and that of his family,
would be destroyed if his past became known? If one

were sure that he was of the type of Jean Valjean, it would clearly be a great sin to betray him. The case would be very different, however, if there were strong reason for believing his present appearance of honesty to be only a mask, and that he was actually awaiting the chance to commit further crimes.

Such instances show how easy it would be to compile a list (which might be indefinitely extended) of cases in which the ordinary rule, "Speak every man truth with his neighbor," is overruled by a greater or more immediately urgent duty.

But now let me confess that I have gone into this matter with great reluctance, and only so far as to show that none of us can be justified in ignoring the principles of Casuistry which deal with the exigencies we often have to decide. The subject is distasteful to me, as I believe it is to most plain-minded and honest men ; and I hold that we should not concern ourselves with it overmuch, but only far enough to "clear our minds of cant" and enable us to see the problem in true perspective.

For it is my deep conviction that mankind suffer far more from laxity in regard to truth-telling than from over-zeal for "extreme" or "absolute truthfulness." Veracity, like honesty, is one of the homespun, everyday virtues which are indispensably necessary in all the relations of life. Probably more harm is done by people's horrible carelessness about whether what they say is true, or whether the effects of their statements will be injurious, than even by deliberate lying. And perhaps more good is to be done by inculcating a due sense of responsibility regarding the import and effect of our words than by the denunciation of liars. I, for one, have long been convinced that the circulation of injurious gossip, and the indulgence of the sensation-seeking love for what (in the elegant vocabulary of the new savagery) is called "the low-down" and "the dirt," constitute one of the commonest and most mischievous of the sins of society.

Formal recitals of duty ought not to be used overmuch; for when they are, they frequently degenerate into mere empty words. Yet I think it could harm none of us, and might do us considerable good, if we were to repeat (once a week, say, in the privacy of our own chambers) those fine old words of the Catechism: "My duty towards my neighbor is to love him as myself; to hurt nobody by word or deed; to be true and just in all my dealings; to bear no malice nor hatred in my heart; to keep my hands from picking and stealing, and my tongue from evil speaking, lying, and slandering."

A little self-examination as to the extent to which we live up to these requirements might be useful. What the Catechism here demands, be it observed, is no exaggeratedly high or saintly standard of duty; it is no more than each man ought to practice, because all men have a right to this order of treatment from their fellows. Yet how different a world this would become if even this unheroic level of plain neighborly obligation were universally lived up to! What a vast reformation would take place in our public life, and what a huge purgation of the tone of society!

Thus have I sought to answer the question "Is Extreme Truthfulness Dangerous?" by admitting that under some circumstances it may be; that in other circumstances it certainly would be; and that in all cases natural justice demands as much truthfulness as is consistent with all the other obligations involved in the particular situation with which we have to deal. In general, the cases that call for deviation from the strict rule are easily discerned. Let me leave the subject, then, by emphatically reiterating my conviction that there is far more need for stricter observance of the rule of truthfulness than for the indulgence of curious speculative Casuistry regarding the exceptions to it.

Chapter V

THE DANGER TO CHARACTER IN SOCIAL SECURITY

Mr. Bernard Shaw began the Preface to one of his plays with a section headed "First Aid to Critics." He did this on the ironical ground that since the production had puzzled the reviewers, it was his duty as a good fellow to tell them what to say about it. I am tempted to feel that it behooves me to undertake something of the same kind, because I have recently had an experience both novel and amusing. Like most public speakers and preachers, I always expect, and generally receive, strictures upon my addresses after they have been given; but in this case, from more than one quarter, I received some highly adverse reflections upon one which I announced on this subject, a week before it was to be delivered! One gentleman first excoriated me (through three typewritten pages) for blaspheming the holy name of Stalin, and implying the monstrous heresy that anything cruel and inhuman could possibly have occurred in that earthly paradise of liberty and justice, the U.S.S.R. He then proceeded to speculate upon the corrupt motives which could alone account for my not believing in social security, and my hard-hearted blindness to the evils entailed by its absence.

Now in face of the impossibility (which one's critics almost invariably forget) of saying everything at once, even on a limited subject, writers and public speakers are forced to rely somewhat upon the memory of those who have followed them through the years. To that memory I confidently appeal when I say that few persons outside the ranks of professional social workers have advocated social security for more years than I have done. Throughout the period of dominance of the Republican Party, from 1920 to 1932, I repeatedly blamed them for their systematic, callous neglect of this fundamental need, which obviously grew the more acute with every year's delay in dealing with it. And in all the many criticisms I have passed upon the New Deal Administration, I never once thought of blaming them for recognizing that this kind of security must be provided.

Let us clear the ground by defining our terms with some degree of precision. In its large literal sense, "social security" of course includes many things that we have long provided; for example, "workmen's compensation" for industrial accidents; or, again, educational facilities. Without the rudiments of literacy, in an age of machinery and scientifically-directed industry, the opportunity for earning a livelihood would for innumerable people be non-existent. By supplying these to every child we take the first indispensable step towards securing his position in the nation's economic life.

But in current discussion, thanks to the developments

of the past thirty years in several countries, we have
come to mean by "social security" such specific things
as insurance against unemployment and sickness, provision for the subsistence of necessitous widows and
their children, so long as the necessity remains; and
pensions for the aged, or maintenance for those of any
age who are permanently incapacitated from lucrative
work. As these things are successively secured and embodied in social practice, the term will no doubt be further extended to cover other modes of sharing the good
things of life and safeguarding people against its
calamities.

In other words, the social conscience of our time, in
country after country, has come to declare its conviction that whenever any person, through genuinely uncontrollable circumstances, economic or physical, is prevented or incapacitated from maintaining himself by
his own exertions, it becomes the duty of the community,
—certainly to remove the disability if possible, and as
soon as possible; but also to see him and his dependents
through as regards the provision of the minimum essentials of life so long as his disability remains.

In this sense, one nation after another—several of
them decades before the United States awoke to the
necessity of action—has responded to the old question,
"Am I my brother's keeper?" with a resounding and
thunderous affirmative. This constitutes one of the most
remarkable ethical advances of our time, which in other
respects, unhappily, has not been conspicuous for moral
progress. Many of us are old enough to remember the

days when no such answer to this question was made by
any nation, and when innumerable sufferers from unemployment and physical disability (including the
wives and children of the victims) were left wholly without any public aid. Whoever remembers those times,
which in most countries continued down to the end of
the nineteenth century, and even later,—especially if
his memory includes the experience of personal hardship
from the lack of such provision (which happens to be
my own case)—must, it would seem to me, have either
a very hard heart or a strangely perverted head if he
can believe in going back to those bad old days, aban-
doning such measures of social security as have now
been established, or refusing to advance further in the
direction of providing them.

I ask my reader to understand clearly that I am here
discussing only one of two equally important questions.
The second question, on which I shall here have almost
nothing to say, is one on which there is room for wide
debate; namely, *how* this provision can best be made.
Social security can, of course, be provided in various
ways. To a large extent, given a sufficiently homoge-
neous and intelligent community, it can be effected by
co-operative self-help among the working classes. This
has been proved by experience in Sweden, Great Britain, and some other countries. In all classes, moreover,
the entire private-enterprise business of insurance is
an installment, and a most important one, of social
security. This kind of co-operation makes effective provision (barring the disaster of currency inflation)

against various kinds of personal accident and disability, against the destruction of property by fire, theft, earthquake, or tornado, and for the contingency of death; the last-mentioned form of insurance being almost invariably undertaken, often at great sacrifice by the insured, in order to provide for the surviving members of his family.

Where these voluntary measures fail, or reach their limit, and the politically-organized community feels called upon to assume responsibility, this again may be done in various ways; *e.g.*, by municipalities or county units; by individual States; or, as is increasingly the case amongst us, by the Federal Government. Here arise important questions both of principle and of expediency. In particular, no man can blink the real danger which attends the monopolization of such services by the Federal Government; for this, together with the increasing system of grants-in-aid to local enterprises, definitely threatens to obliterate all our minor organs of sovereignty, from the State downwards.

Into this large debate I here deliberately refrain from entering; and I ask my critics kindly to take careful note of the fact. For, while I welcome criticism, I confess to a crotchety preference for being criticized upon what I *have* said, rather than upon what I have not said. The point upon which, for the present, I wish to concentrate attention is my unequivocally clear conviction that the thing we call social security absolutely *must* be provided. Here and now, I limit myself to this contention. I insist only that the thing be done, and leave aside the question concerning the best ways of doing it.

On this point I will only say that I thoroughly agree with Mr. Walter Lippmann's excellent statement: "In a free society the State does not administer the affairs of men. It administers justice among men who conduct their own affairs." Starting from this principle, I naturally hold that the fewer the tasks we impose upon government, the better is our chance that those tasks will be honestly and competently performed. The present headlong drift in the direction of thrusting every conceivable task upon government not only means inevitably that many things will be incompetently or even corruptly bungled, but that the government and its ever-increasing cluster of bureaucracies—which needs must be created if any attempt at all is to be made to discharge such multifarious functions—will necessarily expand into a pervasive and grandmotherly tyranny, very alien indeed from the spirit and principles of the American tradition. How little we shall really like this natural consequence of what we have requested or permitted our law-makers to do for us, was betrayed by the hot resentment against improper questions, so called, that were included in the 1940 census inquiry. Yet it is hard to see how the Federal Government could be expected to do the things that many people demand of it unless it possessed the information which such questions would elicit.

All this, however, is aside from my present theme. To that I return, by observing that in any well-ordered community (according to my conviction) no person, and especially no family bread-winner, would be permitted to suffer starvation, or destitution of the other necessaries of life, except through his own deliberate fault. I believe that not only the spirit of humanity, but intelligent consideration for the well-being of society requires that when bread-winners die, or are incapacitated, or are deprived of the means of livelihood through the introduction of new machinery, or through failure of domestic or foreign demand for their product, or indeed through any cause except their own culpable wrongdoing, they and their families should be helped.

Even in the case of culpable wrongdoers, their wives and children cannot with justice, or with safety to society, be allowed to suffer the full economic results of the sins of the fathers. These wives and children are social assets. The same motives which lead us to educate the children at the community's cost (and to do so, remember, whether they or their parents like it or not) should impel us to see that their bodily health is not impaired, and that they are not driven by dire need into delinquency.

Especially should the community take seriously upon its conscience the case of those industrious and often highly skilled persons for whose services the economic demand is destroyed by new inventions. Primarily, the industry which they have served, and which now renounces them, should be called upon to assume this responsibility. This might in some cases be done by means of a graduated and gradually-declining tax upon the economies and profits resulting from the new labor-saving instruments. But so far as the particular industry cannot meet the case, the community must step in and provide such persons with maintenance, with the opportunity of acquiring some new skill which will be marketable, and, as speedily as possible, with honorable and duly lucrative re-employment.

I for one also fail entirely to understand why pensions for old age, already provided in a number of our public services, as well as in many private-enterprise professions and businesses, should not equally be made available to every kind of worker who is willing to contribute his fair share towards their cost throughout his working years. If such pensions are good for those who have hitherto had them, why should they not be equally good for others? A life of socially useful work is just as truly done for the community when its medium is a commercial corporation as when it is done through a political or other public enterprise. That such a life, when its earning power fails, should be permitted to end in penury or humiliating dependence upon relatives, seems to me completely unjust, and to constitute a reflection upon the humanity or upon the economic intelligence of society.

Having said thus much, I now desire to guard myself against a further possible misunderstanding; namely, against my seeming to agree with those who affirm that "society owes everybody a living." I do not say this, because I definitely do not believe it. The doctrine seems to me quite false and unjust. It could easily mean saddling the industrious and productive part of the community with the maintenance of an indefinitely great army of deliberate parasites. It could mean penalizing the thrift of the prudent for the maintenance of habitual spendthrifts, who have culpably refused to save anything out of incomes from which the accumulation of reserves was perfectly possible. We must remember the elementary yet often forgotten fact that whenever a government agency gives anything to people who at the time are not earning it, this can only be done by taking it directly or indirectly from those who have earned it. There is no Fortunatus's purse or conjurer's hat from which public treasuries can be replenished. All that they ever can dispense must come from the pockets of taxpayers present or future. This is in no sense an argument against using public funds for socially desirable objects. It is, however, an overwhelming argument for confining such expenditures rigidly within the limits of justice and efficient economy.

I therefore reject the doctrine that "society owes everybody a living." Let me state instead the four things (apart from the social-security provisions already specified) that I think society *does* owe to everybody: *First*, the indispensable minimum of education, without which even so-called unskilled tasks, in an age of scientific industry, cannot be adequately performed. *Second*, the opportunity of acquiring specialized skill in some line of productive and adequately lucrative work; which opportunity no sort of monopoly, national or local, *capitalist or labor*, should ever be permitted to deny to anybody seeking it. *Thirdly*, the opportunity of utilizing the skill thus acquired. *Fourthly*,— as aforesaid—the necessary minimum of temporary assistance when this opportunity vanishes through causes beyond the control of the worker.

Since I thus strongly advocate social security (without now discussing the question of the best means of providing it), I may naturally anticipate the question why I should speak of the danger to character involved in it. My answer in brief is this: Precisely because I earnestly desire further progress with this indispensable reform, I am anxious to consider the strongest case that can be presented against it, and to urge others not to be deterred from advocating it because of the probability, or even the certainty, that it will be attended by some incidental evils. For one of the tragic features of our human life is the constantly demonstrated impossibility of doing almost any good thing without giving rise to some correlative or resultant ill.

This is the solid core of truth in the case against over-legislation and paternalism in government urged in the nineteenth century not only by so extreme an individualist as Herbert Spencer, but also by so eminently fair-minded a liberal as John Stuart Mill. The difficulty with laws is that they have to apply to everybody, and have to be enforced in innumerable situations and combinations of circumstances which the law-makers cannot possibly know or anticipate. Not seldom it happens that immediately after the passage of a law circumstances change so radically as to make it inappropriate, and so create the necessity for radical amendment. The consequence is that besides the ends they are intended to meet, laws produce many effects which the legislators could not dream of, because at the time they were unforeseeable.

All moral philosophers are agreed that it is never lawful "to do evil that good may come." Unhappily, however, the conditions of human life make it impossible to apply the converse of this. For if we always refrained from doing good because of the certainty, or the overwhelming probability, that evil would come, we could do no good at all. Such is the sad but unalterable fact underlying the old saying that "The road to Hell is paved with good resolutions," and the other maxim that "History is the tragedy of good intentions." Under these conditions we are perforce obliged, when we seek to do good, to use all the foresight we can muster to avert evil consequences; but nevertheless we must be resigned to the certainty that some ill effects beyond our prevision will accrue. In actual life we often find ourselves confronted with nothing better than a choice of evils. In these cases we recognize the duty of treating the lesser evil as though it were a good, and deliberately incurring it.

Now the first reason why social security carries danger to character is this: There is in human nature a force of inertia which, in multitudes of quite normal cases, limits men's exertions to the minimum necessary to attain the ends they consciously desire. And with the mine-run of our humanity those ends often do not extend beyond such merely physical and other material satisfactions as are necessary for the maintenance of life, or are consciously desired on account of their pleasantness.

This inertia explains, for example, why there has been so little social or intellectual progress in those favored spots (such as many of the sub-tropical islands of the South Seas) where the means of life fall almost without effort into men's hands. It also accounts for the many recorded cases of lives of mere idle uselessness among the children of the rich. How often, for example, during the last seventy-five years of our own history, have we not seen fortunes, accumulated through immense exertions on the part of vigorous and enterprising fathers, dissipated or turned to positively anti-social ends by their indolent, self-indulgent, or dissolute inheritors.

Now it is perfectly idle to assume (as many social idealists have done) that the rich or "capitalistic classes" possess a substantial monopoly of vicious tendencies, whereas working people and the poor have a monopoly of virtue. This doctrine has indeed seldom been overtly stated; yet it is quite clearly the unspoken assumption of many socialistic and philanthropic members of the more privileged classes, who never had to earn their own living, and consequently lacked opportunity for knowing the working class as it can only be known by those who for years have been in it and of it.

Equally false and unjust would it be, of course, to reverse this fallacy, and represent the poor or the working-class as more vicious than the rich. The plain fact was well stated a century ago by that early American philosopher-humorist Sam Slick, when he said that "There is a great deal of human nature in all mankind." The psychological elements in the make-up of all men are identical. But different elements and phases of that make-up will be elicited and stimulated by different environmental conditions; and in well-disciplined people all parts of our inherited nature are subjected to the dominance of recognized and freely-obeyed standards of right and duty. This means that instead of acting in accordance with the mere strength and enticingness of a native inclination, such people act from what their conscience discloses as a more authoritative motive, however much weaker it may be.

In the year 1937, I made as careful a study as a summer's leisure would permit of the effects of social security in England, where this system has been progressively developing through more than thirty years. The main fact forced upon me by this inquiry—a fact verified by successive election results, and sadly confessed to me in intimate conversations by leaders of the Labour Party—was that the outstanding and immediate result of social security had been to substitute a bourgeois, middle-class, conservative psychology for the old militant working-class spirit; so much so as to turn the voting majority of Britain to the extreme right politically, at the very time when America and other nations were moving politically to the left.

I recall how thirty-five years ago a highly respected

friend of mine, Stanton Coit (a typical aristocratic humanitarian of the Jane Addams type), was shocked, and not a little incredulous, when I assured him, from personal experience, that among the working class—together with countless examples of truly fine and noble character—there was at least as high a proportion of spendthrifts, wasters, gamblers, excessive drinkers, and bad characters generally as among any class—even the much-denounced "capitalist" one; and that the desire "to get something for nothing," to exploit their fellows, scamp their work, and "wangle" difficult or unpleasant tasks upon others, was acted upon whenever possible by many laboring men. But I made these statements on the basis of years of actual experience; and I am certain that they could not be controverted by any experienced artisan who testified honestly.

Idealistic illusions die hard; and this same generous-hearted gentleman seemed no less distressed when I placed before him the results of my 1937 study of the effects of those improvements in the status of the working class which he himself had zealously and conscientiously advocated for many years. Always the impatient crusader for a better world, fired by each partial achievement to yet keener zeal for further improvement, he felt bitterly disappointed when forced to realize that, once given a tolerable measure of security,—once owning the house he lived in, and knowing that in unemployment, sickness, and old age he would be comfortably looked after—the average workman promptly became the most earnest of conservatives, resolute to do nothing and permit nothing that could by any means imperil the safe harborage he had attained.

It is the demonstration of this fact, indisputable in the light of successive election returns, which explains why not only exceptionally humane and civic-minded employers, but the British capitalist class in general, thus taught by an experience which their American brethren have not yet undergone, have long since become the most ardent advocates and upholders of those very measures of social security to which, when first proposed, they offered the most panic-stricken opposition.

In the light of this experience, reinforced as it is by that of other countries, it is truly surprising that the "die-hard Old Guard" of our political parties have not long since taken the same line as their European brethren, and moved heaven and earth to provide for the great mass of our working classes the same sort of solid stake in the stability of the existing economic order as the working men of Sweden and Britain have secured. For this would be not only the best, but the sole effective insurance of the industrial and managerial classes against labor troubles and disruptive agitation.

I contend that all this has come about simply through the spontaneous natural inertia of masses of men, the mere instinct for "safety first," and entirely apart from any special selfishness or viciousness in individual cases. Naturally, however, when social security measures have been introduced, such selfishness and viciousness have displayed themselves in every possible variety of "chiseling" and cheating, until experience has taught the authorities how to prevent them. For instance, in the early days of the unemployment "dole" in Great Britain, shortly after the first World War, one heard many well-attested stories of girls who, upon becoming engaged to be married, sought and found employment, which they retained just long enough to qualify them for unemployment assistance when they left it. They thus obtained, at the expense of the Government (which means, of course, the tax-payers), what was in effect a marriage dowry, to which they clearly had no moral right, inasmuch as they fully intended to refuse any employment offered them after marriage.

In 1931, the head of a metal-working industry in the Birmingham region of England told me that during a former slump he had been obliged to reduce his factory to a four-days-a-week basis. This was the only alternative to dismissing a number of employees, which he was anxious to avoid doing. But when he explained this situation to his workers, they replied with undisguised candor that they were willing to work three days a week, but not four; because on the three-day basis they would be entitled to unemployment pay for the other three days, whereas if they worked four days they would not receive the "dole" for the other two.

To these illustrations I regret to have to add the case of a member of my own former trade: an ingenious printer, who obtained two days of extremely well-paid work in each of two towns some forty miles apart, from both of which he also extracted unemployment pay for

the remaining four days of the week! My informant
added, however, that a British magistrate had provided
this worthy craftsman with a period of hospitality in
jail, that he might have leisure to reconsider the pro-
priety of his conduct.

Our own immature and amateurish experience of social
security, through the hastily improvised measures of
the past seven years, has likewise revealed a dishearten-
ingly large number of cases, not only of crude political
exploitation by administrators of relief, but of imposi-
tion by individuals and families who dishonestly concealed incomes or resources the disclosure of which
would have debarred them from public assistance. For
instance, I recall reading in the New York "Times" the
story of a family who, while collecting unemployment
relief money in New York City, were purchasing elsewhere a summer cottage, in which they spent the greater
part of a leisure which, to their neighbors, appeared
by no means necessitous.

Such cases, one would like to believe, are few, both in
actual numbers and in proportion to the total of those
assisted. Nevertheless, they do occur. One hears, too,
almost daily, of cases where, owing to the amateurish
clumsiness due to the lack of national experience in
administering our system, men and women of the finest
honesty have found themselves confronted with a painful dilemma. They had to decide whether they could
afford to accept temporary employment, since the penalty for accepting it would be a long interval without
relief after the employment ceased. It is difficult to

blame persons who refuse temporary work under such conditions; but the persistence of those conditions betrays grave unintelligence in the administration of the relief funds.

Hitherto, however, we have barely glanced at the deepest reason which makes social security a potential source of danger to character. Unnumbered biographies of men and women of distinguished achievement show how those hardships and dangers which effective social security removes have been the very conditions that spurred them to the efforts through which they achieved their success. No small part of the reverence we all feel for Abraham Lincoln arises from our deep sense of the extreme poverty and the terrific paucity of educational opportunity over which he triumphed. A distinguished college professor lately told me that he felt beyond measure distressed and perplexed by this ominous fact: that all over the country, graduates of universities are to be found working in minor positions as the employees of men who never saw the inside of a college, and sometimes not even that of a high school.

Security saps adventurousness: that is the plain psychological fact which must be honestly faced in all discussions regarding social security. Persons who have never had to take risks are apt to shrink from doing so in circumstances where those inured to insecurity throughout their lives will go in and (very often) win. It is idle to blink this fact, since every man's experience verifies it.

There is decisive reason, however, for believing in

social security despite its admitted dangers to character. That reason is simply that the good it can be proved to have done far outweighs its incidental evils. The Abraham Lincolns and other great men who have risen above conditions which looked crushing are, in truth, extremely rare exceptions; and it can never be proved that such men would *not* have succeeded had their early conditions been more favorable. The handicaps they surmounted, moreover, have crushed whole multitudes for every one to whom they proved effective incentives. Of the great mass of the unprivileged Thomas Gray's words remain as true as ever:

> But knowledge to their eyes her ample page,
>   Rich with the spoils of time, did ne'er unroll;
> Chill penury repressed their noble rage,
>   And froze the genial currents of their soul.

The danger we have pointed out does indeed constitute a difficulty; but a difficulty which can be overcome, and must be. It simply brings home anew the old lesson of experience, which many people are so unwilling to learn, that "Men cannot be made moral by Act of Congress." As Samuel Smiles expressed it eighty years ago, "No laws, however stringent, can make the idle industrious, the thriftless provident, or the drunken sober. Such reforms can only be effected by means of individual action, . . . by better habits rather than by greater rights."

The better citizen a man is, the more is he prone to be impatient, especially when confronted by some manifest social evil, with the complexity of life and the world; and the more apt is he to over-simplify problems and look for short cuts to their solution. This explains our inveterate habit of assuming that laws can be an efficient substitute for religion, for education, and for the influence of the home; nay, can succeed where all these have failed. It explains why, in the teeth of repeated disappointments, we continue to believe so eagerly in those "statutory substitutes for character" which, in truth, never did exist and never will.

The solution I have indicated, then,—a solution to be gradually worked towards and not to be expected immediately—is, first, to recognize the inevitable limitations of what law can do. We must cease to expect the fruits of character from anything other than the roots of character; and we must remember that unless those roots are planted in infancy, and tended and nourished through all the years of growth, they will in a distressingly large proportion of cases remain non-existent, and in others will wither and die.

As an advocate of social security, therefore, I would urge those whom disheartening experience may have tempted to abandon the idea, to re-examine the problem in the light of broader considerations. Let them remember that an ounce of real self-help is worth a pound of external aid, whether the latter be provided by law or otherwise. Let them work, therefore, no less earnestly for such forms of security as voluntary co-operation can provide, than for those parts of it, beyond the range of self-help, for which recourse must be had to the law.

In connection with every human good, abuses and attempts at abuse are inevitable. But the lesson is as old as Rome that "Abusus non tollit usum"—"the misuse of a thing does not take away its proper use." When impostures occur, punish the offender by all means; and, in the light of experience, change the methods of administration so as to make such offenses impossible or unprofitable. But let us never forget the solid advantages, not only to the individual but to society, which a wisely-administered system of social security has been abundantly proved by experience to produce.

Which considerations, by a natural transition, lead us to the theme of our next Chapter.

Chapter VI

"DON'T EXPECT UTOPIA OVERNIGHT"

No small share of the possible zest and interest of human life is missed by most of us, owing to the unfortunate psychological fact so inexactly indicated by the proverb that "Familiarity breeds contempt." Inexactly, I say; for what breeds contempt is not real familiarity, but superficiality, lack of the observing and inquiring disposition, and the false idea that we really know a thing merely because we have seen it many times, though we have never once brought it to the focus of our attention. Consider, for example, what a country walk may be to a person versed in botany, or long interested in noting the differences between the various kinds of trees, as compared to the boredom which the same walk would speedily bring to others; for instance, to the legendary undergraduate who, when asked to define a leaf, replied that it was "a flat green object which we know all about already." It is this attitude (which we all perforce adopt towards large areas of experience that we cannot investigate) which is really the mother of contempt and boredom.

Thus even the most recent and spectacular miracles of science, which fascinate the most blasé when first achieved, and which never lose their interest for the expert, speedily become for most people a dull, commonplace matter of pressing buttons or turning switches. Every day we use the telephone or the automobile, with never a thought for the prolonged delving into nature's secrets and the miracles of ingenuity which made them possible. We turn the radio on and off, some rejoicing at having heard an inspiring program, others cursing the commercialism and vulgar inanity to which so wonderful an invention is degraded; but few with any thought of the incomparable physical research and inventiveness which created it.

In this fashion we justify the criticism of the writer who said, "I do not wonder at what men suffer; I wonder often at what they lose." The measure of our loss, however, is far greater than has yet been indicated. For, to those who have not allowed their power of insight and appreciation to be dimmed by this superficial and incurious familiarity, immeasurably more wonderful and fascinating than any of the works of man is man himself. No arcanum of nature unveiled by the great pioneer in science, no complex mechanism devised by the most consummately ingenious inventor, can compare in interest, or in baffling mystery, with the mind of the inventor or discoverer. Every novelist and dramatist learns that the study of character, even for purposes so limited as his, soon becomes inexpressibly fascinating and absorbing. Accordingly, the cure for the contempt and boredom to which we are condemned by what we uncritically call familiarity, is that true familiarity which springs from long-continued, well-directed, eagerly interested attention.

This interest, moreover, can be awakened by others besides people of exceptional mentality or ingenuity. Fully as mysterious as intellect, though fortunately commoner (but therefore still more ignored or held cheap), is the triumph of character over native propensity. The daily-verified fact that quite ordinary people can and sometimes do obey and act from an intrinsically weaker incentive, despite the counter-urgency of a strong psychological impulsion, becomes, to those who really consider it, beyond expression baffling and awe-inspiring, by reason of the metaphysical and moral implications involved in it.

Now these two powers, moral and intellectual, together with the cognate capacity of discerning and creating beauty, are the three traits or endowments which differentiate man from all other animals. What is more, they offer the sole explanation of the paradoxical and wholly unprecedented turn taken by man's evolution in contrast to that of all other living beings: a fact, by the way, which adds yet another to the many baffling problems light-heartedly ignored by those who tell us that man differs from other animals "only in degree and not in kind."

The paradox alluded to is the following: that the true evolution of man as such—that is, not as an animal but as a rational and social being—begins at the precise point where that of every other species ends. In all other cases, whenever the conditions of the environment

are such as to satisfy the physical needs and psychic
cravings of the creature, it simply rests in them; it
never dreams either of seeking other natural surroundings, or of changing those to which it is already ad-
justed.

Now this contrast is a very astonishing circumstance,
little as we commonly think about it. We often find ourselves amazed by what seems—nay, what truly is—the
remarkable cleverness, say, of a highly-trained dog;
such, for instance, as those provided for the guidance
of the blind by the "Seeing Eye" organization. What
these animals can be trained to do is simply bewildering.
When one witnesses it, one is sometimes tempted to
think that in their case the line between animal and
human has been crossed, and that their achievements
give evidence of reflective rational thought. Yet not
even such a dog will betray the slightest power of judging or appraising the environment in which it lives. It
will display no consciousness of the difference between
a beggar's shack and a palace, nor any preference for
the one over the other.

The idea of improving conditions by changes in-
itiated by thought—of adapting the environment to
itself, instead of merely adapting itself to the environment—is thus clearly beyond even the most intelligent
of animals. But it is this idea alone which accounts for
human civilization, from its remotest beginnings to its
highest achievements. What is more, it is only when his
powers of thought and initiative are partially liberated,
through the attainment of some margin of leisure and

sufficiency beyond the exhausting demands of an un-interrupted struggle for bare subsistence, that this idea begins to work in man.

In other words, the "divine discontent" which con-demns the actual scene of our existence by comparison with a conceived but never experienced ideal, awakens precisely at that point where every other creature on earth becomes fully contented and quiescent. We must accordingly say (by way of working hypothesis) that everything in the animal make-up of all creatures, our-selves included, which really is evolved from, and there-fore adapted to, a natural environment, is fulfilled and satisfied by what that environment continues to pro-vide, so long as it remains unchanged. When it changes, those creatures which are animals and nothing more can only seek another natural environment that will supply their needs. If they succeed, they survive. If they fail (as the geological record proves to have happened often), they become extinct. Environment and animal-ity answer to each other as container to content, the mold to the plaster.

But if this be so, then the presence in man of an ele-ment which *no* natural environment can permanently satisfy becomes one more of the many reasons which reflective thinkers have always found for holding that man's distinctive nature is unique, in the sense that it cannot have been evolved from anything which preceded it in terrestrial development. In other words, that which makes man truly man—that single, indivisible power which in one application is reflective rational thought, in another is conscience, and in a third aesthetic discernment—is unique in the sense of being an evolutionary new departure, a manifestation of something in the cosmos which had to remain latent until a measure of physical development complex enough to become organic to it, and serve it as a vehicle of manifestation and expression, had been reached: and this point apparently has thus far been attained on earth only in the brain of man.

Into some such train of thought as this one naturally finds oneself beguiled if one takes time to brood over the implications of the word "utopia." I was led into it by reading newspaper summaries of an address delivered early in 1940 by President Roosevelt to the American Youth Congress in Washington. The reports made it clear that the President told his youthful auditors a number of salutary things designed to counteract the undue and disruptive influence which had long been exercised upon them by Communist and other propaganda. Mr. Roosevelt at long last—somewhat belatedly —used commendably plain language about the Russian dictatorship; language which some of us would have liked to hear from him several years sooner. He confessed to the disappointment of the high hopes he had entertained twenty years ago for Russia's development. While reaffirming the absolute liberty of thought and opinion guaranteed by our Constitution to his auditors, as to all Americans, he rightly differentiated this from the attempt to give effect to any such opinion by means of violent and unconstitutional action designed to change our system of society or our method of government.

But it was when he used the simple words "Don't expect utopia overnight" that he reached the deepest note of his address, and epitomized what is probably the most difficult lesson that life compels all of us to learn; a lesson that we find hardest, and in some cases quite beyond understanding or belief, in our youthful days. I imagine that many readers of this speech found themselves tempted, as I did, to suspect that it had needed the experience of the previous seven years to bring the full force of this lesson home to Mr. Roosevelt himself. His very remarkable career in the White House seems to have begun with an incredibly optimistic conviction that he could indeed produce a social utopia "overnight" in the United States, to replace the disorder, depression and discouragement which were rampant when his term of office began. When the bias and rancor of present-day party controversy have passed away, and he and his Administration are surveyed in the dry light of history, it seems probable that the main charge sustainable against him will be this almost boyish hopefulness, which tempted him into rushing measures far too fast, and into being beguiled by the advice of different counselors into sanctioning inconsistent and contradictory measures which naturally proved incompatible with one another.

Consider, for instance, the fact that Mr. Roosevelt started out with wholesale pledges of national economy, and that at first he even tried to fulfill them. Within a few months, however, he completely reversed his course; and by 1939 he stood before the nation as the apologist of a national debt, swelled beyond all precedent solely by the measures he had sanctioned, and so enormous that it produced grave forebodings in everybody but himself. This phenomenon is to be interpreted, I think, not as the mere inconsistency of a careerist politician who will promise anything to obtain power or retain it, but as the vacillation of a mind impatient with economic realities (because profoundly ignorant of them), and so elastic that it leaps to new hopes the instant an old one is frustrated.

But be this as it may, it remains true that the President gave much sound advice to the American Youth Congress; and, in particular, that he spoke wisely in counseling them not to expect utopia overnight. For it is the natural impulse of youth to indulge in this impracticable expectation, and to be intolerantly impatient of the caution, skepticism, and apparent acquiescence in unpleasant or shocking conditions, which are commonly characteristic of age. But since this very quality in youth, at least after it has been wisely disciplined, is the most valuable element in human nature, and the world's best hope for the future, the finest pedagogical tact is required to guide it, and to forearm it against the inevitable frustrations that await it, without either crushing or sapping it.

Inasmuch as in this respect most people seem to be pretty much alike, and Sir William Gilbert's jest about every boy and girl being born "either a little Liberal

or else a little Conservative" is not true (there being
very few *born* conservatives), I hope it will not seem
bad taste if I venture to illustrate the inevitable effect
of the years from my personal experience. I have conclusive evidence, at all events, that my own development
has been paralleled by that of many men whom I have
known; and I also have good reason to suspect a like
development in many other men, who have been among
the élite and the leaders of mankind.

Looking back forty years, I see myself as a young
student of history, politics, and social conditions, driven
into numerous lines of study and inquiry by a devouring
curiosity and a galling sense of ignorance, yet also beyond measure bewildered and indignant at the manifest
wrongs and injustices in the social order. What is more,
this retrospect shows me my youthful self as so convinced that *I knew* how these wrongs could be put right,
that I could find nothing but wicked self-interest and
cruelty to explain the unwillingness of the dominant
classes to accept and apply remedies which seemed so
obvious.

Some share of responsibility for this naïveté of mine
may perhaps be fairly placed upon the socialistic writers and orators with whose gospel my head in those days
was full. For they, who were old enough to have known
better, were cocksure that the social problem was exactly
like a problem in arithmetic or mathematics; that is,
one of which the solution was either known or easily
reachable; and hence youthful auditors or readers were
perhaps little blameworthy for imbibing their certitude.

These writers simply shut their eyes to the mountainous fact that the whole business is infinitely complicated by moral and psychological factors, which never can be reduced to the quantitative terms of exact science and mathematics. All their teachings were pitched in this dogmatic and infallibilist key. And inasmuch as the evils they denounced were manifest and undeniable, it is perhaps not strange that young people should have felt the same certainty regarding the proposed remedies as they felt concerning the diseases that cried for cure. Their just resentment of the inhuman conditions under which they saw myriads of people condemned to live (and many of them lived themselves) predisposed them to accept at face value, without critical investigation, any confidently-proffered cure-all.*

Now the outstanding characteristic of the present younger generation is that *it is exactly like every other younger generation of past history;* most of all, perhaps, in respect of its certainty that it is "new" and "different," has novel standards, and sees the world with an insight and realism not possessed by its parents or ancestors. One needs but to listen to its more articulate spokesmen, and compare their utterances with those remembered from one's own youth, to become fully convinced of this fact. And although not a few of the grosser evils which affronted our consciences forty years ago have now been remedied (as anybody

* This is the justification of a clever remark which I have heard attributed to the former King of Sweden: "If a man is not a socialist at twenty, there's something wrong with his heart. But if he's a socialist after thirty, there's something wrong with his head."

may know by studying the advance of social legislation), nevertheless enough of these old ills remains, and so many fresh and unforeseen ones have developed—sometimes in consequence of the very attempts at remedy—that there is still ample scope for the old idealistic impatience; especially when this is accompanied, as it generally is, by the old cocksure confidence that the remedies are perfectly clear, and that only greed, or lack of good will, or the stubborn conservatism of age, prevents their adoption.

This temperamental quality characteristic of youth remains dominant in some natures until a comparatively advanced period of life. Among other consequences attributable to this fact is the current habit of sneering at people as "escapists" if they are skeptical regarding the social panaceas to which the young are devoted, and more particularly if they occasionally seek diversion from contemporary distresses, and the nagging pressure of social and political maladjustments, in the literature and history of the past.

I do not argue that the term "escapist" is meaningless, or its application in all cases unjust. No doubt there are persons now living who fairly merit this reproach, as multitudes have often done in the past. When, for example, whole peoples (especially those of small nations) have been crushed under a foreign yoke, and enslaved by powers so comparatively omnipotent that no possible human means of deliverance could be discerned, they have sometimes taken refuge in modes of escape that did indeed belong to dreamland. Thus,

for example, they deceived themselves into expecting
the return of some heroic deliverer of a former age,—
some Man in the Iron Mask, some Duke of Monmouth,
some Barbarossa. The apocalyptic literature and Messianic doctrine of the ancient Jews furnishes such an
example of collective escapism. Themselves they could
not save; but they managed to convince themselves that
God would send them a delivering Messiah from heaven.
Following this example, the early Christians pathetically expected "new heavens and a new earth" to be inaugurated by the speedy second coming of Christ upon
the clouds.

Such a lack of realistic appraisal of their situation,
however, is far from being fairly chargeable against the
majority of the authors of literary "utopias." Many of
these books were the work of men entirely realistic in
their sense of the evils that marred the society in which
they lived, but also wise enough to know that only the
smallest measure of their hopes for amelioration could
possibly be fulfilled in their own time. These authors
wrote their utopias solely to provide themselves with
standards for the appraisal and judgment of actual
conditions, and to clear their minds as to the lines of
advance towards improvement which necessity prescribed. They neither ran away from the immediate task
confronting socially-minded men, nor did they expect
to achieve a faultless society at a single stride.

Their idealized pictures of perfected commonwealths
and earthly paradises constitute a fascinating section
of world literature, which has perhaps fallen too much

out of mind. If any friend of mine were setting out on a prolonged holiday, and wished to hit upon a course of reading which would involve just enough effort to be diverting but not enough to be irksome,—a course that promised both agreeable diversion and mental profit— I should recommend to him a study of utopian literature, wider or narrower, according to the time at his disposal. If this were ample, he might begin, say, with the "Works and Days" of the Greek poet Hesiod, and include such a treatise as Plutarch's Life of Lycurgus. The frankly-acknowledged lack of historical basis for this proves that Plutarch used it as a peg on which to hang an idealized picture, painted for the purpose of criticizing the social order amid which he lived. The same may certainly be said of the "Germania" of Tacitus. —But to a less leisured student, the natural startingpoint for such a study would be that oldest and greatest of systematic utopias, the "Republic" of Plato.

The charm of this marvelous old book is felt irresistibly even by those who would most heartily dislike living in the sort of totalitarian State, governed by benevolent despots, which it shadows forth. For it is a mine of wisdom in its ethical analysis and its incidentally expressed or implied criticisms upon the contemporary Athenian democracy; besides being, in its greatest passages (such as the myths of the Cave and of Er the Armenian), a miracle of beauty. Moreover, it clearly grasps an essential fact which seems almost to have vanished from the consciousness of present-day political and economic thinkers; the fact, namely, that no

matter what machinery of government may be established, still a better world will only be achievable
through better *men;* that we shall never get a millen-
nium by machinery; whereas, if the characters and motives of men were improved, a society in which comparative prosperity, contentment and humane relations
among classes would obtain, would almost automatically
ensue, and the temper which makes possible fundamental improvements in machinery would be generated.

Now to call either Plato or Socrates an "escapist"
(as has been done) is wild nonsense. Socrates took in-
cessant part both as soldier and citizen in the life of
his time, and was constantly endeavoring to improve
both the political machinery of his beloved Athens and
the character and motives of the men by which it was
to be operated. Plato's whole life, moreover, after his
master's death, was devoted to the attempt to find,
or to establish, a real working commonwealth in which,
as he said, "kings should be philosophers, and philosophers kings."

A reader who has time only for the principal specimens of the genus utopia will probably overleap the
nineteen centuries following Plato, and turn next to
that delightful little book which has given its name to
this whole department of literature: the "Utopia" of
Sir Thomas More. He will not fail to note that it is an
ebullition of youthful high spirits blended with the
grave wisdom of a prematurely realistic genius. He
will do well to enter into its spirit by reading first the
"Praise of Folly" by Erasmus, so as to perceive the con-

nection between these playful productions of two intimate friends who possessed the finest minds of their
time. The very nomenclature of More's book illustrates
the spirit of fun which prompted it. The name of the
imaginary explorer and discoverer who tells the story
(Hythloday) means Nonsense. The name of the island
and its capital city means Nowhere; and that city ap-
propriately stands upon the River Anhyder, which is
"Waterless." Nevertheless, as with the "Praise of
Folly," every sentence has a serious purpose; and the
book is a standing reminder of the important truth that
there is not the slightest opposition, either logically or
psychologically, between seriousness and fun.

For More in this *jeu d'esprit* was driving at the chief
social evils characteristic of his own time; in particular,
at the impoverishment of the peasantry through the
conversion of arable land into pasture, which displaced
the labor of the peasants; and also against the savage
laws which, instead of recognizing and rectifying this
evil, punished its unfortunate victims for their poverty,
under the pretense of suppressing vagrancy and pre-
venting the multiplication of what, in those days, were
called not unemployed, but "masterless men." He also
takes his powerful fling at the savage folly of war, at
the religious persecution universal in his day, at the
arrogance of kings, and at the materialistic mammon-
worship which was the underlying cause of most of
these, and indeed of practically all social evils. This
same Thomas More, let us remember, was a man who
devoted his life to the public service at a time when, as

he well knew, independence of mind and genuine patriotism were all too likely to entail the fate which actually befell him;—that of execution at the whim of a tyrant, after a trial which was a blatant travesty of justice. It is no wonder that the Roman Church, to whose communion he belonged, has canonized him. The only thing to regret is that this was not done centuries ago, instead of being deferred until our own time.

Two minor and much less remembered utopias will be found well worth the few hours their study requires: I refer to "The New Atlantis" of Francis Bacon and the "Oceana" of James Harrington. Bacon's reason for trying his somewhat clumsy hand at an imaginative composition was his strictly practical purpose of enlisting men in scientific research, by prophetically projecting the allurements of the greatly-improved world he expected science to bring. Harrington, who began writing his work immediately after the execution of King Charles I (when the whole question of what should be the future form of society in England was thrown open), published it seven years later (1656), in the vain hope of converting the military dictatorship of Oliver Cromwell into a bearable and potentially permanent social order, which was to be based upon a just distribution and fair equilibrium of property.

The writing of utopias as such seems to have gone out of fashion in our language after the seventeenth century. Some few echoes of the old strain may be detected in the first two parts of "Gulliver's Travels," but even these (to say nothing of the third and fourth

parts) are too deeply tinged with the savage misan-
thropy and hopeless pessimism which finally subverted
the remarkable intellect of Swift. A partial return to
the old method may be seen in Bulwer Lytton's fantasy
of the eighteen-thirties, called "The Coming Race";
and a relapse into pure satire, combining wittily malicious innuendo with a total absence of helpful suggestion and genuine social insight, in the "Erewhon" and
"Erewhon Revisited" of Samuel Butler.

A full-blown resumption of the old authentic utopian
strain, however, was marked by two extraordinary pictures of a hoped-for socialist paradise, produced late
in the nineteenth century: the "Looking Backward" of
Edward Bellamy (with its astonishingly shrewd prophecy of the radio), and the "News from Nowhere" of
William Morris, that unique blend of poet, artist, and
craftsman. The latter work shows its best insight by
anticipating a shortage of agreeable occupation as the
chief difficulty that would befall a socialist paradise,—
although, of course, without the attendant suffering and
want which such unemployment entails in existing society. It was, indeed, this frankly-confessed anticipa-
tion of boredom in a community in which there was
nothing to want, and everybody enjoyed artistic surroundings of a pre-Raphaelite pattern, which led an
early reviewer of the work to say that, delightful as
such an utopia might seem, he for his part would prefer
to live in the London of Dickens.

Nevertheless, the general characteristic of this entire
literature is that it reflects the thinking of active, prac-

tical-minded men who, so far from being "escapists," threw every ounce of their mind and will-power into grappling with the social evils of their day. Nor will the reader fail to observe that these utopias, although their ostensible purpose is to present an ideal social order purged of all possible ills, are generally conspicuous for the manner in which they propose or imply remedies for the special evils which loomed largest in the periods that produced them.

Our present generation of social critics seem usually to lack the courage or the imaginative and literary skill even to attempt to formulate pictures of what society would become if it were transformed in accordance with their doctrines. It might be really useful if they could be goaded into trying their hands at this undertaking. What is more, as Woodrow Wilson once wisely said, "Many a troublesome reformer would be silenced, or put to better thinking, if he were compelled to present his desired reform in the exact terms of a workable statute."

One profound and noteworthy distinction between modern and ancient utopias remains to be noted. The moderns invariably refrain from facing the question what recourse, if any, would remain available to the human spirit if the projected utopia should fail of actualization. The socialistic ones among them evade this by emphasizing the pretentious fallacy, dating from Karl Marx, of the "inevitability" of the transformation of capitalist into socialist society. All Marxian preaching consists of exhortations to the faithful to help along the inevitable.

The older school, on the contrary (in which we include both More and Plato), were not only perfectly cognizant of this problem, but they simply never expected their ideal order to be integrally realized on earth. Plato would certainly have applied to his own "Republic" the closing words of More: "Many things be in the Utopian weal publike which in our cities I may rather wish for than hope after." Accordingly, they frankly and unhesitatingly took refuge in the conception of an eternally perfect order beyond space and time, whence they drew the strength and courage to endure anything in the way of failure and disaster that human history could bring. The serene certitude with which they held this faith explains the heroic cheerfulness with which both Socrates and More encountered death,—the playfulness of the last conversation of Socrates with Crito (reported in Plato's "Phaedo"), and the jesting of More with his executioner.

It is the misunderstanding of this attitude by the modern materialist, with his equal and impartial scorn for metaphysics and theology alike, which leads him to stigmatize the cause of it by the sneering epithet of "escapism." In this, however, the said materialist is guilty of a twofold injustice. First, he simply denies the existence of the profoundest problem confronting human thought;—that, namely, of the origin of the spirit of man, with its rational, ethical and aesthetic powers, and of its relation to the inscrutable supersensible reality which thorough and realistic thinking cannot avoid postulating as its source. The materialist shuts his eyes to this problem and declares that it isn't there.

In the second place, he undiscriminatingly places under a single condemnation two completely opposite attitudes. One of these is the total despair of human effort and power represented by the recourse to supernaturalism, as in the Jewish Messianic dream and the early Christian expectation of a divinely inaugurated social transformation. The other is the precisely contrary attitude of Plato, Socrates, and More, which derived, from its contemplation of eternal ideal standards of right, the utmost courage and strength for laboring incessantly and cheerfully towards a perfected order of human society, despite the clearest-eyed perception that perfection will never be attainable (development in time being simply incompatible with it), and that the best to be hoped or expected for mankind is partial and gradual improvement, each successive installment of which will in its turn produce disappointment and open ever fresh vistas of still-needed betterment. Nobody has expressed this thought in simpler or more eloquent language than our own Emerson:

> The fiend that man harries
> Is love of the Best;
> Yawns the pit of the Dragon,
> Lit by rays from the Blest.
> The Lethe of Nature
> Can't trance him again,
> Whose soul sees the perfect
> Which his eyes seek in vain.

To vision profounder
  Man's spirit must dive;
His aye-rolling orb
  At no goal will arrive;
The heavens that now draw him
  With sweetness untold,
Once found,—for new heavens
  He spurneth the old.

Now the problem is,—how to produce the wisdom expressed in this attitude, common to the Athenian Plato and the American Emerson, without at the same time eliciting the despairing temper which throws up its hands, wails "What's the good?" and retreats into self-centered neglect of the social problem. I would suggest that it is precisely the old Platonic philosophy (albeit re-expressed in terms congruous with modern knowledge and reflection) which must be aimed at and encouraged. How may I find the fortitude, zeal, and persistence to work whole-heartedly, eagerly, and cheerfully for reforms that I know will fall short of perfection, that I probably shall not live to see, and that are sure themselves, before very long, to need reforming?

So far as experience permits me to discern, this is possible upon two conditions only. One is that I shall first attain the insight to recognize that the truly fundamental problem is that of producing better men and women than I and most of my contemporaries now are; that I shall learn to perceive that the very efforts men make to improve conditions will yield their best effect by contributing to this end; i.e., that not their direct consequences in bettering social conditions, but their indirect, retroactive effects in bettering those who make them, are chiefly to be valued. The other condition is that I shall find myself able, with full intellectual sincerity, to share the Platonic metaphysical conviction, re-worded in simpler but less philosophical language by St. Augustine, that "The City of God lives on for ever, while the empires of man pass away."

Nor may we permit ourselves to fall into the illusion of supposing this to mean that the "City of God" will ever be brought down to earth or duplicated on earth. This insight really means that the more we try to realize the ideal, and the more experience brings home to us not only our own failure, but the inevitable failure of all such attempts, the more do we realize *the reality* of the ideal. We acquire an invincible certitude that there truly is an eternally perfect order to which our deepest nature belongs; or, in Felix Adler's phrase, a "spiritual universe" of which we are members.

Thus in the effort to actualize the unattainable perfection we do two things. In the first place, we effect real improvements in human society which, partial as they are, are nevertheless of inestimable value; and we advance in the direction of perfecting our own personal possibilities. Whereas if, on the contrary, we lamely and meanly succumb to the cheap and easy pessimism which asserts that small installments of reform are not worth striving for, we shut ourselves off from the only kind of action that can really develop our latent potentialities; we commit treason to our fellows; we show ourselves unworthy of the great heritage of good which we enjoy, since we owe every fragment of that heritage to men who accepted the task we refuse; and, above all, we are false to the evolutionary direction of the universe, the further unfolding of which (so far as this earth is concerned) is entrusted to the conscious reason of mankind.

Chapter VII

BEWARE OF GOOD EXAMPLES!

In any scheme of moral education, or any effort to appraise our own or other men's character and conduct—above all, in any effort to forecast the ethical development of mankind in general—two interacting factors have to be considered. One of these is the moral ideal itself, embracing the whole graded scale of ethical values. Fine pioneer efforts have been made by various philosophers, such as Aristotle, James Martineau and Nicolai Hartmann, to chart this in detail. The second factor is the actual make-up of human nature, with its remarkable variations from individual to individual.

It would be unjust and hopeless to expect from any man the perfect fulfillment of the ideal moral law in all its parts. We may be capable of *seeing* the perfect; we are *not* capable of realizing it in practice. Some people can do easily what others can manage only with great difficulty, or not at all. Every man's actual achievement, therefore, must be appraised in the light of the obstacles in his own make-up, as well as in his circumstances, which he had to surmount in order to attain it. Men are not to be condemned for falling short of perfection. They are only to be censured for falling short of such attainment as, given their equipment, a sufficient effort could have compassed.

One of the first results of the psychological analysis which is necessary to a fair judgment of men, individually and collectively, is the discovery that man is by nature not only a gregarious but also an imitative creature. The animal in us is the substratum of the human; and, in the subhuman world, the kind with which we have most in common are the apes. This is the species in which the propensity to mimicry is strongest; so much so that we have actually turned their name into a verb to express this quality. "Aping" means mimicking or imitating. Now, while I have maintained throughout this book that man differs from all animals in kind and not merely in degree, it is yet a commonplace of biological science that everything which is in the ape reappears also in man.

The human child spontaneously copies the language, manners, and activities of those by whom it is surrounded. Probably the most enduringly important part of every child's education is imbibed in this way. How much can thus be achieved is astonishing. While it yet remains unself-conscious, a quite ordinary child can, in this fashion, get a thorough grounding in three languages, without ever realizing their difficulties. This may be seen happening every day in Switzerland and other countries where two or more languages are in current use. Long before it reaches the stage of knowing that there are such things as nouns, verbs, and the other parts of speech, a child will accurately utilize all of them through this process; *i.e.*, through sheer instinctive imitation of its elders.

Now this instinctive tendency remains in us throughout life. It is never eradicated. But it takes subtler forms, becomes more concealed, and often has to be deliberately inhibited, when we reach the age of responsibility, and our interactions with mankind grow more extensive and more complex.

There is no difficulty, however, in demonstrating that the instinct remains operative in us. The proof of this is furnished by the distress and embarrassment which grown-up people experience when they find themselves in a society from which they differ markedly in dress or appearance, bearing or speech. Many a man has felt this chagrin upon finding himself in a company among whom he was the only one wearing evening dress, or the only one who had omitted thus to attire himself. Many of us have felt it when traveling in foreign countries, as soon as we became conscious that we were marked as objects of attention by the foreign accent with which we spoke the language. The *malaise* caused to us by such circumstances, which may range from faint uneasiness to severe distress, attests the operation in us of the imitative instinct.

This propensity towards conforming to our surroundings often has to be overcome. We may override it for reasons of principle, or because our health requires us to follow a special diet, or because the indulgence of the instinct would entail the forfeiture of our intellectual independence. Sometimes the imitative instinct is nullified by the rival tendency, prominent in egotistic persons, towards self-display or exhibitionism. Since this type of conduct is also instinctive, it presumably engenders an agreeable feeling in those who practice it. But in normal persons the need of suppressing the innate prompting to imitation never ceases to be in some measure disagreeable and embarrassing.

Now, like all the rest of our native make-up, this imitative tendency has its good side and its uses. It makes for socially agreeable conduct. It induces ready submission to those necessary conventions which are the lubricants of the social machinery. It renders education possible,—or, at all events, easier than it would otherwise be. For the disinclination of most children to use their brains in prescribed ways, or beyond the small degree needed for their play activities, might prove to be quite insuperable were not the educator aided by the native imitative tendency, and the dislike to appear different from others.

But, also like all the other elements of our animal heritage, this quality has its drawbacks. Being instinctive and animal, it is of course sub-rational. It is therefore undiscriminating. The tendency it stirs in us is to imitate *anything* which is habitual or customary among the persons who constitute our entourage, without ascertaining, or even caring, whether it is right or wrong, wise or foolish, graceful or ugly. This propensity, moreover, conquers—always in some people, and sometimes in all people—the prompting to question or criticize existing institutions and manners, or even to assert a rational preference in regard to them.

I know not how else to explain, for example, the slavish endurance by men, for well over a century, of the miserably unaesthetic, unhygienic, and uncomfortable clothing assigned to them by fashion. Nor otherwise can one account for the sheep-like manner in which women follow every vagary of the mode, even when the dominant style must, for aesthetic or hygienic reasons, be intensely disagreeable to them. For some years now we have seen the ladies going about with objects upon their heads that look like freaks designed for a Hallowe'en or Mardi Gras; and I am told that the sensible women who object to these fripperies find enormous difficulty in procuring headgear that satisfies their own standards of taste and dignity.

The same influence can be seen at work regarding fashions in oratory and literary style. A horde of writers always adopt the mannerisms of the most popular contemporary authors. And every great actor has his host of small imitators.

Now some portion of everybody's conduct, and the greater part of most people's, even when it is not wrong, remains sub-moral, because it represents only this unreflective imitation. The sole question such people ask about anything is, "Is it done?" If it is "done," people find in this mere fact the only sanction they desire for their own action. In the jargon of the present day, such conduct is called behavior according to "*mores*," or "folkways."

The first condition of intelligent judgment is to remember that this kind of behavior must always be distinguished from moral conduct. For the first condition of anything worthy of that name is that it shall represent choice determined by rational conviction. Lord Russell, with his pungent fashion of expressing the bitterness of his prejudices, often lets fall a phrase which is useful for a purpose quite different than he intends. He does this in a passage of his book on "Marriage and Morals," where he defines conscience as "the unreasoning and more or less unconscious acceptance of precepts learnt in early youth," and in the inference he draws from this that a person's conscience "is never wiser than its possessor's nurse or mother."

This seems to me valuable on the *lucus a non lucendo,* or "reverse English" principle. I learned the meaning of that principle in childhood from one of my classmates at school. I asked him why a certain King in English history was called Edward the Confessor; his reply was, "Because he was never known to confess anything." Similarly, I find in Lord Russell's phrase a very precise definition of what conscience is *not*. It is a good description of that inferior substitute which all of us sometimes follow (and some always follow) when the real conscience is asleep, or drugged, or dead.

It is not uncommon for conscience to be lulled into a state of partial sleep or anaesthesia by the hypnotizing influence of our surroundings. Critical attention may easily go off guard or become fatigued. We are liable to be immensely influenced by suggestion. There is a natural tendency to conform to conventions; and within limits this is commendable, seeing that the conventions are often useful and necessary. We seldom trouble, however, to ask whether any given convention is really so, or whether it may not impel us to conduct which our moral judgment ought to disapprove, or whether a better and more useful rule could not be devised. There must needs be arbitrary rules of action prescribed for many contingencies, in order that each person may safely reckon upon the action of others. It matters not in the least, for example, on which side of the road we drive, provided only that we all use the same one. Dangerous as road travel now is, it would be yet more fatally chaotic if each individual were allowed to indulge his whim by driving on the left in a country where the prevalent rule is to drive on the right, or vice versa. But this very necessity for conventions, coupled with the tendency to accept existing ones uncritically, is precisely the reason why bad political practices, low moral codes and unethical religious beliefs and customs have always lasted so long. A mature conscience, we may say, is at least as rare a thing as a mature intellect, if not even rarer.

Plato, to be sure, makes Socrates say that "an uncriticized life is not worth living." I hope that every reader of this book will agree with him. Nevertheless, this was the judgment of an intellectual aristocrat, a uniquely gifted thinker, the most eminent member of the most highly intellectual community that has yet existed. The mass of men certainly do not agree with Socrates on this point. It must be recognized, indeed, that relatively few are capable of the immense and sustained effort required for the effective criticism of life. Human beings in general do not wish to live adventurously or dangerously. They want the comfortable life, alike in the material and in the mental sphere. "Safety first" is a slogan to which, overtly or tacitly, most men have always given their allegiance; and this accounts for the unrebuked persistence of many iniquities.

This is, in fact, the reason why the collective moral progress of mankind, even in the most advanced nations, has been so discouragingly slow. It takes a quite exceptional mind to appraise its own conduct, and that of the group to which it belongs, impartially and with original ethical insight. And it requires a spirit still rarer to be able to secure the acceptance by others of its own moral discoveries or innovations.

Perhaps the greatest of the practical difficulties in this matter is the distressing fact that even our good customs, as Tennyson said, may "corrupt the world"— not, of course, because they are good, but because they are *customs;* for this means that they are simply handed on as traditions or taboos, and become stereotyped codes for the many who never dream of asking whether they are right or wrong. Not only in remote ages, and not only among contemporary savages, but in our own community we can observe this conformity to established modes of behavior which are never evaluated. And we may notice the storms of protest that are sometimes aroused by the most trivial departure from an habitual custom, even though no hint of moral wrong or harm is produced by it. Witness the uproar of controversy that was provoked by the proclamation of the President in fixing Thanksgiving for 1939 *on its usual date,* the fourth Thursday of November. There happened to be five Thursdays in that month; and the common thought-less assumption was that the *last* Thursday of Novem-ber is the only "correct" date for Thanksgiving Day. The President violated the letter of this routine habit for no other purpose than to preserve its utilitarian purpose, by leaving a few more "shopping days" avail-able between Thanksgiving and Christmas. Yet to judge from the hubbub this aroused, one would almost have thought that he had committed sacrilege or treason.

Thanks to this rigid conservatism of obedience to custom, good or bad, it has come about that many thinkers have altogether denied the existence of an in-trinsic difference between right and wrong, and a real power in man which discriminates between them, and commands him to follow the right. They say that all so-called morals are in reality only *mores;* that nothing is really good or bad, but only custom makes things to be thought so.

This denial is absurd; for, as we have seen, the authority upon man of the moral judgment and its verdicts is on all fours with the authority of reason and its findings. If our general education had advanced to the point where the moral power was exercised even to the extent that the rational power has been freely and fruitfully exercised in science, this denial could never

have been made; or, if made, it could not have persisted. It is thoroughly shallow and superficial, because
history certifies that there actually has been moral progress. The question, moreover, can be brought to the test
of every thinking man's experience. Concrete moral
judgments are constantly passed by the very men who
deny the existence of a "moral faculty" or of any
objective difference between right and wrong. Thus
out of their own mouths their theory is refuted, and
the reality of what they deny is established.

Now the training of reason can only proceed by way
of preliminary submission to authority and imitation of
examples. The education of every child requires an
initial stage of docility and obedience; a stage in which
he believes things on the unquestioned authority of his
teachers. There is no other way by which human beings can advance to maturity of understanding, or
attain to mastery of the subject-matter they study, or
of the art of learning itself. Yet it is obvious that the
final purpose of education would be frustrated if this
last stage were never reached, but the pupil instead
remained forever in his original condition of docile sub-
missiveness. The proper function of authority is to render itself unnecessary, and bring about its own super-
session, at the earliest possible moment. Thus the wise
Francis Bacon remarks that "disciples do owe unto
masters only a temporary belief, and a suspension of
their own judgment until they be fully instructed, and
not an absolute resignation or perpetual captivity."

My present purpose is to maintain, and if possible to demonstrate, that the process of moral development should take a similar course to a like end; and that our education in this department is not completed until independent originality is achieved. The child must, indeed, follow examples. The grown man should not. If he does, or so far as he does, he proves that he is not fully grown.

But here an obvious question is to be anticipated. "Is it not better," I shall be asked, "that the many should follow good examples rather than bad ones, seeing that they will follow something outside themselves in any case, and that they cannot or will not reach the ethical maturity of which you speak?"

Before answering this question, one may be permitted to point out that the last assertion is a gratuitous assumption based upon a misunderstanding. I am far from agreeing that it is impossible for the many to reach ethical maturity. The undisputed fact that they do not do so at present is no proof that they cannot. This misunderstanding arises from failure to discriminate between moral and mental maturity, or to observe the great difference between the qualifications required for the saint and those necessary to make the master in science or philosophy. The capacity for goodness in motivation and action is, I am convinced, much commoner than the capacity for high intellectual achievement. Many most genuine saints have been entirely undistinguished for mental eminence. I believe that the mine-run of our humanity turns up a thousand possible saints for each potential Einstein or Newton that it yields us.

But to come now to our question. So long as people, whether by reason of youth or (in later years) through lack of the necessary effort or the right teaching, remain at the stage where they needs must be followers and imitators, it is an obvious truism that good examples are better for them than bad ones. But this does not change the fact that the end and aim of all moral education should be to raise them above the stage of following examples; precisely as in art the goal of education is to produce creative artists, and not copyists; and in science the purpose is to produce original researchers and discoverers, and not mere assimilators of what is already known.

As authority for this assertion that our purpose should be to outgrow authority, all the great masters of ethical discernment and development could be cited. It certainly was not the fault of Socrates if the young men imitated him or believed things simply because he asserted them. No doubt they did this, because young men always do. Yet Socrates constantly urged them not to act thus. He declared that he "would have them to be thinking of the truth and not of Socrates." It was an affront to his deepest convictions for any man to accept even them upon the strength of his belief in them.

Nor, certainly, was it any fault of Jesus Christ, or of the line he took in spiritual matters, that his followers down to this day have substituted the imitation of his acts and words for the assimilation of his standards of valuation, and principles of action. Yet this marks precisely the difference between false and true discipleship to any great man. Jesus struggled and labored against the false kind, and begged people to use their own judgment independently. "Why even of yourselves judge ye not what is right?" Fortunately, his earliest competent disciple, St. Paul, did understand and apply this portion of his master's teaching.

When we fix our minds upon the best-authenticated portions of the teaching of Jesus, and interpret these (as they should always be interpreted) by the light of the commentary upon them furnished by St. Paul's line of thought and action, we see that the whole Christian movement was intended precisely to emancipate people from routine and code, from authority and external observance, by inspiring them with freely-accepted standards of valuation and springs of action, in order that they might become, in the great phrase of the New Testament, "a law unto themselves." There are no passages in the Bible better worth studying than those portions of St. Paul's Epistles which deal with this theme. He expounds "the perfect law" as "the law of liberty." "Stand fast," he urges his followers, "in the liberty wherewith Christ hath made us free."

In the effort to expound and make clear a doctrine which was then startlingly novel, he carefully imparts a new meaning to a current word. Judaism had been a religion of obedience to "the Law." It had come to consist in the minute observance of a multitude of precepts

and ritual practices, many of them morally meaningless. To all this St. Paul deliberately opposed the
doctrine of "grace," which he defined as meaning spiritual self-determination; the attainment of autonomous
insight into what is good; the doing what one's own
conscience proclaims to be right, even though most people think otherwise; and the neglecting of many things
other people think right (such as dietary taboos and the
observance of days), because one's own deliberate judgment proclaimed them superfluous. Yet he would have
his converts bear always in mind the rule that one should
not, without great reason, do anything that might
"cause a brother to stumble."

But again I shall be asked—as indeed I have been—
"Why should you think the following of examples dangerous? Why is it not a good thing? If the action performed by some great man was right when he did it,
how can I be wrong in copying him?" The full answer
to this involves the profoundest principle, not only of
ethical action, but of all free, spiritual and genuinely
personal religion. To put it as it was challengingly
expressed by Emerson, "Nothing is at last sacred but
the integrity of your own mind."

This saying, to be sure, may sound anarchistic, or
dangerously individualistic. But if so, it is because due
attention has not been paid to the meaning of the word
integrity. That word means *wholeness* as well as *gen-
uineness;* and we must add (as Emerson clearly taught
in his essays on "Self-Reliance" and on "Spiritual
Laws") that it must also mean wholeness and genuine-

ness according to one's own bent, one's individual uniqueness, and the differentiated form of ripened maturity prefigured in that uniqueness. Integrity in this sense can never be attained anarchically, or in solitude, but only by social action and interaction. It is the resultant of a man's maximum possible exertion of helpful influence upon others, and his maximum possible reception of helpful stimulus from them. The scholastic maxim, "Quidquid recipitur secundum modum recipientis recipitur,"—"Whatever is received is taken in according to the receiver's mental make-up,"—is in one sense a fact; in another and a higher sense, it is the very standard Emerson inculcated.

The same conception which we have traced in Socrates, Jesus, St. Paul, and Emerson, underlies the classical statement of Immanuel Kant:

"Imitation has no place in morals. Examples serve only to encourage to moral practice—to put beyond doubt the possibility of performing those duties unremittingly commanded by the law—and to exhibit to sense, in a tangible and outward substance, what the legislation of reason expresses only in the abstract and general; but their use is perverted when their origin in reason is overlooked, and conduct regulated upon the model of the example." *

According to all the high authorities we have cited, the essential demand laid upon each of us is to sound, as it were, an original note in the symphony of the world's spiritual music. Each of us is to contribute to the achievement of the universe through humanity that

* From "The Metaphysic of Ethics."

fraction, however slight, which only he can produce; for
if he fails in this, the total accomplishment will remain
forever incomplete. Now, whatever else may be possible
to an imitator, this clearly is not. Kant, moreover,
offers a second reason for declaring that "imitation has
no place in morals"; namely, that every occasion calling
for moral action has its unique phase, delicate adjust-
ment to which is requisite to render action upon it truly
ethical.

Nobody denies, of course, that there are certain broad
obvious duties that may be fulfilled by mere routine
acts; as when one writes a check for a contribution to
a Community Fund, or to some particular philanthropy
which has evoked one's sympathy. If men are hungry
they must be fed; if naked, they must be clothed. To
the provision of material requirements, we shall be told,
only a charitable motive is requisite. But even here discrimination is required. Precisely because the hungry
and naked are human personalities and not animals,
even the means of physical sustenance and protection
must be supplied for the sake of their effect upon that
in them which is not physical. If we desire, as we should,
to express respect for their souls and to elicit a response
from them, we must individualize our benefactions, so
that they shall make the right appeal to those affected.
There are ways of being "charitable" which insult men
and women, and arouse in them a just resentment. Too
much of our so-called philanthropy has always borne
this taint. It provided or bestowed the animal sustenance
as though *for* animals, and distributed its spare clothes

and cash with a churlish and embittering condescension. The charity of a Gradgrind may well be more hateful than his enmity. A Mr. Bumble's way of distributing "parish relief" may make it poisonous.

In the whole calendar of saints there is none more universally beloved and admired than St. Francis of Assisi. He is the poet of the devout life, and has long commanded as much affection and enthusiastic appreciation outside the Roman Church as within it. It may seem ungracious to criticize and point out the error of so beloved a man, or to indicate the like mistake made by that saint in fact, though not in title, Bishop Jeremy Taylor. Yet I cannot but think that both of them erred, and Thomas à Kempis with them, in their interpretation of Christianity as consisting in the *imitation* of Christ.

Thanks to this misleading idea, St. Francis fell into the fallacy of adopting as a virtue that "apostolic poverty" which in the case of Christ and his first followers was either a mere necessity imposed by their circumstances, or perhaps something that did not really exist; —for there is some reason for thinking that it was an illusion produced in the mind of St. Francis and other readers of the pre-critical period, through their misunderstanding of the Oriental and figurative language used in the Gospels. St. Francis took as his bride "the Lady Poverty." He lived in abject squalor, and would not allow his followers to own any possessions whatsoever. Yet Christ had never said that his disciples—even those who took nothing with them on their missionary journeys—should not receive payment for their work. His Apostles manfully insisted, as he had done, that the laborer is worthy of his hire.

What St. Francis failed to realize was that the renunciation of property is no remedy for abuses of property. The ethical problem concerning wealth is only solved by learning how to use it so as to promote the common good, and to be spiritually independent of it while possessing and using it. He alone is mature in this department of ethical practice who knows, like St. Paul, "both how to want and how to abound"; who possesses, but is not possessed by, his money and his worldly goods. As Dr. Inge truly said, Christ's main contribution to the theory of wealth was his insistence that riches are "grossly overvalued."

The failure of St. Francis's method was made clear by a painful fact which emerged within a generation or two of his death. He had promulgated a constitution for his monastic Order which strictly prohibited its members from acquiring possessions. But nothing could hinder wealth from being lavished upon the Order collectively; and as its members had never mastered the secret of the art of rightly using wealth, they proceeded promptly to misuse it, at least as badly as any of the other Orders had done.

Jeremy Taylor is one of the greatest masters of our literature. So sublime is his style and so profound his insight that Emerson justly called him "the Shakespeare of divines." Among his works is a voluminous narrative and interpretation of the life of Jesus, entitled

"The Great Exemplar." This phrase epitomizes the
error I am criticizing. If I am right, the work should
instead have been entitled "The Great Inspirer." All
the difference between sound and unsound ethical guidance lies here. Even though the statement may appear
paradoxical, I maintain that the imitation of Christ is
not Christian—not true to the genius of Christianity.
For whom did Jesus ever imitate? And where would his
greatness have been had he been an imitator? When,
moreover, did he ask to be imitated? We read in the
Gospels that he bade his followers "Learn of me," but
never that he said to them "Copy me."

I am not attempting by this argument to disparage
in any way the charm of hero-worship. This is one of
the greatest inspirations under which aspiring youth
can fall; and, though it necessarily undergoes modifica-
tions in our later years, when what John Morley called
"the exciting splendour of the dawn" has become a paler
and a soberer light, by which we see more clearly the
human failings and limitations of our heroes, it nevertheless remains a source of strength and "a joy for
ever," even to the oldest man. Assuredly I have nothing
to urge against it. To the contrary, I loathe the envious
meanness of many recent attempts to strip the haloes
from great figures in history, and, under pretense of
exposing truth, to besmirch and belittle them. Only with
people in whom greatness is dead could this pettiness
be possible. I am but pleading for discrimination in
hero-worship, and for a right understanding of what
Emerson justly called "the *uses* of great men."

Emerson, it will be remembered, tells the story of a boy who, after much admonitory repetition, was driven to cry out in desperation, "Damn George Washington!" (I strongly suspect that that boy's name was Ralph Waldo Emerson.) I think many a man will be able to understand and sympathize with the lad. His exclamation was not in the least intended to be disrespectful. It only meant that the poor, inarticulate, harassed boy realized that he had to be himself, and that he could not meet this demand upon him by imitating even the greatest and best of men. If he had been mature enough to express his thought completely, I think he would have put it thus: "I am not of course cursing Washington. I am only cursing your foolish habit of forgetting that Washington's circumstances and problems were his own, and not mine."

This is, at all events, a valid answer to many of those who urge examples upon us. *You* have not Washington's problems, or his duties, or his opportunities. It is even barely possible that you may be inferior to him in genius. But whoever you are, and whatever your tasks, you can draw immeasurable benefit from him by imbibing his breadth of mind, his unconquerable fortitude, his unweariable patience. Your true "use" of Washington is to make these qualities your own. Then, equipped with them and forgetting him, you are to face your own problems with original insight.

One of the most valuable fragments of the literature of this subject, to my thinking, is the essay entitled "My Station and Its Duties," contained in the "Ethical

Studies" of the philosopher F. H. Bradley. What it is right for me to do in my station can only be discerned by the insight developed through a careful study of its demands. General rules always need specialized modification to adapt them to particular cases. The more exactly right some great man's handling of his problem was, the more must it fail in precise applicability to mine. By all means let me con his problem and his handling of it; not, however, to spoil my own performance by imitating him, but to improve it by adapting my action as plastically to my exigencies as his was adapted to the conditions it had to meet.

To illustrate from a different field: every wise teacher of English will admonish his pupils not to try to imitate the style of Shakespeare or Milton or Emerson. He will urge them to learn the works of these masters by heart, to soak themselves in them, to regard them not as a task to be endured, but as a feast to be enjoyed. But then he will add, "When you yourself have to write, forget all about them, and express what you have to say in the shortest, clearest, and simplest way you can. Discriminating critics will perceive well enough that you have read these masters. They will feel something of them in your style. But they will above all things rejoice that you are not imitating them." Thus is it also in morals. The enlightened onlooker will be far more pleased by seeing the influence of Socrates and Jesus in a man's deeds than by hearing him quote their words.

Emerson rightly enough says, "Trust thyself." But what reason does he offer for the counsel? Here there

is a certain ambiguity. His oracular statements convey
an appearance (though not the reality) of contradic-
tion, and therefore need reconciliation. For the precept
of self-reliance, he seems to say, the reason is this:
"Thou art one organ of the Over-soul, the universal
spirit." Elsewhere, however, he rightly stresses the
uniqueness of individuals; and it is in this fact that the
best reason for self-reliance is to be found. So let us
rather say, "Be yourself (or, better, *Become* yourself
—make actual what is latent and hidden in yourself),
because it is your destiny to be a unique member of
the spiritual universe, an unprecedented synthesis of
the universal elements of man's higher nature, and thus
to make a contribution to the total achievement that can
come from nobody but yourself."

It is clear, as we have said, that this cannot be done
by imitating anybody. That procedure, carried beyond
the point to which it is admittedly necessary for educational purposes, is fatal to the very achievement for the
sake of which education is supplied. In order that one
may become a man, one must, in St. Paul's words, "put
away childish things." This does not in any sense mean
parting from the spiritual company of those to whom
we have initially looked as examples. It means that we
must cease to utilize them in this fashion; we must
abandon all thought of imitating them. Instead, we must
now draw upon them as inspirers, as living fountains
of that universal yet endlessly differentiated spiritual
life which we are to quicken in ourselves.

Only in this fashion, I hold, shall we be able to make

the proper use of our native tendency to imitate. The correct discipline to be imposed by reason upon this spontaneous, instinctive propension is to utilize it as a means for our education in order that we may pass beyond it, and become (as we may through diligence and good fortune) persons in whom our own juniors, in their turn, may profitably find objects of imitation during their ethical apprenticeship.

But if we ourselves remain imitators and example-followers, our juniors, with the unerring and disconcerting clarity of youth, will see us as *imitations* of those we have followed. This discovery will put a speedy end to our possibilities of usefulness to their education and development. For it is not possible, especially for aspiring youth, to admire or emulate copiers of others. Their healthy instinct is to adore the originality of which they themselves are as yet incapable; and no man can be exemplary to them who has not himself outgrown the status of a follower, even of the best examples.

CHAPTER VIII

MUST VIRTUE BEG PARDON OF VICE?

THE NOTION that "seeing is believing," coupled with the proneness of uncritical minds to misinterpret what they see, explains the extreme ease with which human beings become the victims of illusions. Let us begin by reminding ourselves of one of these illusions which is widely prevalent in regard to history.

The immense diversity of the externals of human life which characterizes uncivilized times as compared with the ages of civilization, and the striking contrasts between the different types of civilization from ancient times until now, often conceal from us the vitally important truth of the fundamental identity of human nature in all times and places. The common obliviousness to this fact constitutes the illusion to which I refer.

Any real comprehension of history requires a clear understanding of this situation. When we look at the strange figures to be seen on Egyptian or Chaldean monuments, or at pictures of Greeks or Romans "in their habits as they lived," we incline to feel that some impassable gulf of alienness divides us from such people. The Chaldean's square-cut beard, strange armor and rigid posture, and the singular attitudes and incomprehensible activities of the Egyptian as painting and sculpture disclose him to us, make us forget that the originals of these portraits were immeasurably more like us than different from us. We find extraordinary difficulty in realizing that they and their kind were moved by thoughts and feelings, emotions, propensions, desires, hopes and fears, completely identical with our own.

To be sure, this illusion vanishes before thorough study. But the majority of men never have time or inclination for such study. This is unfortunate, because the more closely we con and comprehend the records of far-off times and lands, the more does the impression of difference fade. Our great Egyptologist, Dr. Breasted, proved to us how among the Egyptians, nearly five thousand years ago, ethical standards— such as the idea of impartial justice, and the equality of all men before the law—were as clearly perceived to be necessary and binding as they are among us, and that the vices against which these standards had then to be maintained were the same as those against which we struggle today.

We need but to read the easily accessible works of Plato and Aristotle to realize that the Greeks, for all the strangeness of their language, costumes, religion, and customs, were yet men and women made up of and actuated by the same instincts, emotions, and psychic inclinations as ourselves. The pages of Tacitus and Livy make it abundantly clear that the politicians and soldiers who swayed the destinies of the Roman Republic and Empire were motivated by the same ambitions and rivalries, the same jealousies and greeds, and occasionally by the same promptings of lofty and self-sacrificing patriotism, as are exhibited in every page of our own history.

We must not, indeed, minimize the differences either between communities or between individuals. And we must never forget that the elements of the common human nature are imparted to each person in some uniquely differentiated measure. Nevertheless, the differences are like the various picture-patterns upon tapestries, which yet are all woven of the same stuff. This stuff, moreover—the common matter of our humanity—is a baffling compound of elements of littleness and greatness. The primordial part of it consists of an animal substratum, wherein we find—in full completeness, so far as we can judge—the entire nature and full range of motivations which underlie the feelings and activities of the higher apes and other advanced mammals. But supervening upon this substratum, transfusing and transforming and disciplining it, is the mysteriously novel human endowment of reason, conscience, and aesthetic power.

It is in the endlessly varying degrees to which these distinctive gifts are actualized that individuals and communities have always differed, and presumably always will. But we must beware of overlooking or forgetting the background of identity against which these differences are deployed. When we study some primitive tribe, whose language is devoid of verbs and abstract nouns, and who have never learned even to count up to ten, and compare it with a community like that which literature and history show us to have existed in Athens in the Periclean Age, or with the extraordinary men and women who are to be found assembled at any international gathering of scientists, the staggering and apparently unbridgeable contrast makes it hard for us to realize that the essential make-up of all the groups is the same. Yet this beyond question is the case.

Moreover, among mankind in all times and communities, the animal substratum of their common nature has tended to overbear the high human endowment interblended with it. Indeed, to this day, some statisticians tell us that although individuals act reasonably, collectivities never do; and therefore that predictions based on the expectation that collective action will be expressive of blind egoistic folly will generally prove trustworthy. There is a measure of truth in this statement; and this is the reason why progress in the ethical essentials of civilization (as distinguished from the progress of mechanical inventions, arts and sciences) is so distressingly slow.

But we must not allow the statisticians to make us forget the painful truth that even individuals only act reasonably at some times. Every man who makes the most moderate attempt to strive towards ideals finds to his cost and sorrow, as St. Paul found, that there is "a law in his members" which fights against the higher "law of his mind." The animals that we have been for millions of years put up a mighty struggle against the men we are only now beginning to be.

This is also the reason why we discover the same manifestations of egotism, jealousy, and pettiness, the same
resentment of every kind of superiority, in all periods
of history and in every land that has traceable records.
Indeed, I was set upon my present theme by hearing a
young man remark that among his business associates
he found himself constantly ridiculed and scoffed at for
expressing respect for ethical ideas and standards. This
was a peculiarity in him which to his associates seemed
self-evidently to attest either naïveté or hypocritical
affectation. It is possible that the young fellow who
told me this was hardly aware how old a story he was
repeating. His words impressed me the more, however,
because it happened that on the previous evening I had
witnessed Mr. Maurice Evans's notable performance of
"Hamlet," so that the familiar words addressed by
Hamlet to his mother were ringing anew in my ears:

> Forgive me this my virtue;
> For in the fatness of these pursy times
> Virtue itself of vice must pardon beg,
> Yea, curb and woo for leave to do him good.

What is more, this attitude of general public contempt or skepticism toward all pretensions to a standard
of conduct more exacting than the prevailing one,
was no more a novelty in the days of Shakespeare than
it is in the America of 1941. The proof of this can be
found in the most ancient literature,—the pages of
Plato, in particular, being replete with evidence of it.
Every reader of "The Republic" has felt the powerful

depth and truth of the great myth of the Cave: that cave wherein men were so fettered by the necks that they could look only before them and not behind, and therefore did not know that the things whereon they gazed were only an assemblage of shadows cast by the light from behind. But among these captives a few, a very few, somehow escaped from their bonds, turned their eyes away from the shadows, and saw the light and the realities behind which projected them. These were able to struggle up into the world of realities which the shadows reflected; until at last they attained the vision of that Sun of Reason and Righteousness which is the true source of all light in this our lower world. But when they returned and endeavored to make known what they had seen, and how the captives were deceived, they were met with scorn, fury, impenetrable misunderstanding, and incredulity.

Here we have a parable, not only of Plato's philosophy and the reception accorded to it by the unthinking many, but likewise of the entire career of Socrates; just as in the glorious story of his trial and death we have the proof that the parable faithfully depicted the facts. Grecian story also records for us the lot of Aristides, deservedly surnamed "The Just." His very integrity probably caused his banishment; men voted against him not because they disliked being treated justly, but because his character accused them and showed them up to themselves.

It is clear enough from the New Testament, moreover, that Jesus anticipated a similar fate for his own followers; since he is reported to have forewarned them, "Blessed are ye when men shall revile you, and persecute you, and say all manner of evil against you falsely for my sake and the Gospel's." He, too, had experienced the sneers of the worldly-wise, and found himself confronted with the scornful repudiation of his teaching by "his mother and brethren."

No literary artist has ever drawn a more powerful and varied picture of this ever-recurring situation than John Bunyan. A great part of the "Pilgrim's Progress" is a series of illustrations of the persecutions lavished upon the handful of men who took seriously and endeavored to live up to the religion which the persecutors themselves professed. Seeing this religion sincerely practiced exposed these people to themselves, and filled them with a vehement hatred of those who forced the painful contrast upon them. The story of "Vanity Fair," of the trial of Christian and Faithful, and the martyrdom of Faithful, is a true picture of the kind of hostility in the teeth of which practically all human advancement, in all times and lands, has had to be won.

Now Bunyan lived at a period which in many respects was very like our own, and in which, consequently, the opportunities for making the observations to which we owe the grand picture of "Vanity Fair" were exceptionally abundant. England in those days was undergoing just such a reaction against moral earnestness, and just such a debauch of skepticism concerning all pretensions to it, as the past quarter-century has witnessed. The Puritans from 1642 to 1660 had

had their brief and unhappily abused period of dominance. Not satisfied with the suppression of real vices, they had undiscriminatingly crushed many quite innocent and even laudable expressions of the common desires for happiness and artistic satisfaction. They had closed the theaters, and made it criminal to give or to witness performances of "Hamlet," "Lear," and "Othello." They had made of Christmas a season of gloomy penance instead of kindly jollity. They had banished the maypole and the old country dances. They so completely destroyed the fine musical culture which had before prevailed that for more than two centuries afterwards the English remained under the reproach of being an unmusical people. In short, they had acted generally upon their grotesque principle that anything pleasant or beautiful, anything that made people happy, must *ipso facto* be sinful.

The result of all this was that the Puritans incurred the hatred and resentment not only of people whose tastes and characters were actually vicious, but also of the great multitude of ordinary citizens who were neither especially vicious nor especially virtuous. So deep was this anger that these people were willing to allow the inevitable reaction against "the reign of the saints" to run to very undesirable lengths before they recoiled against its excesses. It happened, moreover, that the restored King, despite great superficial charm and a veneer of culture and fine manners, was one of the most cynically selfish wretches, one of the most worthless wasters and roués, who ever disgraced a throne. His Court became a center at which every vice was fashionable; and his coterie set the tone of sneering at any virtue whatsoever, and disbelieving in its reality. Ostensibly a member of the Church of England, with secret but finally indulged leanings towards Roman Catholicism, Charles II was in reality a materialistic atheist of the school of Thomas Hobbes, but quite devoid of the patriotism and other virtues of that school.

The writers and dramatists of the day did what the bulk of such people always do. Partly from a propension to loose living, but far more from a sycophantic desire to curry favor with those in high places, and thereby gain money and success for themselves, they took their tone from the Court of Charles II, and produced a literature which remained unparalleled in its foulness, moral degradation and skepticism, until the similar cult of filth that has sprung up in our own day.

Like that of our own day, this declension of literature and drama was kept in countenance by a philosophy of moral nihilism, the beginnings of which can be read in the works of Hobbes, and its culmination in those of Mandeville. The latter, a Dutch physician whose mature career was spent in England, and who wrote our language with great felicity and charm, presents such a degraded estimate of human nature as had never been reached, in the whole history of literature, until the contemporary insanity of behaviorism. Man, according to Mandeville, is and can be nothing else than a pleasure-seeking animal. Consequently, all forms of disinterested conduct, or any kind of moral virtue, are psychological impossibilities; and the profession of them is a hypocritical affectation.*

It should give encouragement to the many who are dismayed by the seeming eclipse of moral standards in our own time to remember that whereas many instances of such degradation have occurred in history, they have invariably been followed by revivals, both of a sounder philosophy and a more civilized level of practice. The spiritual nature of man cannot be permanently eclipsed, for the simple reason that it is an indefeasible reality; and accordingly any temporary suppression or denial of it is bound to provoke a reaction.

Thus in the seventeenth century the disease produced its own antidotes, in the form of voluntary societies for the reformation of manners, and in a counter literature, among the writers of which were not only clergymen and professional moralists, but also brilliant men of letters. These turned the weapons of the degraded dramatists and poets against them. A remarkable instance of this was the book by the preacher Jeremy Collier, published in 1700, under the title, "A Short View of the Profaneness and Immorality of the English Stage." Herein he called a spade a spade with exemplary plainness, and attacked the chief offenders by name; with the striking result that old John Dryden, the master poet and dramatist of his time, publicly admitted that Collier

* The best-known of Mandeville's works propounding this doctrine is "The Fable of the Bees"; but it comes out even more blatantly in a less familiar book called, "An Inquiry into the Origin of Honour, and the Usefulness of Christianity in War."

had justly accused him, and professed his penitence for the harm that he had done.

Thus after nearly forty years of scornful satire poured upon the everyday virtues of marital fidelity, common honesty, and even ordinary decency, a new school of writers sprang up and effected a much-needed disinfection of the manners and tone of society. The most widely popular of these were Addison and Steele. We still read with inexhaustible pleasure their delightful commentaries upon everyday character and manners in "The Tatler" and "The Spectator." They put a stop to the leakage from the sewers into the *belles lettres* of their day, and succeeded in evoking a general disgust against the filthiness which had been fashionable in the preceding generation.

The manners of the eighteenth century remained bad enough in all conscience; and the complacency with which it accepted the illiteracy, moral degradation, and economic exploitation of the poor, is to us inconceivable. We are appalled upon realizing how little the consciences of such outstanding men as Bishop Butler, Dr. Johnson, and Edmund Burke seem to have been disturbed by these unbearable evils. Nevertheless, it is both true and notable that the literature of the eighteenth century, almost throughout, is one sustained attack upon the personal vices which prevailed among the middle and upper classes of society.

This fact furnishes a striking contrast to the literature of the period from 1660 to 1700, which, with lamentably few exceptions, had been a pandering to the prevalent viciousness of taste and practice. Even Fielding, plain-spoken as he is, and scathingly as he satirizes the priggish and mercenary moralism embodied in certain characters of Richardson, is as solidly on the side of decency, just dealing, and honest industry, as are those sermons in pictures, "Marriage à la Mode," "The Rake's Progress," and "The Idle and the Industrious Apprentice," of his admired friend Hogarth.

Never again, in fact, from the time of Dryden's repentance until our own days, did drama and fiction frankly abandon their high prerogative of improving instead of degrading the taste, manners, and conduct of their spectators and readers. This remains true, despite the fact that during the first three decades of the nineteenth century there appeared once more in the upper circles of British society a festering center of corruption, the nucleus of which was that peculiarly repulsive person, the Prince Regent, afterwards King George IV. The lowering of the tone of social life, for which this new irruption from the Augean stables was responsible, was the very cause which produced, by way of reaction, what we now think of as the primness and prudery of "Victorianism."

This is a truth so little realized that it may be well to pause upon it for a moment. The majority of people born since the end of the nineteenth century seem to be entirely unaware that the "Victorianism" against which they have reacted so violently was itself just such a recoil against a previous period of debauchery as history shows it to have been. The fact is unquestionable, and the evidence for it is easily accessible. Not only in literature and the arts, but in the whole tone of public and private life, and more especially in the quickening of the social conscience against the prevalent evils of illiteracy, moral degradation, and poverty among the working people, the Victorian period, on both sides of the Atlantic, was one of steady improvement and moral advancement.

It cannot, indeed, be denied that the period was over-puritanized; and, as always happens at such times, there was a great deal of hypocrisy, since over-much pretension to virtue is the best camouflage for secretly-practiced vices. For in those days social ostracism would have penalized the open avowal of many vicious practices which nevertheless continued to be secretly indulged.

Now hypocrisy cannot be successfully defended, even by so clever a satirist as Samuel Butler. Yet I hold it no offense to good morals to maintain that the state and tone of society are better when the vices of the vicious have to be sedulously concealed, especially from the young, than they are when these vices can be flaunted for the corruption of the young without the offender incurring the danger of ostracism or any other social penalty.

The pursuit of this thought brings us directly to the difficult practical problem which nowadays confronts every man and woman who desires to maintain, I will not say an exalted or saintly standard of virtue, but even what forty years ago would have been called "ordinary decency"; that is, the traditional standards of family life and honor, of temperance in conduct, honesty in business, and cleanliness in speech. The current vogue in literature and drama, and the widely-tolerated standards of social conduct, now fall so abysmally below these very moderate levels that those who seek to uphold them feel themselves constantly put out of countenance and constrained to adopt a defensive and apologetic tone. Nowadays, in fact, virtue constantly feels compelled to beg pardon of vice.

What is a young man to do when he finds himself in the predicament of the youth whose words I have quoted? He does not wish to be a prig, or even to seem one. He has to recognize the genuine difficulty that too violent or outspoken opposition to the prevailing base practices may seriously injure his prospects of business or professional advancement. Is it his duty to incur this economic martyrdom? Is he under obligation to submit to ostracism from his social set for making himself the evangelist of higher standards of conduct and taste?

Or what is a young girl to do who detests (as it can hardly be doubted that thousands secretly do detest) the drinking and smoking habits which prevail among her kind today, and the South-Sea-Island standards of personal adornment which the fashion imposes? If her practice constitutes too conspicuous and aggressive an example of abstention from these excesses, she may well feel herself in danger of missing those normal and legitimate fruitions of life to which young women naturally look forward.

The answer to these questions (which we shall endeavor to give in a moment) is clear enough in principle, however difficult its practical application may prove in individual cases. Virtue must never condescend to beg pardon of vice. So paradoxical a reversal of all right and reason involves what Hooker called "the singular disgrace of nature, and the utter disturbance of that divine order whereby the pre-eminence of chiefest acceptation is by the best things worthily challenged."

But the initiative towards reversing this absurd situation should come from older people, and particularly from those who are relatively secure in regard to professional, economic, or social standing. Such persons should lead the way, alike by practice and by outspoken utterance, in making clear what in their judgment is virtuous and what is vicious. The time is more than ripe for a revolt against the tacit assumption that these questions are to be settled by counting heads, or by deference to the authority of popular and financially successful individuals. It is time for a general protest against the decivilizing assumption that anything whatsoever becomes "right" provided only that enough people practice it.

A heavy challenge falls upon the vast army of men and women who hold academic, pedagogical and clerical positions, to join in a concerted drive against the baseless philosophy of which all the various current manifestations of animalism are but so many expressions. The popular literature and the prevalent manners of today cry out their underlying dogma, that men are but animals who can seek only the satisfaction of their appetites and impulses. Any pretense to the contrary is regarded either as self-deception or as sheer hypocrisy. This is the secret formula of what, with appropriate vulgarity, is called "debunking," not only of the characters and reputations of great men and women in history, but of those standards of decency, right and dignity, which thousands of people have revolted against as unbearable restrictions upon their just self-expression and proper freedom.

That this debased estimate of human nature is grotesquely false, all history shouts at us; or rather it would do so if our ears were not deafened to its voice by the still louder braying of the manifold mechanisms which broadcast the current immoralisms. But the speediest way of proving its falsity, and the one nearest to hand, would be an analysis of the concrete moral judgments uttered every passing day by any representative spokesman of those who profess to believe in it. Such persons constantly condemn the actions and motives of others by labeling them "insincere," "hypocritical," or "camouflage for secretly-indulged vices of their own."

But how can there be any point in such condemnations, unless it be previously agreed that sincerity, frankness, candor, and the eschewing of the implied vices, are *duties* with which men can and ought to comply? Yet if they are duties, it automatically follows that men are something other than animals; for there is nothing in the merely animal nature which could render possible the conception of duty or the recognition of its authority. And if men can fairly be blamed for not complying with these standards, it can only be upon supposition that they possess the power to comply with them; and this means that they are not creatures of materialistic or any other sort of external determinism.

In short, the professed repudiators of all moral standards reveal nothing but their own irrational inconsistency; for every one of the standards they repudiate is implied in the criticisms they pass upon other people.

Nietzsche, who commended an essentially erroneous philosophy to the world by the merits of great literary power and intensely realistic insight into human littleness, dwelt much upon the resentment of the underman against greatness. It was, indeed, his intense repugnance to this common failing which inspired his furious contempt for democracy and his enthusiastic advocacy of the claims of that mythological personage, the Superman. But the measure of truth which Nietzsche's judgment undoubtedly contains constitutes no proof that democracy is wrong. It merely demonstrates how very far short we fall at present of realizing the best possibilities of democracy; but this, of course, no true democrat has ever doubted. Before we can have a truly admirable democracy, we shall have to produce a generation of aristocrats; that is to say, persons who so

disinterestedly love the best that they are willing to
subordinate themselves to superior manifestations of
it in others.

The self-confidence of vice when kept in countenance
by numbers, and its attitude of sneering superiority to
the virtue of individuals supposed to be lonely, or
minorities supposed to be insignificant, is the chief contemporary manifestation of that "resentment of the underman against greatness" which Nietzsche denounced.
It is a self-betraying jealousy against those who are and
do what the scorner secretly knows he ought to be and
to do,—a disguised confession of their superiority and
his own inferiority.

But vice, despite its secret misgivings, *is* kept in
countenance by numbers. And so again we come to our
question, "How is this unnatural condition of things
to be overcome?" I would answer, By a truer and
stronger self-confidence upon the part of those who
know that the many are wrong, and by the banding together of the minority which is thus convinced. If, for
instance, at every rowdy party during a holiday season,
all those who detest the excesses so commonly indulged
in could recognize each other, and could join together
to manifest their detestation, I believe that a surprisingly sudden and extensive change would be witnessed.

A current anecdote (in all probability based on fact)
illustrates this situation. It is the story of a college girl
who attended, in a friend's room, the sort of meeting
which even among "co-eds" is designated as "a bull
session." The party being assembled and the door

locked, this girl asked her hostess, "Are you quite sure
that nobody else is coming?" "Yes," was the answer.
"And are you certain that nobody outside will know
what goes on here?" Again the answer was in the affirmative. "Well," said the first speaker, "then thank God
we need not smoke!"

I am convinced that if all the girls who really hate
drinking and smoking, and only indulge in these practices because they fear the social consequences of refusal, could muster courage to wear a button or badge
whereby they could recognize each other, these practices
among young women would speedily become as uncommon, and be thought as offensive, as they were in Victorian days. I also believe that if all the young women
whose native good taste makes them abhor the disgusting practice of painting their lips and fingernails like
Fiji Island savages could recognize each other, these
imbecile fashions would soon become as obsolete as by
every principle of common sense and human dignity
they ought to be.

A similar surprising alteration would, I am sure, be
brought about in any company of men in a business
house or factory where, as things now stand, one who
boldly upholds honorable ethical standards will be
sneered at by a dozen, while the rest remain silent
through cowardice or self-distrust. If but a few of this
last group would conquer their pusillanimity and follow their consciences by siding with the protester, the
apparent majority against virtue would be greatly re-

duced, and might easily be revealed as actually a minority.

These considerations furnish the greatest of all reasons for the existence of ethical and religious fellowships. Churches and kindred societies, at all events when they are true to their professed principles, afford to the individual who is thrown into the conflicts of life the assurance that he does not stand alone, even when he seems to do so. They reinforce him by the knowledge that a large number of people recognize the validity of the decrees of his own conscience; and thereby he receives spiritual support and help in fighting his battles. Truly did William Morris say that "Fellowship is life, and lack of fellowship is death." This is true whatever the nature and objects of any given fellowship may be, —even if it be one of pirates or gangsters; but above all is it true in the case of associations which stand for the ideal of right. Hence the soundness of Felix Adler's watchword: "Fellowships we want that will hold not religion as a duty, but duty as a religion."

Here, however, I once again find myself using a word against which, I am assured, the younger generation are in revolt. They have no patience (said my informant) with the word *duty*, or the idea for which they assume it to stand. They prefer to talk about *responsibility*, and are willing to heed exhortations to them to act responsibly. To this I can but answer, in the first place, that these two words are properly identical in meaning, and that to imagine otherwise is to betray a grotesque ignorance of the significance of everyday language. In the second place I would add that whatever may be the case with the pampered youth of some particularly favored class, the word "duty" has never become unpopular with *real men*,—such, for example, as firemen, policemen, and the men of the Army and Navy. All of these still speak proudly and self-respectingly of "going on duty," and react as angrily to any charge of dereliction of their duty as ever did any of their Victorian or Puritanical ancestors.

If, then, there really is, in the circles of our "gilded youth," a revolt against the word "duty," this can only mean that the parents, teachers, and clergy, under whose influence these circles have grown up, have neglected *their* duty by allowing this to occur. The remedy for this neglect must be effected through sounder teaching (beginning in the nursery) both in discrimination of the meaning of words, and in discipline in those habits of action which are the roots of virtue. There would surely be little difficulty for intelligent parents or teachers to instruct a child regarding what is *due to it*, and what is *due from it* to others. This, and this alone, is what the word "duty" means; and every human being is *responsible* for rendering what is due from him or her.

The particular "disease of the age"—and of so many other ages—which we have here discussed is due in its present phase to two causes: one being the doctrine of human animalism; the remedy for which, as we have throughout insisted, is a truer philosophy, which all who understand it are responsible for teaching. The other cause I take to be that amazing fad of the modern

education which falsely pretends to be "progressive,"
which consists in "deferring to the personality of the
child" long before it is possible for the child to *be* a
personality, except incipiently.

As a remedy for this, there must be a return, not to
the errors and excessive severities of the past, but to
what is sound in the idea of discipline; by which I understand an educational catering to what experienced
adults know the child *needs,* instead of an anti-educa-
tional pandering to what it consciously *wants:* the
same rule, in fact, for the child's mind that everybody
agrees should be applied to its body.

By following these two lines of thought and action,
we shall hasten the advent of a state of things in which
children, no longer "spoiled," will cease to grow up
into yet more spoiled adolescents and ruined adults; a
state of things in which virtue will no longer feel constrained to beg pardon of vice, because vice itself will
be socially repudiated, so that those who cannot be
really cured of it will at least find themselves constrained to conceal sedulously their practice of it.

CHAPTER IX

LIFE'S DEEPEST CRAVING

THERE ARE times when, to our overwrought emotions, the chaotic maladjustment of human affairs seems to extend even to the realm of nature. The severe winter of 1939-40, for example, which throughout the Northern Hemisphere was the harshest and coldest for more than half a century, would certainly have been classed by the superstition of our forefathers as in some sense an effect of the wars raging in Europe and in China. The occurrence of Easter here * in weather more wintry than that of Christmas at least chimed with our feeling that "the time is out of joint" more than ever before.

This feeling, however, reflects an illusion which the slightest glance at history suffices to correct. That human life is shot through with tragedy, and that "man is born to trouble as the sparks fly upward," is a conviction which thoughtful people have never, in any age, been able long to escape. For this, remember, is not a thing which pessimists have affirmed and optimists denied. It is common ground between them. The difference in their views consists in their contrary explanations of the fact, which both recognize; and in their opposite beliefs as to whether any remedy or compensa-

* At Chicago in 1940.

tion for it is now available to man, or may be expected, or is indeed possible.

Pessimism, both according to the exact etymology of the word and the present views of those who profess it, is the conviction that not only are the frustrations, sorrows, pains, and other sufferings of life inevitable, but that they vastly overweigh any happiness or good fortune which may incidentally occur; that in human life sorrow and suffering are certain, joy and happiness uncertain, contingent, and rare; and that neither now nor in any foreseeable future will this cease to be the case, either for the individual or for mankind collectively.

Words are used so carelessly nowadays that any insistence upon their precise original or present meanings would probably seem ridiculously pedantic. Since, however, some regard for the meaning of the terms we use is essential to clear thinking, one may be permitted to point out that the words "pessimism" and "pessimist" in their full and exact original meaning *may* be justified; since there have been and still are men who, at least in theory, hold life to be absolutely and irredeemably evil, though they contradict themselves by remaining alive.* But the terms "optimism" and "optimist" are not properly applicable in any strict sense. Both these names for schools of thought or modes of feeling are Latin superlatives. "Optimism" thus means strictly that all is for the best in the best of possible worlds. It would oppose an unqualified good to the unqualified evil

* See on this point Chapter XII.

proclaimed by the pessimist. But the plain facts of life make it impossible for any sane man to say this seriously. To call a person an optimist, therefore, if we really know what we are affirming, and use our words as vehicles for thought instead of substitutes for it, is to insult his intelligence.

Certainly no man ought to be called an optimist simply on the ground that he is opposed to pessimism. What those who are commonly called optimists may and do affirm is this: that for the majority of individuals, as well as for the human race collectively, the good of life can, and does, outweigh its evil. On a calm survey of our own experience and that of others taken as a whole, we conclude that the good we have been privileged to experience preponderates over the ill. One who holds this conviction would be prepared, not perhaps to re-live his actual life (since this idea involves such contradictions as to be inconceivable), but to face a future of equal length, if he could be assured beforehand only of proportions of good and evil therein equal to those in his past. On those terms he would be prepared to endure the evil for the sake of the good. This attitude, of course, is not strictly "optimism." It is rather one of faith in the essential and fundamental goodness of life, despite all its admitted evil. And with this conviction I explicitly identify myself.*

It may be that in this attitude toward life there is involved an instinctive or subconscious conviction

* My reasons for doing so are set forth in Chapter XII, "Why Life Is Worth Living."

(which perhaps few persons trouble to think out) that the evils men suffer are relative and transient, whereas the good they experience is absolute and indestructible; that in some profound way evil belongs to time and good to eternity. Whether such a belief is philosophically justifiable I shall not here discuss. I believe, however, that, as a fact, this conviction has operated throughout history in reconciling people to their sufferings.

At least, one cannot easily explain otherwise not only the irrepressible hopefulness which has colored the religion and characterized the history of the Western World, but the very same quality of temperament and attitude in the Chinese people, who never had the Western religious doctrine to buttress it. Their collective sufferings have certainly been not less, and probably much greater, than other divisions of the human family have had to endure. Yet Dr. Lin Yutang assures us that they are still the same merry, light-hearted, cheerful people as they always were. And how otherwise than by some such subconscious belief can we explain the fact that, for all its professed pessimism, the Hindu people, both before and since the days of Buddha, have clung to life and perpetuated themselves as eagerly as any other?—and this despite the fact that myriads of them have lived in unspeakable squalor, at a stage of poverty far below the worst level that disgraces the West; and, what is more, the majority of them have always been treated as outcasts and pariahs by their brethren of the recognized castes.

The difficult, and perhaps insoluble problem to which this chapter and Chapter XII are addressed, is whether this hopeful attitude, with its fundamental faith in the goodness of life and the soundness of the universe, is justifiable upon a balance of all the relevant considerations.

Let me approach the task by the following line of argument: There are two ways of trying to understand ourselves, our characters, our capacities, our deeds, our temperaments, and our valuations of life. The one which has been most dominant for many years has been prompted by the procedure of physical science, to which the notion of *causality* is fundamental. Now causality means roughly that we look to the past to explain the present; since anything presently existing is regarded as the effect of one or more causes, operative either the previous moment or (as the case may be) a myriad years ago. This principle of explanation has proved so immensely fruitful for the purposes of physical science that we cannot wonder at seeing men attempt to apply it universally.

Nevertheless, as Felix Adler insisted with great insight, this mode of explanation fails us at the level of human personality. For those qualities which deserve to be called truly personal—or ethical, or spiritual—are characterized by mutual interdependence, by their simultaneous and reciprocal operation; so that the essential characteristic of causality—precedence and sequence in time—is absent from them. Or, to put the matter more simply, my influence upon you emanates from me at the same moment as your influence upon me emanates from you. Thus the two streams cross each other, and neither can properly be described as cause or effect of the other.

Without seeking to delve further into this abstruse matter (which, however, will confront us again in Chapter XIV), I would point out that it does constitute a reason—one of many reasons—for not limiting ourselves, when we are endeavoring to understand what we now are and how we now evaluate life, to explanations of the kind dealt in by men of science (in this case, biologists and psychologists). For we find, at bottom, that these explanations always fail to explain anything human. However true we admit them to be, we feel in them a certain irrelevance or inadequacy. That we are descended from animals which were not men; that not only our bodies but the new human powers in us have developed through the medium of a struggle to maintain life against adverse surrounding conditions; —all that we know of the development of the world and of man compels us to proclaim as true. Yet we cannot refrain from feeling how very far it is from accounting for us, even though it should account adequately for all other animals.

We observed in a previous chapter that the proper evolution of mankind (which is summed up in the word "civilization") begins precisely where that of all other creatures ends: namely, at the moment when every physical and psychic craving is satisfied and every biological need met by the resources of the natural environment.

Nevertheless, we readily concede to the man of science one point upon which he may truly insist. In order to decide whether there really are elements in our make-up peculiar to us, and not exemplified in any other animal, we must first apply to ourselves, and carry as far as they possibly can be carried, those principles and reasonings which account to us for the lives of other creatures. For that we too are animals is a fact so certain that nobody has ever doubted it; not even Fundamentalists like the late William Jennings Bryan. Even they admit, as all Christians have done, that man is an animal—*plus;* that the qualities, powers, and characteristics which to them seem evidences of special divine action in originating humanity are superimposed upon, and interblended with, an animal substratum.

The identity thus admitted between mankind and other sentient creatures extends throughout our bodily life and throughout the psychical cravings and emotional promptings which are correlated with it. "Function," it has been said, "is the psychic correlative of structure," in ourselves as well as in all other forms of life. Hence it results that in all sentient beings the existence of a structure points to the need of exercising the correlated function, and foreshadows a craving to do so when, for any reason, the function is thwarted. Even though in our own case we are burdened with the task of devising means for satisfying some needs which nature meets in other creatures, still the need in our case is equally imperious. An instance in point is the necessity for bodily warmth and protection against inclement weather. Nature clothes the bear and the eagle, as she does all her creatures except man, from her own resources. But she leaves in man the need she has refused to meet; and it is one that he must either satisfy or perish.

Again, in respect to food and drink, the need for exercise, the play of that "animal spontaneity" which is the source of the countless activities classed under the head of "sport," the complex system of cravings and emotions correlated with our sexual organization and its functions, the instinctive clinging to life and repugnance to death: in each of these we find in ourselves all the same phenomena that we see exemplified in every living creature which we have opportunity to examine.

Now if the story ended here, or if what followed upon it in mankind could be described even plausibly as a mere variation on the general animal theme, which could be classified with the variations on it played by other species, then the case of those who hold that we differ from other animals only as they differ from one another —that is, in degree but not in kind—would be unanswerable. But this is far from being true. For the difference between even the men of the remotest Stone Ages and the animals nearest to them—the anthropoid apes—turns out to be of a kind such as does not subsist between any other two species of living beings. Stone Age man is already an inventor, maker and user of tools. Indeed, through vast lapses of time, this is the sole evidence which compels us to class him as man at all. But the existence of these undeniable artifacts, all plainly devised for operations that only man can perform, and that only man could think out in advance so as to devise means for performing them, is conclusive evidence, even to those most eager to assimilate man with other creatures, of man's uniqueness.

What is more, even in the Stone Ages, man likewise betrays himself as an artist and a religious animal. Far back in paleolithic times he painted on the walls of caves, and engraved upon weapons, implements, and ornaments of stone and bone, images, often beautifully artistic, of the animals with which he was familiar. Now —as Mr. Chesterton once humorously put it—if we found anywhere pictures of men painted by apes, or if we discovered anywhere instances of other creatures bestriding man as man bestrides the horse, or taming him as he tames the dog, these would indeed give some color to theories of human animality which, given the data as they are, are simply absurd.

In these facts of tool-making and artistry, then, we have proof of the occurrence of an event which I know not how to describe otherwise than as a miracle. By this I mean something which certainly did occur; which occurred once only; and upon which we are unable to throw even the faintest glimmer of explanation: I mean the appearance in the first men, or the first animals which varied in the human direction, of powers which have since blossomed into the full range of reason, conscience, and the sense of beauty, with all their products. These powers have never appeared in any other species

whatsoever. Or, if it be alleged that in some species
they exist in rudiment, still they remain in those other
creatures only the same today as they were millions of
years ago; they have in *no* case undergone any evolution
whatsoever, save in the case of man.

But primitive man, as we have said, manifested himself also as a religious creature. He buried his dead
with reverential care, and placed in their tombs food,
tools, and weapons, for their use in an imagined after-
life. Thus, even in those "fathomless years forgotten,
wherever the dead gods reign,"—even in his immeasurably remote infancy—he already merited the famous
characterization of him by Sir Thomas Browne: "Man
is a noble animal, splendid in ashes and pompous in the
grave, solemnising nativities and deaths with equal
lustre, nor omitting ceremonies of bravery in the in-
famy of his nature."

From the standpoint of a scientifically-educated civilization, there is something pathetically foolish in this
practice of interring the food and implements of earthly
life in the tombs and tumuli of the dead. Yet the custom
is plain proof that even at its beginnings, humanity,
however dimly and blindly, apprehended in itself a
quality of worth and dignity completely *sui generis;*
that quality which later led to such explanatory legends
as we read in Genesis, about God communicating his
own nature to man alone among all the creatures that
He made. In this, as in all the parallel myths with which
the archives of anthropology abound, what interests us
is not at all the fanciful explanation, but *the fact which*

it was thus endeavored to explain: the surmised presence in humanity of something divine and inviolable,
the recognition of which as a fact is proved by the very
existence of these myths.

Thus even when we do follow the scientific procedure,
and attempt to account for ourselves as we now are by
leading up to the present from the past, we encounter
the stubborn fact that the very remotest beings with
whom present men can possibly be affiliated felt as we
feel about the uniqueness of the species to which they
belonged. They discovered that there was something in
themselves which was not to be accounted for by such
explanations as sufficed to satisfy their curiosity about
all the rest of the world and its contents. Their "explanations," both of themselves and of the world, were
of course mere myths and legends. They could be nothing else, because they were the products of imagination
working *in vacuo;* imagination unballasted by knowledge. The significant point, however, is that one order
of explanations *did* satisfy them about the rest of the
world, whereas a quite different sort had to be invoked
to account to them for themselves.

Let us glance now, however, at the second way of
approaching the problem to which we alluded. This is
to begin with ourselves as we now are, and work back-
wards, instead of beginning with what is remote in time
and working forwards. It may sometimes be helpful to
recognize that the man is the fulfillment and explanation of the boy, instead of always harping on the fact
that the boy is father to the man. Aristotle always in-

sisted that only the crown and flower of any natural process could explain the process. Any course of evolution is to be judged by its final outcome, not the final outcome by its obscure beginnings. The plant explains the seed, rather than the seed the plant. Humble origins throw no discredit upon any worthy fruition. To the contrary, fine end-products dignify the humblest origins.

Moreover, it is to be remembered that we do at least know ourselves, as we know nothing else, at first hand and from within. Our consciousness is infallible in testifying to its own states, however numerous and grotesque the errors into which we may fall when guessing at their causes; whereas, whatever we may know about man of the Stone Age, or about animals, is at best less immediate and less indubitably certain than our self-knowledge.

Now among these immediate and indubitable certainties is the fact that we spontaneously and instinctively join in celebrating such observances (instituted by men like ourselves) as Easter and Christmas, and, in our own nation, the Fourth of July and Thanksgiving Day. All of these are expressions of gratitude for, or of aspiration towards, satisfactions that could not be felt or recognized as such by any creature at the merely biological level.

Our national observances commemorate the achievement of our claims to liberty and self-affirmation, and bear witness to our recognition of our dependence upon a universal order which only reason can apprehend.

The mid-winter and the spring festivals attest the prophetic hope of some unprecedented efflorescence of human potentialities in a new-born child, and the daring parallel between a new birth of nature and some ideally transformed condition of human life, clearly apprehended, although never experienced. All of these are expressions of our nature which, however they may sometimes be degraded, are yet intrinsically spiritual; that is, rooted in the super-biological elements which are distinctive and definitive of humanity.

Another way of expressing the uniqueness of man is to say that at the animal level life is propelled forward by forces acting from the past, whereas at the human level it is lured forward by attractions from the future; which attractions exist only as possibilities in our minds, not as facts that are anywhere visible. Since, then, these idealized possibilities can only be apprehended by a self-conscious intelligence, the very fact that we, and we alone, can be influenced by them proves once more the uniqueness of our endowment.

In saying that life below the human level is propelled forward by forces from the past, one does not forget, of course, that many instinctive animal acts do provide effectually for future conditions. The point is, however, that nobody supposes the animal in doing them to be conscious of the purpose for which its acts prepare, or to foresee their fruition. The naturalists tell us, for example, of a certain kind of wasp, which prior to laying its egg makes most elaborate preparation for the accommodation of the larva it will never see. It has to select a suitable caterpillar, sting it in such a way that it will be paralyzed without being killed, and then to deposit its egg upon its victim, in order that the larva when hatched shall be surrounded with the kind of food it needs. Nobody supposes, however, that in performing these teleological acts the wasp understands what it is about or does what it chooses. It does blindly what it must, and can do no other.

In species far more highly endowed than these wasps, the lack of prevision with which elaborate actions are gone through is completely proved by the performance of the acts under conditions in which they are unnecessary or useless. Chimpanzees, for example, are one variety of the animals nearest to man,—those very anthropoid apes, our possible "ancestors," sometimes pointed to in support of the contention that the difference between us and them is one of degree only and not of kind. Yet the excellent psychologist Köhler, who devoted years to the study of their mentality, tells us that these creatures, at certain seasons, would sedulously build the nests, which are necessary to them in the state of nature, *inside* the comfortable and thoroughly-equipped houses that he had provided in order to study them.

Or consider the beavers, the earliest barrack-builders, who erected their elaborate apartment-houses, with specialized chambers, possibly before the existence of humanity; and who know so well how to meet the needs of their amphibious life by the construction of elaborate dams. Yet these skilled architects and engineers will obey their dam-building instinct in captivity, erecting across the floor these impounding barriers for rivers that will never flow there. Man, on the contrary, not only foresees whither his instinctive acts will lead, but devises ever more elaborate means towards ends which no instinct, but only his unique mentality, impels him to seek.

Now if, as all science testifies, the human part of us is the newest and latest evolved, it would seem reasonable *a priori* to expect what we actually do find: a sort of rivalry, or internecine warfare, between the human and the animal within us, and a frequent victory of the older and tougher animal elements over the newer and less solidly established human ones. All the more would this be expectable since the maintenance of our bodily life, which is indispensable if the higher part of us is to live at all, is largely in the hands of those mysterious instinctive powers which dominate animality, and over which our human consciousness can exercise no control. Our respiratory, cardiac, and digestive functions are so wholly independent of our consciousness that they continue in sleep, or when we are under anaesthetics, or in a state of coma; and, so far from conscious attention improving them, every one of them becomes impaired when we attend to it.

It would perhaps be fanciful to say that this life within us, of which we know little except that it lives and works, is "a very wise life," as I once heard an eminent philosopher call it. Science would adjudge such an expression anthropomorphic, and sternly ban it.

Nevertheless, when we cut ourselves, or are otherwise wounded, our blood-corpuscles certainly do act in what seem very ingenious and inventive ways to repair the damage. Medical science knows only the fact that they do this. Why they do it is unknown. The doctor's art merely takes advantage of the known fact by removing obstructions from the action of what was called of old the *vis medicatrix naturae*, the curative power of nature itself, which is always the true healer.

Being thus complex, humanity is subject to all the needs, desires and cravings characteristic of animals, plus those which correspond to its distinctive make-up. Now, the question is which of these is deepest and most dominant in us. Were we dealing with any species other than our own, and so obliged to answer without the advantage of self-knowledge, we could hardly doubt that those needs and cravings which are rooted in animality, since they are by far the oldest, and plainly indispensable both to the maintenance of the individual and the perpetuation of the species, must be the strongest, and must invariably predominate whenever they conflict with the impulsions of the novel human part of us.

Not only so, but when we survey such evidence as survives from the vast prehistoric periods, and add to this that record of "crimes, follies, and misfortunes" called history, our first superficial impression is that this is indeed the case; that man has always been "a wolf to man"; that animal self-assertion, egoistic greed, and blind lust have always overridden the dictates of conscience, and frequently even the self-regarding promptings of rational prudence.

These, indeed, are the very facts which make it plausible to interpret life in terms of pessimism. Despite their obtrusiveness, however, it is quite superficial to think only of them, and ignore the thin, feeble, often-reversed, yet persistent and increasing current of the stream of higher life and motivation which flows through this vast desert. For we must take into the reckoning not only the broken skulls and limbs collected from prehistoric caves and tumuli, which witness to the prevalence of battle and murder long before the dawn of history, but also those votive offerings in tombs, those lovingly devised pictures, figurines, and other evidences of affection and reverence, which remain from those remote times. Into the reckoning also must come the protests of conscience—at what Breasted called its very dawn, in ancient Egypt—against cruelty, graft, corruption, exploitation, and oppression; protests which were uttered and written down many long centuries before even the earliest of the prophets of Israel had arisen to give them still deeper interpretation.

This increasing emergence of the distinctively human element called conscience, moreover, is not only attested by the great figures who are universally recognized as the driving-force of man's highest progress,—by prophet and saint, by Buddha, Socrates, Jesus, and their nearest counterparts and emulators in many lands and times—but just as strikingly by the universal, sometimes involuntary and reluctant, reverence felt for them by the multitude who have no thought of emulating either their principles or their conduct.

Once more, however, we have to decide this question not only by reference to history, but also by self-examination and by our estimate of our contemporaries. Here it is that we discover the really conclusive evidence of the paradoxical truth: that that element in us which is latest evolved, and therefore presumably weakest, lays claim to a sovereign right to govern and override the boundless cravings of our older nature. And it does actually succeed, sometimes in all men and always in some men, in getting its way with us, defeating and suppressing the clamorous mob of our instinctive psychic impulsions. That we can and do act from motives which are morally strong, but psychologically far weaker than the desires which have to be suppressed to make way for them,—this is the real proof of the superior nature in man.

The paradox, however, is not less effectually illustrated in cases where the purely moral element does not enter. Even the necessary satisfaction of our physical needs is increasingly made subservient, as civilization and its refinements advance, to desires and ends which are human in the sense that they are possible only to a self-conscious and self-determining intelligence. The gourmand, for example, does not eat only to gratify an animal appetite, but much rather to indulge the aesthetic taste of a rationally-regulated palate. It was not the animal "motive-pleasure" of repletion, but the mentally anticipated "resultant-pleasure" of these aesthetic satisfactions, which inspired the scientific development of the culinary art and the elaborate craft-mysteries of the wine-maker.

An analogous transformation also characterizes the human manifestation of all the needs and cravings we share with the animals. Thus, with us, the necessity of warmth and protection against the weather has led not merely to the adoption of *any kind* of protective covering, but to the evolution of a sartorial craftsmanship which, in all ages, has cared even more for decency and elegance, for personal embellishment and artistic display, than for mere comfort. The history of fashion in all lands and ages bears this out; and it might be profitable if some student possessed of the necessary leisure would re-investigate it from this standpoint.

Equally noteworthy is it that the volcanic impulsions of our sex-life, so clamorous in their claim upon us, have been not less effectually subordinated to ideational forces. Always and everywhere among mankind, from savagery to civilization, there has been a recognized and emphatically-asserted distinction between love and lust, the permitted and the prohibited, to which nothing in the life of other animals corresponds. Every form of legal or religious regulation of sex relations and marriage institutions, from oldest to newest and lowest to highest, equally attests the power in humanity of an ideational force strong enough to bridle and restrain the most imperious of all somatic cravings. It is noteworthy, too, that nowhere have such regulations been

stricter or better observed than among peoples whom
we call savages.

When, moreover, we survey the life of our own times,
is not our very sense of social injustice, our pity and
wrath at the empty and frustrated lives of myriads of
our fellows, the plain proof that we all desire for ourselves, and therefore feel that justice demands for
others, some kind of fulfillment that has nothing to do
with our bodily make-up? We cannot bear the thought
of men being treated like animals; not even like pet
animals, or the pampered denizens of zoological collections. That a dog or a horse should starve or suffer
bodily pain moves us to pity, and to indignation if the
unnecessary suffering is caused by human cruelty or
carelessness. But when a human being endures starvation, or pain wantonly inflicted, we are moved to something far deeper. A feeling of outrage is awakened, as
though something worthy of reverence had been pro-
faned.

When we see in the slums of our own cities, or among
the "poor whites" or the impoverished negroes of the
South, men, women, and children cut off from the intellectual and aesthetic heritage of civilization, the spectacle shocks and accuses us, even when we know that
these unfortunates are not deprived of anything necessary to their bodily life. Often, to be sure, they suffer
this deprivation also. But when they do not,—when
their needs for food, shelter, and clothing are sufficiently
met,—still if their state is that of slaves, even pampered
ones; or, yet worse, of the kind of degradation so dra-

matically presented in the play "Tobacco Road," the
spectacle moves us to unspeakable horror and indignation.

Hereby we confess that human life has claims—because it has potencies and responsibilities—which do
not relate to the sense-world at all. They could not have
originated there; and the satisfactions correspondent
to them cannot be found there. Now the deepest craving
of every human life relates to claims of this order, and
to the latent powers in every person which should be
exercised in their fulfillment.

But this is to say, in other words, that every human
life needs its Easter experience; meaning its ascension
to a plane of action and fulfillment which, because it is
aesthetic, rational, and ethical, is properly described as
spiritual and eternal.*

This claim interfuses with and raises to its own level
the consciously-controllable phases of our animal existence. For in us the functions correlated with bodily
structure, however imperiously they clamor for fulfillment, are yet not to be satisfied with *any kind* of fulfillment. Whatever our failures and fallings, we know
that what we need is not lust but love; not mating but
marriage,—*i.e.*, the interfusion of complementary personalities in such wise that each is enriched, and lifted
nearer to the level of its best possibilities. The instinctive desire for the perpetuation of our kind is not satis-

---

* On this subject, *cf.* the chapter on "Resurrection" in my book,
"The Emerging Faith" (1937).

fied at the human level by offspring of *any* sort, but
only by creatures, derivative from us, on whom our love
and nurturing skill may be lavished, so that in their
spiritual and personal qualities and achievements we
may expect to behold the fulfillment of potencies latent
and aspirations thwarted in ourselves. Nothing stirs us
more to anger, or is more justly called inhuman, than
the conduct of men and women who are "parents" only
in the sense in which cattle and carnivores are parents.

The deepest craving of human life, then, is for
the effectual realization and expression of what is distinctive and unique in our several personalities. The
tragedy of failure in this is finely expressed in the following beautiful lines by Oliver Wendell Holmes:

> A few can touch the magic string,
>   And noisy fame is proud to win them;
> Alas for those who never sing,
>   But die with all their music in them!
>
> Nay, grieve not for the dead alone
>   Whose song has told their heart's sad story;
> Weep for the voiceless, who have known
>   The cross without the crown of glory!
>
> O hearts that break and give no sign,
>   Save whitening lip and fading tresses,
> Till Death pours out his cordial wine,
>   Slow-dropped from misery's crushing presses,
>
> If singing breath or echoing chord
>   To every hidden pang were given,
> What endless melodies were poured,
>   As sweet as earth, as high as heaven!

And thus we verify, as the distinctive element of our humanity, that creative or evolutionary striving which originated and develops civilization, and illustrates in it the spiritual elements which are eternal. We crave that as the result of our having lived there shall remain for ever some trait or trace of good in the spiritual universe (which, so far as this earth is concerned, means human society) which originated with us, and but for us would not have been there. Nor is this an egoistic aspiration for our *names* to be known or remembered. When we truly understand ourselves, we realize that what alone matters is the achievement of the end, the making of our distinctive and permanent contribution, and not its attribution to us.

Here, then, I hold, we unveil the deepest meaning of the symbolism of Easter. To achieve for ourselves and for all men this fulfillment of our nature's deepest craving is truly "the Resurrection and the Life." And if the grand words of the Fourth Gospel may be paraphrased, I would venture to add: He that liveth at this level, though he die, yet shall he live; and whosoever liveth and achieveth this, shall never die. For this is to live in the Eternal Order, which is above time, and endures for ever.

Chapter X

THE DUTY OF HAPPINESS

THE TITLE of this chapter was suggested to me by a
sentence from a once-popular book by the late Lord
Avebury (Sir John Lubbock): "The world would be
better and brighter if our teachers would dwell on the
Duty of Happiness as well as on the Happiness of
Duty." It may be supplemented by another quotation
from that curious modern mystic James Hinton, who
writes as follows in his book on "The Mystery of Pain":
"It is not only our right, it is our duty to enjoy and to
be happy. Pleasure does us good if gratefully and lovingly accepted; the nature often expands and blossoms
under it as under no other influence."

Before and since the publication of the Declaration
of Independence, but especially since, abundant stress
has been laid upon the "right" to happiness. But from
a much earlier period (as we saw in Chapter III), the
tribe of ethical philosophers has been divided between
those who regarded happiness as the end of life, the
measure of right, the chief good or *summum bonum*,
and those who have found the standard and criterion of
right in something else. The former school was represented in antiquity by Aristotle and Epicurus, and in
modern times (to name only writers in our own lan-

guage) by Hobbes, Paley, Bentham, Mill, and Herbert
Spencer. Some of those who maintain this view today
can scarcely be called ethical theorists at all; they are
mere nihilists, like Lord Russell, who insists that "outside human desires there is no moral standard," and
therefore that each man should do what he himself
wants to do.

The school opposed to the view that happiness constitutes man's chief good also numbers exponents of
the highest eminence, beginning in antiquity with Plato,
Zeno and Epictetus, and including in modern times
such great names as Kant, Green, Lecky and Martineau. Now the fact that these thinkers have denied
the claim of happiness to be the supreme end of life,
and the standard of morals, has caused them to be regarded as severe ascetics who dislike or disparage happiness. Such a view, however, is only possible to those
who have not read them critically. It is in fact completely false and unjust. Without exception, they would
have endorsed the words of that austere moralist Bishop
Butler: "Happiness is what all men naturally desire."

We shall do well to begin by clearing up a slight
confusion involved in the idea of men's having a "right"
to happiness. A "right" denotes a relation that can
only subsist between *persons* of kindred moral and rational nature; and this means, so far as life on earth is
concerned, between fellow-men. My "rights" are those
privileges and opportunities which it is your duty to
accord to me, just as your "rights" define and measure
my duties toward you. It is meaningless to speak of

"rights" against the material world, or against living creatures which are below the level of rational and moral consciousness. When an earthquake destroys a city, or a tiger devours a man, we are indeed confronted by tragedy; but such a tragedy as it would make no sense to describe as a breach of right.

Since, moreover, the term "right" connotes a duty on the part of other human beings, it follows that we can only have "rights" to what it is in their power to accord to us. All thinkers are agreed that it is never a duty for a man to do what it is impossible for him to do. Since, then, it is in general beyond human power to guarantee happiness, it follows that to speak of a "right" to it (unless with careful qualification) is fallacious.

The true task of those moralists who denied happiness to be the supreme end was to establish the position that the true end of life must be something which it lies within our power to achieve. Not only the Intuitionists of the old Platonic school, but even the wiser Utilitarians, such as John Stuart Mill, sought to justify this position.

It is always possible to learn much from good men whose general philosophy one cannot accept. Here, then, we may go to school to the Stoics. Gloomy as their system often became, and unacceptable to us as its pantheistic basis may be, they were yet right in maintaining that nothing contingent can be the true end of life. That end must be something independent of the vicissitudes of fortune, and dependent only upon our own character and effort: which means that it will consist in something that we may *be*, rather than something we may *do* or *acquire*.

Experience abundantly proves that when men directly aim at happiness for themselves, they generally miss it; so that when this happens, the man who self-centeredly makes it his single goal is bankrupt and without resource. But although happiness is contingent upon a multitude of circumstances we cannot control, it certainly does not follow that it is not eminently desirable. Nor does it in the least follow that a teacher who advises the pursuit of something else is a foe to happiness. All those ethical philosophers who find the criterion of right and the goal of life in something other than happiness will agree not only that happiness is a good, but also that the realization of their ends will be accompanied by it. Happiness, they would say (and this generalization is as much psychological as ethical, and is abundantly verified by daily experience), is a *by-product* of the disinterested pursuit of other ends. It ensues when those other ends are sought for their own sake, and not for the sake of the happiness they may entail.

The position from which we set out, then, may be stated as follows: Nobody can guarantee happiness to others or assure it to himself. Everybody, nevertheless, naturally desires it. But if it be directly sought for oneself it is almost invariably missed. Our earthly life is shot through with unavoidable sorrows, and we constantly find ourselves plunged amid circumstances which are uncontrollable. But for these very reasons it becomes our duty to do all we can to promote the steady and enduring happiness of our fellows, and to do nothing to hinder it. Moreover, our own best chance of being happy is to strive to make others so.

Many people, however, will feel that the phrase I have borrowed from Lord Avebury involves an absurdity. To *command* happiness, by talking of a "duty" regarding it, they will maintain, is nonsense; and I admit that it makes sense only within limits,—the limits it will here be my task to define. I would remark, however, that the same criticism has been brought against the command to love. The dictum of the Bible, "Thou *shalt* love thy neighbour as thyself," has been attacked or ridiculed, as ordering men to do something which it is wholly beyond their power to do. "To tell me I ought to love somebody," such a critic will say, "is like telling me that I ought to enjoy a square meal. I either can or I cannot. If I can, I naturally shall, and shall need no orders to do it. But if I cannot, no amount of exhortation can make me do it."

It is easy to see the basis of these criticisms. Love, it is felt, is the outflow of spontaneous feeling. No doubt it will be admitted that there is such a thing as natural affection; *e.g.*, in children for parents, in parents for children, and in all normal people for their kindred and their country. Undoubtedly, as life proceeds, there develops a spontaneous love for friends, and the specialized kind of love associated with the attractions and functions of sex. The objection, then, amounts to this: that we love when we cannot help doing so, but we cannot force ourselves to love when we do not.

Plausible as this may appear at first sight, it is not difficult to see the answer to it; which is, that it ignores the extent to which those instincts and propensions which we share with the animal world are controllable and transformable by the higher and distinctively human elements in us. Undoubtedly, the drive of the will in us is deeper and more primitive than reason, and our psychic life is rooted in instincts and spontaneous feelings. Nevertheless, ideational forces—the dictates of reason and conscience—react powerfully upon these. Feelings can be subjected to and modified by standards created or discerned by thought. To say that morality is a matter *merely* of feeling is really to deny its existence. It is in truth an affair of the regulation of feelings and impulses by rational convictions. What is more, this may be (in the case, say, of children or primitive people) effected at second hand, through convictions which are not at all present to the consciousness of the persons directly concerned. They may be merely the subjects of a discipline imposed by others—a discipline which does indeed embody and effectuate the convictions of those who impose it, but which the young or the primitive will conform to simply from habit, or from reverence for their mentors.

By means of such discipline, the elemental attractions and repulsions of instinct can be effectively bridled and guided. The extent to which, and the conditions under which, they shall be indulged or resisted are determined. Through such influence, those spontaneous sympathies and antipathies which would prohibit affection may gradually be nullified, and it is possible even for genuine love to grow up where there had formerly been indifference or hate.

Anthropologists have long since shown us the striking manner in which this fact is illustrated by the marriage institutions of primitive tribes. The constant, manifold, subtle inculcation of the tribal standard upon individuals from infancy, exercises so powerful an effect upon them that when the strong sex-feelings evoked by biological maturity come into play, they seldom or never flow into channels which the tribal law forbids. Thus among endogamous tribes—that is, those in which the rule prevails that marriage selection is permitted only within the community—the difficulty caused by persons falling in love with people outside the defined circle scarcely ever arises. Where, on the contrary, the tribe is exogamous (*i.e.*, only marriage with outsiders is permitted), it very rarely occurs that people's impulses make them desire to violate this rule.

Now similar considerations apply to the problem of happiness. Undoubtedly it is true—tragically true— that happiness and unhappiness are subject to contingencies mainly beyond our control. "Nature," as Emerson said, "does not cocker us." The workings of the great world seem entirely indifferent to our desires, and fortune is as blind as justice ought to be:

Streams will not curb their pride
The just man not to entomb,
Nor lightnings go aside
To give his virtues room;
Nor is that wind less rough which blows a good man's barge.

Death may come to our beloved friends, our relatives, our children, as uncontrollably as lightning and tempest to the skies. Slight accidents, or unpredictable bodily changes, may destroy our sanity, undermine our moral character, or make us helpless burdens upon the kindly services of others. Nor are these disasters limited to the operations of external nature. In our own time we have twice seen the criminal insanity of a handful of men precipitate upon the whole world an immeasurable disaster, recovery from which may take many generations.

Nevertheless, there are two considerations which modify this general truth and make a vital difference to its bearings. The first of these is that human action, the expression of men's ideas and purposes, can in great and growing measure control outward events. And the second is that the very attitude of will and mind which we ourselves adopt towards the course of events may change their aspect; because it either strengthens or enfeebles us in grappling with them, and thereby in so far determines them.

William James, in his well-known lecture entitled "Is Life Worth Living?" illustrated the matter by the following instance:—

"Suppose ... that you are climbing a mountain, and have worked yourself into a position from which the only escape is by a terrible leap. Have faith that you can successfully make it, and your feet are nerved to its accomplishment. But mistrust yourself, and think of all the sweet things you have heard the scientists say of *maybes*, and you will hesitate so long that, at last, all unstrung and trembling, and launching yourself in a moment of despair, you roll in the abyss. In such a case (and it belongs to an enormous class), the part of wisdom as well as of courage is to *believe what is in the line of your needs*, for only by such belief is the need fulfilled. Refuse to believe, and you shall indeed be right, for you shall irretrievably perish. But believe, and again you shall be right, for you shall save yourself. You make one or the other of two possible universes true by your trust or mistrust,— those universes having been only *maybes*, in this particular, before you contributed your act."

Quite rightly does James insist that such situations, in which the faith and courage of the individual make all the difference to the outcome, are of daily occurrence. Almost every task we undertake is different in its meaning for us, and in the result we achieve, according as we believe in our own power to compass it, or are daunted and enervated by the apprehension that it will overwhelm us.

We commonly think of the cleavage between ourselves and the universe as being more complete than it really is. We stand on the one side (so we feel), and on the other side lies the whole vast cosmos opposed to us; between being a clean-cut, bottomless gulf. Of course this is not so. It is incorrect to think of the world *minus* yourself as complete. Yet it is not unnatural for us to think so. We are so small, so insignificant even in our own eyes, that we are tempted to think ourselves like the fly on the coach-wheel. All the same, the mood in which we face life is a part of the sum-total of reality; and, as regards the minute margin of the world at which we can interact with it, that mood is frequently the decisive factor of our own fortune, and in some measure even of the great world's destiny.

One of the many paradoxes with which life confronts us is this: that it demands of us an ever-renewed series of efforts to achieve what logic would pronounce impossible. And often enough this logic cannot be refuted by the formal procedure of the reason of which it is the expression. For that reason, canalized in its forms and modes by the necessities of action, looks upon the world as an assemblage of clean-cut, static objects, and perforce ignores what Bergson called "the fluid continuity of the real." So that if we harkened to its dictates, and never attempted the apparent impossibilities it vetoes, we could never progress or succeed. Logic tells us that a is either b or not b, but takes no account of the possibility of a *becoming* b. For logic, I can either swim or not swim. If I can, I need not learn; if I cannot, I shall sink in the water and drown, and so can never learn.

Fortunately, life is wider and deeper than formal logic; and the reason embodied in logic is not the whole of our personalities. It is a rationale of the world as it appears to the discursive intellect, a partial statement

of the conditions which have rendered possible the existing state of things. It cannot foresee results into which
factors of life other than the discursive reason, or the
known uniformities of the outer world, must enter. For
it, the creations of genius are impossible before they
occur, and inexplicable afterwards; nor can it allow for
the possible achievements of heroic and desperate courage. The act of creation transcends all the categories
of science. What the next picture by Rembrandt, or the
next play by Shakespeare, would be was unpredictable
even by those who knew all that could be known about
those men, and were familiar with every detail of their
previous work.

With regard, then, to our present problem, it stands
thus: It is our duty to aim at happiness for others
(which means, let us note clearly, that what we shall
be seeking *for ourselves* is something other than happiness). But we need happiness ourselves in order that
we may be a source of it to others; for, as Ruskin well
said, "No man who is wretched in his own heart, and
feeble in his own work, can rightly help others." And
yet, with regard to both objects, we can never fully
command or guarantee the conditions upon which they
depend.

The pessimist, therefore, will tell us that the whole
idea of a *duty* in this matter belongs to dreamland,
since we are impotent to assure happiness either to ourselves or to those whom we love better than ourselves.
On this last point, the pessimist, of course, is emphatically right. But in his implied, unavowed conclusion,

"therefore it is idle for you to attempt either to be happy yourself or to confer happiness on anybody else," he is quite as emphatically wrong.

With just as good reason he might argue on this basis regarding health or business success. Nothing lying in the future can be certain—with this only exception: that if we permit the uncertainty of what is future to paralyze our present effort, we make impossible the attainment of whatever goal we may desire. How can I know that within six months I may not be stricken down by some fatal disease? Of course I cannot know this. But if I act upon the assumption that I inevitably *shall*, I shall certainly spoil the next few months for myself, and very possibly (for all I can know) succeed in hypnotizing myself into contracting the malady. But if, on the contrary, I say "I will cross that bridge when I come to it," meantime keeping my body in rational exercise and my mind in deliberate cheerfulness, I shall have at least some interval of unimpeded activity and comparative freedom from distress. And even if, at the end of the six months, the disaster should befall me, my chance of being cured and surviving will be at the possible maximum instead of the minimum.

It has by now become a truism that every business commitment is a venture of faith: faith in the dependability of other men and their undertakings; faith in the unchanging order of nature—*i.e.*, in the unprovable proposition that the same effects will follow from the same causes in the future as in the past; and faith in our own power to continue to guide events as we have hitherto done. Whenever we speculate, with money or with action, we are uncertain of profit, or even of not losing our ventures. But to refrain from action in all cases because of the possibility of loss is itself to act;— and to act foolishly.

The true end of life, we say, is certainly not happiness, because that depends upon an innumerable series of unforeseeable and uncontrollable contingencies; so that, were it so, it would be very difficult in the case of totally unhappy people to assign a convincing argument against suicide. Nevertheless, the real end of life, however defined, must be something of which, in so far as it can be attained, happiness will be the accompanying *atmosphere* and *overtone*. When this fact is clearly understood, it destroys that appearance of gloom and harshness which attaches to ethical doctrines that contradict the notion of happiness being the end.

I am moved to emphasize this point, because some years ago, after I had delivered to a class a course of lectures on "The Moral Philosophy of Aristotle," I was horrified to find that I had produced upon some of my hearers the impression that I "disliked happiness." I attribute this grotesque misunderstanding to the controversial exigency which compelled me to stress the uncertainty and frequent unattainability of happiness in order to justify my rejection of Aristotle's doctrine that "eudaemonism" is the chief good and end of life. I share with the great masters of whom I am a pupil the conviction that the end of human life is something which we are to *be,* rather than something which we may *do* or *have.* All the same, being neither a Manichee nor a Puritan, I love to be happy; and, by natural consequence, long to see those happy whom I love more than myself. And I hold that it is our duty deliberately to aim at the happiness of others.

Despite the fact that our best-laid plans "gang aft agley," the notion that one can *never* make other people happy by deliberately planning to do so is a gross exaggeration. True indeed it is that a self-seeker, hunting happiness only for himself, will almost inevitably miss it. To realize this, one needs only to think of the hectic crowds of rootless expatriates, with no manly tasks or social purposes to ballast them, who used to haunt the gambling centers of the Riviera. But it is no less true that he who deliberately endeavors to promote the happiness of others will generally succeed in some measure, and will experience joy himself in proportion to his success.

Some people have been perplexed by the alleged impossibility of defining happiness; because (they say) there seem to be as many varieties of it as there are individuals. In this matter, too, one man's meat is another's poison. At the risk of writing myself down a crank, I must confess that I am daily bewildered at seeing other people made happy by means (such as jazz "music," surrealist "art," and certain radio programs) that make me miserable. But the perplexity abovementioned is quite gratuitous. It arises from a confusion between happiness itself (*i.e.,* the inner state of consciousness) and the outward means which produce it. Thus the alleged difficulty need not deter us from recognizing some universal elements of happiness, and some very simple rules upon which we may profitably act.

By way of general definition, we might offer this: *Happiness means any state of consciousness, or combination of states of consciousness, the continuance of which is spontaneously desired by their possessor.*

When we can say with Faust,

> "Then dared I hail the moment fleeing,
> 'Ah, still delay, thou art so fair!' "

surely that is happiness. And as two of the necessary elements in all such states of consciousness, we may set down, first, harmony between internal and external conditions (or what Spencer called "correspondence between organism and environment"), and second, the society and co-operation of other persons similarly in harmony with their circumstances and with ourselves.

It is this last consideration which compels us to speak of a *duty* in the matter. I cannot, indeed, guarantee happiness to anybody; but I can guarantee unhappiness if I behave towards him in certain ways. Any fool or knave can make a family miserable. We may see this done every day, with the completest possible success, by people who succeed in nothing else. It is therefore necessary to say "Thou shalt not make thy neighbor unhappy." The casuist and hair-splitter may make merry over the difference between "not creating unhappiness" and "creating happiness." Practical men will recognize that the difference is negligible, since the determination to avoid occasions of unhappiness will speedily beget that of seeking occasions of happiness.

It is an old but true story that those whose experience and circumstances give them the most right to be pessimists are usually the world's most shining optimists. The author of the Fourth Gospel showed true insight when he represented Jesus as saying—with the prospect of Golgotha before his eyes—"These things have I spoken unto you, that my joy may be in you, and that your joy may be fulfilled."

To me it is impossible, when brooding over this subject, to avoid the thought of one of my most beloved literary idols, Charles Lamb. His whole life lay under the storm-clouds of tragedy, and was in truth a march through the Valley of the Shadow of Death. The intermittent insanity of his sister Mary, who in one of her mad fits had killed their mother, compelled him to devote the whole of his mature life to her, and to deny himself the joys of marriage and fatherhood. Had he been as black a pessimist as Schopenhauer, men would have confessed that the circumstances of his life gave him justification. Yet he was the very contrary. He loved, with a true and discriminating affection, whatever is lovable in people, and in the myriad things, great and small, which make up the satisfactions of human life. He always rebuked whining in others, and found his highest happiness in making others happy. He distilled the last drop of joy from every moment of life.

Who can ever forget his beautiful reflections on "New Year's Eve"?—

"In proportion as the years both lessen and shorten, I set more count upon their periods, and would fain lay my ineffectual finger upon the spoke of the great wheel. I am not content to pass away 'like a weaver's shuttle.' Those metaphors solace me not, nor sweeten the unpalatable draught of mortality. I care not to be carried with the tide that smoothly bears human life to eternity; and reluct at the inevitable course of destiny. I am in love with this green earth; the face of town and country; the unspeakable rural solitudes, and the sweet security of streets."

When we regale our palates with the delicate and lovely humor of Lamb's Essays, and still more richly with the hearty gusto of his personal letters, we see that no man ever more perfectly exemplified the duty of being happy—by being so under conditions which would have furnished a plentiful excuse for unhappiness —and also the duty of making others happy.

Especially was this illustrated in Lamb's relations with little children. They adored him, as he adored them. There is a letter from Mary Lamb to Dorothy Wordsworth in which she tells this: "John Hazlitt's little girl was so fond of Charles that, when he was expected, she used to stop strangers in the street and tell them, 'Mr. Lamb is coming tonight!'"

If I could think that my presence had ever meant as much as *that* to a little child, my deathbed would be a happy one.

And an old woman, who in childhood had seen much of Lamb in a small country town near London, told the following to his biographer Lucas: There was in their circle a deaf man, who, like many deaf people, was rendered irritable and peevish by the strain of constantly trying, and generally failing, to hear what others said. "Mr. Lamb and Mr. Richard never got on very well," said the old lady, "and Mr. Richard did not like his teasing ways at all; *but Mr. Lamb often went for long walks with him, because no one else would.* He did many kind things like that." *

What a contrast between the "optimistic" Lamb and the "pessimistic" Carlyle, who—for his sins—disliked Lamb, and who tells us that "all the statesmen of Europe" could not "make one shoeblack happy"! Carlyle, however, had in mind a shoeblack who was a moral lunatic, a creature of unlimited and uncontrolled cravings. Ordinary human beings are luckily more restrained in their yearnings. Indeed, I boast the acquaintance of some shoeblacks whom I am sure anybody could make happy,—provided, of course, that they did not read "Sartor Resartus" to them.

There have been whole ages of the world in which it seems to have been thought almost sinful to be happy. Many of the extravagances of Catholicism in the Dark Ages and early Middle Ages—such as its self-flagellating asceticism, its desert monasticism, and its cult of celibacy and virginity—have carried this implication. The same was true of Puritanism, which was, indeed,

* Cf. E. V. Lucas, "At the Shrine of St. Charles."

the lineal descendant of this phase of Catholicism. The Puritans thought that God was incapable of sympathy with laughter. They envisaged him as a sort of magnified and intensified Presbyterian elder, who objected on principle to pleasure. The stinging epigram of Macaulay is as true as it is pungent: "The Puritans disliked bear-baiting, not because it gave pain to the bear, but because it gave pleasure to the spectators."

Though an occasional survival of this temper may still linger among us, yet the world in general has happily grown out of it. We no longer regard children as specimens of total depravity, created only to inherit eternal punishment, as St. Fulgentius and Calvin did. We think it consistent with righteousness and "our duty towards God" to take towards children the attitude which Jesus Christ took—an attitude that many of his followers strangely seem to have thought highly unchristian. We recognize that it is our duty to make children happy; and intelligent parents and teachers understand that it is possible to do this, not only without injury to the children's moral and mental development, but actually as a help to it. My plea is that this duty does not become extinct when the children grow up; and that we should extend the same attitude towards our adult neighbors.

One of the chief reforms which seem necessary in this connection is to recognize and insist upon the possibility of happiness in and through one's work. Many educators and others are devoting their thought and energies to the redemption of leisure. People ought to have culture, they tell us, and learn to enjoy fine things, in order that their leisure may bring them real happiness and develop their higher powers.

All this is, of course, quite right. Nevertheless, it implies too often that work itself is a curse. Unwittingly we carry on the ancient Biblical tradition, that the primitive divine state of man was a state of idleness, and work was a penalty imposed by God after sin. "In the sweat of thy brow shalt thou eat bread." The fact is that hours of work ought to be as happy as hours of play; and they actually are so when men have tasks that accord with their powers, and perform them under just and friendly conditions.

I once read a discourse delivered by the late Mr. Charles Schwab to a gathering of college boys, in which he told them that they would have to choose between succeeding and "having a good time." "You may do one or the other. You cannot do both," he said. This unfortunate way of expressing—or rather misrepresenting —what he really had in mind seems rooted in the old Biblical idea. By way of emphasizing my opposition to it, I would say that it is only by working hard and succeeding that anyone can possibly have "a good time." The Garden-of-Eden legend is untrue to human nature. We need the sweating of our brow in order that we may enjoy our bread. Too much idleness would be a far greater curse than too much work. What Mr. Schwab really meant is plain enough: namely, that people who go in for fun to the neglect of their work cannot succeed. But in that case they do *not* "have a good time." Those who act thus have perhaps a brief season of hectic pleasure; but they pay for it afterwards by years of misery and self-condemnation. And anybody who merely saw Mr. Schwab, or heard him speak, would rightly have felt certain that he had had a far better time in and through his work than he could have obtained in any other way.

To practice our duty of promoting the happiness of others we must study their individuality, as an artist studies the features of a person whose portrait he is to paint, and a teacher explores the mind of a pupil he is to educate. Thus must we study the soul—the unique combination of volitional, psychic and mental qualities —in those with whom we have to deal; for thus shall we learn, like a wise physician, to prescribe for the individual case.

Nor shall we fail to find our own spirits flooded by joy through this activity; and our joy, in turn, will be a fruitful factor in creating the happiness we desire to bestow, and in evoking a mutual love which is itself the truest happiness.

A modern dramatist has said that life does not cease to be humorous because people die, or cease to be tragic because they laugh. Despite its sorrows, life is good, joyous, and happy. Man is great despite his littleness; for it is only the greatness in him that shows him how little he is. That life is richest and best which is ever aware of the sunshine behind the clouds, which perceives the hidden god in the clay images of our fellow-men, and "begets the smiles that have no cruelty."

And the happiness which we ourselves experience, to say nothing of that which we bestow upon others, comes most near to "the quality of virtue" when all things around us conspire to make us unhappy. The theme here discussed, therefore, incongruous as it may appear to some in a time of war which loads us all with sorrow, seems to me most appropriate of all at exactly such a time.

CHAPTER XI

SEVEN KINDS OF LOVE

I T IS a curious circumstance that the deepest and most certain knowledge we human beings possess is that which we find it hardest to define in words and grasp with conscious understanding. The very basis of all our thought and all our valuations of life consists of "dumb certainties." These are truths which we experienced before our infant consciousness had developed into self-consciousness. Nay, without the experience of some of them—parental love, for example—we could never have lived to become self-conscious beings. Precisely, therefore, because we knew these things before we could know that we knew them; precisely because they are so self-evident, so deeply presupposed in all our thinking, that it has never occurred to us even to formulate, and still less to question them, we find ourselves bewildered and unable to answer if they are ever disputed. Which of us would not be reduced to a puzzled silence if he were asked, for example, *why* he considers flowers or sunsets beautiful?

I imagine, too, that if my reader were asked to state in a few words what love is, he might find himself as deeply puzzled as I confess to having been when I first put the question to myself, and endeavored to decide how to answer it. I am still troubled by this state of doubt, because I know not how to proceed with my present theme without attempting, however rashly, to formulate a definition of love. The difficulty of this must excuse the imperfection of the attempt, which I offer rather in order to provoke discussion and elicit amendments than with any notion that my tentative effort can be final.

I begin by assuming the soundness of that fundamental conception which is accepted by all varieties of the analytic school in psychology; that which is common ground between Freud, Adler, Jung, and other exponents of this school, however widely they differ in their interpretations of it. This assumption is that there is in man (as in all living forms whatsoever, animal and vegetable alike) an original life-energy which is deeper than consciousness. It is also older, since it is manifested in the life of plants, which are presumably unconscious; and it must also be regarded as the originating cause of consciousness throughout the entire range of animal life.

The primitive life-energy in question has been variously named "élan vital," "libido," "will-to-live," and "will-to-power." In every phase of the struggle for existence, this it is which sustains the struggle. This energy seizes upon whatever opportunities for self-expansion and self-enrichment are furnished by the bodily organization of each individual and species, and by the environment each confronts. It modifies the organism itself; —certainly by the use and disuse of particular organs

within the limits of individual lives, if not also by heredi-
tary transmission. It ever strives to adapt itself to the
environment; and at the higher levels of animal and
human consciousness, it strives also to change the environment in conformity with its desires.

For our present purpose it is unnecessary either to
choose between the different names by which various
thinkers have designated this primordial energy, or to
go behind the fact of its reality. Even at the animal
level, the relation of the psychical to the physical is utterly mysterious; and no less mysterious at the human
level is the relation between the mental or spiritual
and the physical. Nobody can explain it; whence it
follows that philosophy and psychology can offer nothing better than the contradictory guesses of different
schools of speculation. The ground common to all these
schools, however, is a fact of experience; something that
we can all verify by merely attending to our own emotions, volitions, and thoughts: the fact, namely, that
the psychical and the physical are inseparably blended
and perpetually correlated, yet without being identical.
A nerve-movement is one thing, and a pleasant or painful sensation is another. The conveyance of this sensation to the brain is one thing,—a physical process; the
thought or volition thence arising is another thing,—
a mental fact. The nature, however, of the nexus between the sensation, the thought, or the volition, and
its physical correlatives, is inscrutable.

Being in this condition of inevitable ignorance, we
have to choose, more or less arbitrarily, between regard-

ing the body as the source and cause of all that is included under the term "consciousness," and regarding the central life-energy as the source and cause of its physical instrument, the body. Between these equally unprovable hypotheses, I personally lean to the second. To me it seems more reasonable to suppose that an energy which is common to *all* forms of life, and was manifested in vegetable forms in ages long anterior to the evolution of animal bodies, should be regarded as the cause or source of the infinitely various kinds of bodies it animates, than as the product or effect of any or all of them. Tentatively, therefore, and with full readiness for correction should countervailing facts ever be discovered, I hold with the poet Spenser:

"Of the soul the body form doth take;
For soul is form and doth the body make."

By the word "soul," however, nothing more is meant here and now than the above-mentioned psychical fact called "élan vital" or "libido." Our present theme only requires us to begin with existing and recognizable psychological data. It does not demand any attempt at metaphysical derivation of these.

With this understanding, I submit the following as a tentative definition of love:

Love is that phase or direction of the original life-energy which craves and seeks the enlargement and enrichment of its own nature by appropriating to itself, and blending with itself, kindred or congenial psychic elements of whatever character.

An excellent psychologist, the late Dr. McDougall, listed the primary needs of all animals, including man, as follows: Food and drink, warmth, shelter, work, play, and love. Corresponding to these needs he assigned appropriate "instincts"—meaning inborn or unlearned tendencies to react in specific ways to specific stimuli. These he enumerated as food-seeking, homing, and constructive instincts; instincts of curiosity, self-assertion, and acquisition; and the gregarious and mating impulses.

I do not forget that even the use of the word "instinct" is frowned upon and vetoed by some psychologists. Others, who sanction the word with the foregoing definition, would classify the spontaneous propensions or impulsions of human nature somewhat differently than McDougall does. But with this family dispute among the specialists we need not concern ourselves. It suffices us to recognize that all the elements enumerated and named by McDougall are actually in our nature, however they may be labeled or classified.

The subject of love is clearly related to the last two items in McDougall's list of instincts; *i.e.*, the gregarious and the mating impulses. It is important to note that even primitively, at the animal level, we discern the equal operation of both these instincts or propensions; and that only one of them is in any wise connected with the organization, the functions, and the psychic phenomena of sex. Equally primordial and imperious (in those species in which it appears at all) is the gregarious impulse, which is a craving for the comfort,

safety, and happiness of association with numbers of
the animal's own kind.

It should further be specified that within the general
sphere of that part of the love-impulse which *is* associated with sex, the pairing or mating instinct is again
distinct from the parental instinct. To lump these
widely unlike things together under the title of an
"instinct of race-preservation," as is sometimes done,
is to create a misleading confusion by identifying two
unconnected sets of impulsions and activities. In some
animal species, the male displays no trace whatever of
any parental instinct. Yet in such species the mating
impulse is as strong as in any other; as must needs be
the case, indeed, since without this no species could continue to exist.

Now man, biologically considered, is a gregarious
animal. He therefore displays all three of the types of
impulse and behavior related to the general theme of
love; *i.e.*, the societal, the mating, and the parental instinct. The biologists account for this by pointing out
the necessity for it entailed by the long infancy of the
human species; and to the joint operation of all these
three impulsions they would refer the supreme rank of
man among animals as regards intelligence. For man,
at birth, is the most helpless of all creatures, and remains helpless relatively longer than the young of any
other creature.

This, however, is but another way of saying that love
—self-giving and self-spending love—was originally,
and remains permanently, the condition without which

there could have been no human evolution. These varieties of instinctive behavior were all displayed by the apes, prior to the advent of humanity; and they continue to be equally manifested today in chimpanzees, and in all the varieties of apes which are anatomically nearest to humanity. This very fact shows that they throw no light on the transition from the anthropoid to the human level. That evolutionary new departure is called a "mutation,"—one of the many fine words used in science to denote those facts which the experts have to accept but are unable to explain. This, let me add, is no reflection on science, since facts of this character will persist in occurring, and must be indicated somehow. But it does behoove non-expert thinkers to remember that many such terms are only labels for our ignorance, and not to mistake them (as is often done) for explanations which dissipate ignorance.

The point that now concerns us, however, is this: that the preservation of this "mutation" from highest ape to lowest man, once it had occurred, and its permanent engrafting into the race, depended absolutely on self-spending love, and on the co-operation of both parents in the nurture of the young.

Let us keep clearly in mind, then, that what we call love (and have roughly defined as the expression of the impulse to self-expansion and self-enrichment by blending the self with kindred or congenial psychic elements of whatever nature) is related not to one only, but to *three* primordial animal tendencies: the gregarious, the mating, and the parental; and that of these three only

one—the mating impulse—is necessarily and inseparably connected with the physical functions and psychic
phenomena of sex.

Two other general considerations remain to be noted
before proceeding to the detail of our analysis. The
first is that the animal origin of anything human sets
no limits to its possible development after it has become
transformed and transmuted by its blending with that
nature in man which is distinctive and unique. Suppose
it to be true, for instance (as some scientists hold), that
intelligence at first evolved merely as an aid to food-
seeking. It may have been so. But this has not prevented the intelligence thus originated from maturing
into a power which weighs and analyzes distant stars,
determines the ultimate constitution of matter, and engenders such thoughts as those of Aristotle and Jesus,
of Shakespeare, Newton, and Kant.

A second consideration, also relevant to our theme,
is this: that any power, the fulfillment of which depends
upon its entering into relation or combination with a
responsive power elsewhere, while its intrinsic nature
will remain unchanged, will yet manifest different qualities, properties, or aspects, according to the nature of
that with which it interacts. It is, for example, the most
familiar of chemical facts that a compound exhibits
properties entirely unlike those of its elements in their
separateness, and quite unpredictable prior to experience of the effects of the combination.

This law would seem to hold true in the psychic as
well as in the physical realm. For while love is certainly

an expression of a phase of the original life-energy, yet
it is never called love, or thought of as such, except in
relation to some object. It is platitudinously obvious
that we cannot very well love without loving something
or somebody. But when we do this, even though it be
for the first time in our lives, we immediately become
aware that we are giving release to something that from
the beginning was latent in our nature and integral
to it.

These preliminary explorations of our theme will, I
trust, have made at least two things clear. One is that
the possible objects of love are indefinitely numerous.
The second is that the character or quality of the love
will in each case be differentiated by the nature of its
object, and by the nature of the relation between the
lover and that object. Our present undertaking is to
analyze out and contrast seven kinds of love. But the
reader will understand clearly that the enumeration of
these does not exhaust all the varieties of love. A complete psychological analysis would augment the number enormously.

Yet however numerous the kinds of love, they must
needs all possess some characteristic in common, since
otherwise it would be absurd to call them all by the
same name. At the human level this constant characteristic is found, I believe, in the fact that all varieties of
love find their objects (*a*) in persons, (*b*) in objects
created by personality and permeated with it, or (*c*) in
objects to which a personal nature or origin can be

attributed, either literally or through the exercise of poetic imagination.

The last two classes of possible objects of love may sound somewhat vague and indefinite. But I think they will cease to seem so if we specify further that they include all creations of men which may be objects of love, and all objects of beauty or interest in nature which either have a quasi-personal character (as animals have), or which—like flowers, landscapes, sunrises, the ocean, the moon, or the starlit heavens—can be poetically personified, or can be regarded literally (under the influence of certain theological doctrines) as the meaningful creations of a divine person or persons, whose imprint and sign-manual they will then be construed as displaying.

These distinctions may seem fussy or pedantic. But what I am driving at is this: Ordinary speech and the haphazard carelessness of common thinking regard love as mainly, if not exclusively, a sentiment involving sex. Freud's theory does the same; for which blunder it was most brilliantly reduced to absurdity by Professor McDougall. As the first step, therefore, towards correcting this error, I set down the reminder that we can, and actually do, love all manner of objects—animals, phases of nature, music, literature, poetry, the creations of plastic art, and the like—in relation to which the idea of sex is simply ludicrous. Nor can it be said that to speak of "love" in such connections is to make a forced or figurative use of language. We may do so with literal appropriateness. If anybody thinks, for ex-

ample, that devotees of music or literature speak only
figuratively when they talk of their "love" for them,
he can know little of the depth and power of the feelings concerned.

My reason for pointing out that these quasi-personal
objects, or things created by and imbued with human
personality, may be objects of love, is to show how very
wide-ranging is the propension expressed by that term,
and therefore how boundless is the craving for the enlargement and enrichment of our personalities by the
assimilation and interblending with them of congenial
objects or elements. My seven illustrative types of love,
however, will be confined to personal relations. I do not
contemplate analyzing further the kinds of love which
arise through attachment to objects treasured as expressions of personality, or through the poetical or theological transfusion of natural objects with personality.

Let us now proceed, then, to our first "exhibit," by
considering those types of love between human beings
which either are altogether independent of sex, or in
which the special quality arising from difference of sex
is wholly distinct from that associated with the mating
impulse.

As "independent of sex" I would class all relations
of love between persons of the same sex. Everyday experience shows that men can really and genuinely love
other men, and that women can truly love other women;
that the kind of love exemplified in these relations can
exist in the complete absence of any known or recognized tie of blood-kinship; and that such love may be

as pure, deep, lasting, and life-enriching as any of the kinds which do involve sex. This is one of the most certain and most beautiful phases of human experience. In some ways, perhaps, it may be considered the highest type of love, because at its best it is the most utterly disinterested of affections, richest in pure self-giving, and most frequently poured forth without thought, and even without possibility, of recompense.

It is noteworthy in the life of boys and young men that, at the very stage of their development when the emotional attraction of the opposite sex is most newly and powerfully felt, this fascinating and thrilling delight in loving others of their own sex is also manifested. And, perhaps as a result of its non-sexual quality, this kind of love is less liable to ebb and flow, less transient and variable, than the sort of fascination in which sex-attraction predominates.

A man may speak with confidence about the friendships of men, especially those originating in boyhood, because his assertions in this connection are based upon and verified by his own experience. I believe, however, that what I have said respecting them is equally true (though possibly not as *frequently* true) regarding friendships between women. Here, however, a man's judgment can only be based upon observation, testimony, and inference; it therefore cannot have the full assurance and certitude which only personal experience can yield. For there is a sense—there is a sphere—in which men and women can never fully understand each other, because they do not share the same world of experience. I refer to that area in the life of each which the other cannot enter because it is created and defined by their differences of organization and biological function.

I urge this caution upon myself and upon the reader, because no less a person than Edith Wharton, after writing an eloquent and enthusiastic description of the friendships of Alexander Hamilton, declared that this relation between men is the noblest and grandest of human experiences, and that in the lives of women there is nothing comparable with it. With the highest respect for Miss Wharton's authority, I find myself unable to accept this statement; for I believe that I have actually witnessed cases of friendship between women which were every whit as deep, true, and lasting, and as inspiring and exalting to those concerned, as any friendships between men have ever been.

As my first specimen, then, I submit that the love which may subsist between men and men, or between women and women, is one kind of love clearly independent of sex. This sort of love, which is the very stuff of friendship, may conceivably owe its origin (in the racial, evolutionary sense) to the gregarious instinct; since that is a force of attraction between members of a species which embraces the whole kind, irrespective of sex. If, however, we accept this theory of its origin, we shall do so only because we could not well understand the possibility of this type of love unless some ancient instinct, surviving in us from animal ancestry, provided for it a psycho-physical basis or substratum. For the essence of the love exemplified in friendship is its selectivity, its preferential discrimination of its individual objects; whereas the gregarious instinct at the animal level is an undiscriminating, undifferentiated yearning for the society of any specimens whatever of the creature's own kind. What is more, this primitive form of the instinct persists likewise in us; as is proved by the longing for any sort of human fellowship which awakens in persons condemned to prolonged solitude.

But now let us consider a distinct class of cases of love, the peculiar charm and beauty of which are indeed due to difference of sex, but in which that difference has still nothing to do with the specific attraction which is the dynamic of the mating instinct. The most conspicuous types of this class are the love between brothers and sisters, that between mothers and sons, and that between fathers and daughters. Each of these owes its distinguishing peculiarity and unique quality to difference of sex. Yet each of them is so completely distinct from the mating instinct that the intrusion into it of this factor would be its perversion and destruction, and would be regarded by all sane people as a manifestation of criminal insanity.

Here, I submit, we behold three types of love, the reality of which is proved by universal experience. The specific difference between each of them and its nearest counterpart is manifestly due to the varying psychology of sex, operating in each case in ways which are unmistakably real, though it would require long and deep study to specify them in detail. Clearly, however, the love between brothers and sisters differs from that between brothers and brothers or between sisters and sisters, just as the love between fathers and daughters, or between mothers and sons, differs from that between fathers and sons and mothers and daughters.

Thus far, then, we have listed four kinds of love: First, the type which subsists between men and men, and between women and women, without possessing or needing the cement of blood-kinship; second, the distinctive love between brothers and sisters; third, that between mothers and sons; and fourthly, that between fathers and daughters. The basis of each of the last three is the fact of blood-kinship; but in all of them alike this force is crossed and modified by the subtle psychological influence of sex difference. These three types fall naturally into a class by themselves, despite the interesting and charming unlikenesses which impart to each of them its unique quality. These contrarieties between them we all know by experience, however difficult we might find it to specify them with precision. The reality of the differences, however, is spontaneously, if unconsciously, admitted whenever we recognize the painful void that exists in the lives, for example, of "only" children; of girls without brothers, or boys without sisters; of mothers without sons, or of fathers without daughters. If the differences (clearly due to sex) between these analogous relations were not very real, there would be no such void in these people's

lives;—except, of course, in the case of the "only"
child.

In the present analysis I shall undertake no study
of the love which *is* associated with the mating instinct;
partly because I have treated of it elsewhere, but
mainly because it is almost the only branch of the
subject which has been widely studied, and is well depicted in psychological and general literature. Any
reader who may be interested in my own thoughts concerning it will find them presented in a small book
entitled "The Fine Art of Marriage," and in various
chapters of my other writings.

Neither shall I take space to specify the potentially
beautiful and mutually enriching quality of the love
that may subsist between fathers and sons, and mothers
and daughters; between brothers and brothers, and
sisters and sisters. These varieties within the common
species are, I agree, fully as worthy of analysis as those
to which I am directing attention. A complete human
life certainly needs the experience of all of them.

The fifth differentiated type of love to which I
would direct attention is that which may subsist between men and women unconnected by blood-kinship,
and yet is not due to and not affected by sex in the
mating sense. Interesting instances of this type are
often to be observed between what are colloquially
called "in-laws." For example, the relations—often
most agreeable and mutually enriching—between a
man and his wife's sisters, or between a woman and her
husband's brothers, well merit a psychological analysis

that would throw light on their specific character. In the broader sphere, this type of love is exemplified also between men and women who are simply good comrades or friends, without even the artificial legal kinship which arises from marriage among their relatives.

Regarding such friendships, in which the thought of mating never arises, two things can be confidently affirmed. One is that they can and do happen; and that they often continue through many years, unperturbed and unshadowed by any influence which could spoil them or change their character. The multiplication of such friendships is one of the good results of the new association and co-operation brought about by the opening to women of occupations and professional careers formerly monopolized by men. The second point which needs mention concerning them is this: that if the cheap cynicism were justified which sneers at these friendships, or slanders them by implying that they merely camouflage those relations which law and social standards prohibit, then the whole idea of equal opportunities for both sexes, and the consequent stimulating rivalry of men and women in cultural and professional pursuits, would be an impracticable dream.

It is admittedly true that friendships of this order frequently carry with them a special type of dangerous possibilities. But so do many other human juxtapositions, which, nevertheless, nobody thinks either of sneering at or of banning. These dangers in life are the very conditions and opportunities for the testing and development of character. Without them the strengthening of moral fibre would be impossible. Their due appraisal requires us to bear in mind the fine discrimination of Milton: "I cannot praise a fugitive and cloistered virtue, unexercised and unbreathed, which never sallies forth and seeks its adversary, but shrinks out of the race where that immortal garland is to be run for, not without dust and heat." The tragedies that sometimes occur in such relations, through the frailty of individuals, however lamentable, are more than offset by the many good results in moral development which accrue where the danger is surmounted.

The sixth type of love which we must briefly characterize is that more generalized, but far from sufficiently exemplified affection called "the love of our neighbor": a kind of love which every ethical religion has inculcated, and which the fine insight of Aristotle perceived to be the one trustworthy and durable foundation of a democratic society. So rare is this type (at least beyond the limits of the smallest communal groupings, or when it is not reinforced by traditional blood-ties of tribe or clan) that the seers who have perceived its moral bindingness and social necessity have held it necessary to command it. But in the precept, "Thou *shalt* love thy neighbor as thyself," we seem to confront a paradox. The elucidation of this, accordingly, requires careful thought.*

The paradox, as we have seen, is this: Love is taken to be a purely spontaneous sentiment—something that

* This subject was admirably treated by Sir John Seeley in his famous book, "Ecce Homo." See also Chapter X.

merely happens, or fails to happen. You "fall" into love; and if later you "fall" out of it again, the relaxed standards of the present day regard this as merely a fatality, which constitutes sufficient cause for the dissolution of a marriage; the old ties of duty and responsibility being considered merely superstitious. On this view, you either love a person or you do not. In neither case, it is assumed, has your will anything to do with the matter. But if this were so, what would be the sense of annexing, as Seeley puts it, "an imperative mood to the verb 'to love'?" To *command* love, it is said, is like commanding the weather, or telling a person that he "ought" to enjoy some article of food or drink which, in fact, is completely distasteful to him.

We cannot enter here upon the question how far duty, honor, and social responsibility ought to be counted upon to maintain bonds originally created by love in cases where the merely passion-inspired love has ceased to exist. But we can, I think, resolve the paradox of a commanded neighbor-love in a different way. We have seen in the preceding chapter how education, beginning in infancy, can influence feelings that only awaken at puberty. Here we may illustrate the process by referring back to that gregarious instinct which every student of the psychology of animals and of men admits to be part of our native make-up. But if it is so, then obviously it must lie in our nature to find pleasure in the society of *any* specimens of our kind, unless or until some artificial influence arises to pervert the natural attraction into suspicion or dislike, or into a no less alienating feeling of superiority or inferiority.

Otherwise expressed, the psychological fact is that all the prejudices and enmities which divide people into hostile groups are due to adventitious and preventable causes, whereby men's original natural feeling towards each other is poisoned or perverted. Experience and observation have long since proved that all the forces of so-called race-prejudice, hatred of foreigners, and antagonism of class, party, or sect, are due to such artificial causes. For these alienations never arise among children until they are injected by suggestion from elders, or until such causes of quarrel as regularly arise among all children are illogically intensified by being referred to the superficial differences in question.

But if this be a true reading of our psychic make-up in its natural and unperverted state (and either this must be the case, or else it would be false to call man a gregarious animal), then the commandment to love our neighbor as ourself will find rational justification in the facts of psychology and biology. For what that commandment requires is clearly no impossibility. It demands only the removal of those adventitious influences, engendering suspicions and hostilities, which pervert the stream and divert the flow of an original natural impulse.

Implied in the commandment "Thou shalt love thy neighbour as thyself," is the ethical demand that we shall prove our love to him by valuing most especially in him those characteristics and capacities wherein he differs from us; for certainly our self-love is lavished mainly on what we believe to be distinctive of ourselves. So far, then, from putting an impossible strain upon human nature, this is really a command that we should return to it,—by removing obstacles which prevent our nature from operating according to its original constitution.

Our arrival at this sixth kind of love—a kind so rare as to require the introduction of a moral imperative to render it operative—leads us on to the seventh kind I have in mind; and this will complete our selection of instances. This seventh specimen is what Emerson called "the Celestial Love," and what the religious seers have always termed "the love of God."

Reduced to the prose which must be employed for the analysis of experience, this means the love of that universal Ideal which is partially and variously manifested in the fine qualities of fine people. We only truly honor those we love when we see beyond what they are to what they might be. Our mental eye beholds their fine qualities perfected, and all the faults and limitations due to the common animal nature eliminated. This insight it is which can render every variety of personal love an enrichment of personality; not only by its effect in enhancing the joyousness which is love's normal overtone, but by the incentive it affords to self-improvement and self-transcendence. For he who loves, having painted this idealized picture of the object of his love, will feel the obligation of acting in ways calculated to turn the idealized picture into an achieved reality. "My love for him must make him a better man," such a one will say. And the recipient of this love will respond duly to its influence by resolving, "I must become a better man in order that I may deserve such love."

Thus on final analysis it turns out that the highest phase of every type of love is our concern for those ideal possibilities which the clairvoyance of affection divines beyond what is already actualized in the loved person. Unless our affection really inspires its object to seek these nobler heights of attainment, it is of less than the right quality. A love that leaves its object unimproved, and still more one which drags it below its already achieved level, is both perverted and perverting.

I have been led to write upon this theme because of my conviction that those ideally right relations among all human beings, to the discovery and establishment of which ethics and religion are devoted, conceivably could, and some day possibly may, transform the entire human family into a society of friends and lovers. Such a fellowship, if ever it were actualized on even a limited scale, would deserve to be called heaven. The misery in which the whole world is now engulfed makes the idea of such a society seem fantastic. Nevertheless, those who have tried the experiment know that to devote one's life to the effort even to understand what are the first steps towards this far-off goal, is in very truth to breathe something of the atmosphere of heaven, even while we have to live amidst the hell kindled by human perversity.

CHAPTER XII

WHY LIFE IS WORTH LIVING

Among the attributes of the human mind, an illimit-able and insatiable curiosity is certainly to be counted. Not content with posing to itself the bound-less range of questions to which it is possible to hope that answers may some day be found, men also devote much time and ingenuity to the consideration of others which it is inherently impossible to answer. It is well to clear our minds on this point; because if the idleness of such questions is not recognized, the vanity of all attempts to answer them may lead men to a cynical skepticism like that of Omar Khayyam. One set of these queries deals with matters which must remain inscru-table either for lack of access to the relevant data, or because they transcend the powers of the human mind.

Let us glance at a few instances of questions of this character: Our astronomers make very precise maps of that face of the moon which is always turned towards the earth whenever the moon is visible. But this happens always to be the same face; the reverse side of the moon is inaccessible to observation, and questions concerning its topography are therefore unanswerable.—Whether the physical universe is finite or infinite cannot be ascer-tained. Either alternative seems unthinkable; yet no

third possibility had occurred to anybody until Professor Einstein hit upon the suggestion that space may
be "finite but unbounded": an oracular statement which
to the lay mind makes the enigma more impenetrable
than ever.—Consider, too, the many books which have
attempted to answer the question whether life, such
as we know it on earth, exists on other bodies in space.
More than fifty years ago I remember hearing my
father discuss a book dealing with this question; and
in October, 1940, I saw a new work on the subject announced. Now, all the astronomers can do is to calculate
what are the mathematical probabilities regarding the
existence of other planetary systems like our own. They
cannot even say whether the nearest planets in our
own system are the abodes of life or not. Controversy
still continues, because astronomers still differ, as to
whether there is life on Mars. I understand, however,
that those who assert the affirmative claim visual evidence
only for the existence of vegetation. Even this is controverted by their opponents. But if we are thus
inevitably ignorant concerning the conditions on our
nearest planetary neighbors, what are we to say regarding the guesses about other solar systems, the very
existence of which is a matter solely of mathematical
probability, unverified by any observational evidence
whatever?

Or consider, again, the perennially absorbing question whether our individualized, self-conscious personalities continue to exist and retain their self-identity
after death. Whole libraries could be filled with the

literature devoted to this question. Within the past
three decades those who answer it affirmatively have
even produced minute (albeit somewhat contradictory)
descriptions of the conditions under which men's posthumous life is lived. And yet, whether there is such a
life at all is really only a matter of religious faith or
philosophic speculation; that is, it cannot possibly be
a matter of knowledge.

Here, then, we have several instances of a kind of
problem to which only some inconceivable extension of
our factual information, or the development in us of
mental powers at present non-existent, could possibly
enable us to find solutions.

But there is another class of questions which I, for
one, have long ventured to think of as pseudo-prob-
lems. By this I mean that they are questions only in
form and not in fact, because only one answer to them
is really possible. And this answer is actually given in
practice by everybody, including those who seek dialectical diversion by pretending to reject it and formulate another answer in words.

Of this class of sham questions, the old one, "Is Life
Worth Living?" is perhaps the most salient example.
Although men have written serious books under this
title, the query is in truth a sham one. For everybody
answers it in the affirmative, from the first instinctive
act he performs at the moment of birth, down to his last
instinctive struggle against the approach of death.
Our whole physical and psychical organization testifies
that we are embodiments of a will which is deeper in

us than reason; and the maintenance of our life is certainly the first, though just as certainly not the only, expression of this will. No verbal assertion by anybody that life is not worth living, for himself or others, is really worth the breath consumed in making it. For he who utters this assertion contradicts himself by the very fact that he is alive to make it.

The only way of affirming the worthlessness of life which is intellectually respectable (whatever it may be morally) is the act of suicide. If a man kills himself after declaring life to be not worth living, he at least proves that he believed what he said.* I strongly agree with the general moral judgment of the Western world over the past two thousand years, that suicide, *if and when committed by a person fully responsible*, is the most revolting of crimes. We must always indulge the charity of adjudging the self-slayer temporarily or permanently insane, since otherwise we should find ourselves constrained to condemn him for the last and worst treason and disloyalty to humanity and the ideals which command it. But even such an act, though it attests the individual pessimist's logical consistency, still expresses a judgment only upon his individual case; it can throw no sort of light upon any other case, or upon human life in general.

The question I here invite the reader to consider with me is very different from the idle one which I thus dismiss. Our question is, "*Why* is life worth living?" This sets us upon the quest for rational justification of

* Cf. Chapter IX, above.

an inevitable practical belief. The one we dismiss is a really idle pretense that this practical belief is not held, and that a counterfeit question is a genuine and an open one.

What we shall attempt, then, is a task analogous to that undertaken by philosophers when they inquire *how* knowledge is possible. Many a fluent charlatan has jeered at these inquirers on the erroneous assumption— itself a proof of complete ignorance—that they were asking *whether* knowledge is possible. That it is possible is a self-evident fact, which the mere posing of the true philosophic question fully acknowledges. For no man who has paid any attention to the processes of his own thinking would trouble to ask any question whatsoever unless he believed that a right answer to it were attainable; and such answer, when found, would of course be a piece of knowledge. The philosophers, therefore, starting from the undisputed fact that knowledge exists, have devoted their efforts to investigating those factors in our mental constitution which render it possible. So far from this research being the foolish waste of time that it has sometimes been declared, no inquiry could possibly be fraught with more vital interest and importance.

And the same may be said of the question we are to consider. But in attempting to tell *why* they find life worth living, men have given almost as many answers as there are extant religious creeds or philosophic systems. Nay, every religion and every philosophy is, in one sense, an answer to this question. And taking such answers collectively, we find that in the Western world at least they have usually boiled down to this: "Life is worth living because my own particular belief regarding God or the universe is true. If I did not believe this, life for me would not be worth living; and if you deny it, neither can it be so for you, though for a time you may delude yourself into thinking that it is."

Such was the gist of a famous and subtle volume— "Is Life Worth Living?"—published in 1880 by William Hurrell Mallock. This author was a Roman Catholic. He was a scholar of considerable attainments, master of a brilliantly attractive literary style, a consummate debater, and the author of a series of genuinely valuable works on social and economic matters. His treatise on the worth of life was one example of a trick which he repeated in several subsequent volumes. It consisted in an extremely clever counter-attack upon the Positivists, and the agnostic school of Huxley, Tyndall, and W. K. Clifford, which was then at the meridian of its celebrity. Mallock's book was widely read and discussed. (Among other comments which it elicited was the famous retort of "Punch" to his question: "It all depends on the *liver*.")

What I have called Mallock's trick consisted in applying the agnostics' own methods of skeptical analysis, and their own standards of evidence and verification, to a question, the answer to which (as he alleged) the agnostics themselves took for granted. He undertook to show that their system (however much against their intention) really destroyed the validity of all value-judgments, and left no standing-ground for the conservation of those values upon the reality of which the worth of life does indeed depend. As an *argumentum ad hominem* it had great strength, quite apart from the brilliant literary qualities which render all Mallock's books such delightful reading. But when he turned from verbal sword-play to construction, and undertook to show how the worth of life *can* be conserved, his strength failed him. For what is his answer? Simply this: If we can convince ourselves that we can reasonably make the venture of faith required for believing in the infallibility of the Pope and the divine authority of the Roman Church, as expressed in all its beliefs and practices, *then* we shall truly find life worth living; but otherwise not.

The obvious retort was shouted in chorus by Protestants and other non-believers in Catholicism: "But, in fact, we *do* find life worth living." To this Mallock answers in effect, "That is because you are illogical. But presently you will wake up and perceive into what a morass of fallacies you have fallen. Then you will know better."

This publication, as I have said, made a great stir and elicited many answers. I still have in my library one specimen of these, a work which in its day was widely popular. It is a series of sermons entitled, "Is Life Worth Living?—An Eightfold Answer," by John Clifford, who for many years was the leading light of the Baptist Church in Great Britain. Dr. Clifford, of course, is as contemptuous as one would expect a good

Protestant to be of Mr. Mallock's "Popery." But his own answer to the question is simply Mallock's over again with a slight variation: "Life will be worth living only so long as we can believe in the scheme of salvation which Evangelical Protestantism has elaborated."

At first sight it may seem rather surprising to find so thoroughly free a thinker as William James restating the argument in practically the same terms. He did this in a lecture from which we have already quoted.* It was originally prepared, I believe, for delivery to the Ethical Society in Philadelphia, and is to be found in his volume entitled "The Will to Believe, and Other Essays." Even James has to look outside of the present life for grounds whereon to affirm its worth. It becomes worth living, he says, only when we trust the hopes prompted by our spiritual instinct, and affirm our personal immortality in a spiritual world which transcends present experience. We have to live and act (he says in effect) either upon the supposition that these things are real, or upon the supposition that they are not. Neither alternative can possibly be proved. But when this is the case, and we are confronted with what he calls an "option," the course of wisdom, he insists, is to choose that one of the two unprovable alternatives which is most in the line of our desires and interests.

I call attention, then, to this fact: All such answers amount to saying that life on its present merits, life within the limits of what is now experienced and verifi-

* See above, Chapter X.

able, either is not worth living or cannot be proved to be so. For they all tell us that only something superadded to it can make it so. It is this position that I propose to controvert.

Before doing so, let me make it clear that I am far from denying the reality of that spiritual universe in which James believed. On the contrary, I likewise believe in it, and have stated my belief, as every reader of this and my earlier books will know, in a form not dissimilar to his. Nevertheless, I hold it quite unsound to make the worth of life here and now depend upon such considerations. I contend that, as a fact verified in experience, life is worth living here and now to the man who believes in no spiritual universe and no personal immortality; and this whether his reason for disbelieving in them is that he has considered and rejected the arguments in their favor, or simply that he cannot understand those arguments, or that he happens (as has been the case with millions) never to have heard of them.

My case is that such a man, by merely living, still more by working nobly for public causes (as multitudes holding such negative beliefs have done), both affirms and illustrates the worth of life. We may regret his intellectual misfortune in the narrow restriction of his outlook; just as we might sympathize with another man s inability to appreciate music or to enjoy fine literature. Nevertheless, I for one still maintain that he is fully justified in his affirmation. And history proves that life has been lived zestfully, faithfully, and often heroically, by millions of men whose outlook was confined entirely to the present life. The early Hebrews, upon whose minds the conception of personal immortality had never dawned, and some of whose earliest and noblest prophets were devoid of this belief, are a salient case in point.

Surely logic requires us to show life to be worth living "at the worst," as Zangwill says—*i.e.*, taking the world on its lowest terms—if we are to prove that it is worth living at all. Grant, for the sake of argument, that what the materialist takes for the whole of life is really only a part of it. Still if we found ourselves forced to condemn that part, which is all that any man's experience can verify, how could we hope to justify the whole? For that whole, after all, so far as it outruns the experience which we all share with the materialist, can only depend upon faith or inference. And is it not a strange logic to reason, as many do, that *because* this life shows a surplus of evil as compared with good, *therefore* another life *must* contain a preponderance of good over evil?

Such, however, is the kind of reasoning by which the burdensome problem of the evils of life has been met by theological thinkers; and not by them alone. Pascal frankly based his whole argument for Christianity upon a wager; and James, as we have seen, follows him in doing so. Of the two contradictory propositions, "God exists" and "God does not exist," one must be true; but neither, says Pascal, can be proved by reason. Therefore, "*Il faut parier*—You must bet." And seeing that you have everything to gain and nothing to lose by backing the affirmative proposition, and living accordingly, to do otherwise would be the decision of a fool.* Bishop Butler, so famous for his development of the thesis that probability is the guide of life, would have us assume the existence of God on a low degree of probability, and act accordingly. But surely this is a dangerous resource. It is admittedly unprovable that there is for mankind collectively, here and now, more good than evil in the world, or that the good is destined to triumph and the evil to be overthrown in man's earthly experience. Now all scientific reasoning proceeds on the assumption that the future will be like the present, or will become different only through the continued action of forces now in operation. By what warrant can this sort of logic be reversed in arguing from an actual present to a possible future life? As Bishop Butler himself well said, "Why should we wish to be deceived?"

Countless people in the modern world have turned away from these disputes about God and immortality. They have not, of course, disproved these doctrines, for to do so is impossible. But certainly they do not find them convincing; and the weary cynicism, like that of Omar Khayyam, which is now so widespread, appar-

---

* The "joker," if I may speak so flippantly, in Pascal's argument is the silent assumption that, if God exists, He must be the God of Catholicism, and therefore that the traditional scheme of Hell, Purgatory and Heaven, and the sacraments as indispensable to salvation, must be true. That there may be an ultimate spiritual reality quite unlike the God of the Creeds is a possibility Pascal never contemplated.

ently renders the subject uninteresting. Instead, many have tried to comfort themselves and others by the thought that, in the long run, the human race will come to enjoy a clear balance of good over evil.

This seems to be the position of Dr. Eustace Haydon, who, in two of his books which I have read, looks forward to an earthly paradise with all the unwavering conviction and fervent zest of an Evangelical Protestant's anticipations of heaven. Yet, judging by all the results of progress down to date, this is at least as shaky a basis for affirming the worth of the present life as the older beliefs. Two obstacles to our entertaining it are mountainously obvious. The first is that it is quite uncertain, and would remain so even if we could envisage the ultimate harmonizing of all the diverse interests, aims, and psychic propensities of men. To believe in it, therefore, is a matter of faith; and one does not easily see how such faith can be justified by those who object to other beliefs being accepted on faith. It is at best an *Aberglaube*, or (in the etymological and not the offensive sense of the term) a superstition.

The other obvious objection is yet more serious. It is this: that if the belief in a future earthly paradise be true, still all we should learn from it is that life will some day be worth living to one or more generations of our remote posterity. Surely, however, what we are seeking is valid reasons why life is worth living here and now, to ourselves, as we actually find it. There is at least some measure of truth in George Tyrrell's statement that "We live for ourselves, and not for a

posterity that never comes." Our only data for appraising the worth of life are found in our own experience
and in our knowledge of the life of men in past ages;
including, incidentally, the men of the Old Stone Age,
who, practically without weapons, had to encounter the
saber-toothed tiger and the woolly mammoth; and who
by doing this victoriously, and by enduring the Ice
Ages in their caverns or igloos, conclusively attested
their own belief in the worth of life at what to us would
seem its worst.

The tacit assumption of all the arguments, theological and secular alike, which we have thus far considered, is that what gives life its worth is happiness.
I contend that all history disproves this assumption;
notwithstanding the truth (which I fully admit) of
Bishop Butler's dictum, that "Happiness is what we
all naturally desire." Happiness, moreover, has been
assumed to be something quantitative and measurable,
something of which the factors are known, and at least
potentially controllable. Or, at the very least, men have
thought that happiness would inevitably be produced
by providing such knowable and controllable factors.
It was this assumption which led Jeremy Bentham to
formulate his famous standard for morals and legislation: "The greatest happiness of the greatest number."

But it is only necessary to look this dogma clearly
in the face in order to see that the utilitarianism based
upon it was a delusion. Society can, indeed, partially
control (but *how* partially the economic cataclysms of
the past decade have shown) the supply and distribution

of such commodities as may give happiness, or prevent
unhappiness, by ministering to the physical and animal
part of us. It can also place intellectual and artistic
satisfactions at the disposal of people intelligent and
educated enough to appreciate them. But whether any
or all of these things will assure happiness to any given
person cannot be known, because this depends upon incalculable factors. Real happiness (as we saw in Chapter
X) depends upon spiritual facts and personal relations,
which society cannot control; and which, when they do
exist, lie at the mercy of all the vicissitudes of nature
and fate.

This truth is brought home to us every time we contemplate the spectacle—witnessed and bemoaned or
ridiculed by moralists and satirists in all ages—of men
rich and successful, powerful and famous, yet still unhappy. "Call no man happy until he is dead," said the
shrewd Athenians, as Herodotus records. Only material
and external things are even partially controllable; and
happiness, with that which makes or destroys it, cannot
be ensured by externals.

It happens most fortunately, however, that this argument cuts both ways. It is wholesome to remember that
those externals which are commonly thought necessary
causes of happiness, and the deprivation of them, which
might seem to ensure unhappiness and misery, often
prove in practice not to produce their expected effects.
Just as it is an error to suppose that wealth and great
possessions or power must make men happy, so is it,
luckily, no less an error to suppose that poverty and its

concomitants must necessarily destroy or prevent happiness.

I was set upon this train of thought by the accounts our American newspaper correspondents have lately sent us,* with such hearty and generous admiration, of the fortitude and courage, the mutual kindliness and good humor, they have witnessed among the British, and especially among the Londoners, during many weeks of merciless bombing by the German Air Force. The truth of these glowing newspaper accounts has been confirmed for many of us by private letters from our friends in that country.

Now I am a born Londoner, and my own and my wife's kith and kin are among the millions who are enduring this ordeal and displaying these qualities. Hence I shall hardly fall under suspicion of depreciating the morale thus displayed. I would point out, however, as a fact in which we may all rejoice, that this sort of courage belongs, if not to all peoples, at least to many varieties of humanity. It is by no means limited to any one or two peoples. We too often forget, for example, that the Chinese (who certainly deserve all that Dr. Lin Yutang has written in their favor) have been displaying the same high qualities in equally admirable fashion for more than three years. We should remember, too, how much of the same fortitude was displayed in various cities of Spain during its long internal war.

A letter from an old friend, Lord Snell, tells me that on September 15th (the day of the greatest aerial

* Written in October, 1940.

battle over London) he was engaged to deliver a discourse to one of the Ethical Societies in that city.
Shortly after he had begun to speak the air-raid warn-
ing sirens were heard; whereupon he broke off in his
address to ask the audience whether they wished to
leave and seek cover in a nearby air-raid shelter. Not
a single one of them stirred; Lord Snell continued and
completed his discourse, and the service finished in the
regular way. I have also received a diary of a week's
experience of air-raids. This was written by a little old
lady of seventy-six, my friend for more than forty
years. She is a retired school-teacher; and it was actually written in the dug-out in her own garden during
a midnight air attack. In the course of it she remarks
that she and her companions felt reasonably safe from
falling shrapnel, "but of course a direct hit would be
the instant end of all of us." Yet her journal is written
with all the calmness of her ordinary letters and conversation, and with several touches of humor. A letter
from my brother, whose house stands (or stood)
directly in the path of enemy aircraft approaching
London from the North Sea, remarks in character-
istically British fashion, "As you can perhaps imagine,
life over here is somewhat keyed up just now." One
would hardly describe this as an over-statement.

I share to the full the admiration of these qualities
which Americans have so generally and so generously
expressed. Nevertheless, I would point out that the
surprise expressed at them betrays our habitual under-
valuation of the high potentialities of ordinary, every-

day human nature. It strikes me as unfortunate that our power of divining what our fellows have it in them to be, or to become, is either so slight or so little utilized. For the fact is that in the midst of tragedy we always become aware of elements of nobility and greatness in people that only tragedy can call forth; and when life goes sunnily we forget—or we never learn—that those elements are there. It is with our knowledge of our fellows as it is with our knowledge of the stars. Only in the darkness of the night can we see those majestic gems of the firmament which nevertheless are always there. Whoever, for example, has really known and shared the life of the poor, must testify that among them can always be found examples of that neighborly kindliness and mutual helpfulness, that courage and fortitude and humor, which have been so admiringly commented upon in the Londoners.

The point I would stress is that a fuller realization and juster appreciation of the inherent greatness latent in human nature generally, would have made this phenomenon of high courage among civilians under bombardment not indeed less welcome, but less surprising. Lord Snell, in the letter before mentioned, said that when he was in America he heard many comments on the decadence of Britain; and he added, "I hope that under similar circumstances America would display no more signs of decadence than our people are doing." I am very sure that we should not.

It is at times when some great peril is shared by a multitude, and still more by an entire nation, that peo-

ple come to feel what George Eliot called "the mystic
stirrings of a common life that makes the many one."
When such a unifying influence is absent, we are absorbed in our personal affairs, obsessed by our individual cares and perplexities, or rejoiced by some happiness, either purely personal or shared with only a small
intimate circle. At such times even the crowd that
jostles shoulders with us on a busy street may seem
spiritually remote and alien to us. But the whole
psychic quality and atmosphere of our life changes
when we and that crowd lie under the shadow of a common disaster. We become aware of a community of
feeling which breaks through all the barriers of class
and sect, of age and sex and culture-level, and brings
the fundamental humanity in each of us into unison
with that in all. And when the shared tragedy is that
of war, it naturally evokes a vivid realization of the
value of those institutions and ideals for the sake of
which the peril is endured. It is no paradox in fact,
though it may be so in form, that life is never so
intensely worth living as when we most vividly realize
how well worth dying for are the values it enshrines.

Secure possession dulls us to the worth of our best
blessings. The threat of their loss brings it newly home
to us. Thus it is that men have come to realize the true
worth of life on beds of incurable sickness, or on the
rack,* or at the stake. They have discovered it on

---

*Benjamin Jowett, the famous Oxford scholar, when asked the old
question whether a good man could be happy on the rack, answered,
"Well, perhaps a very good man,—on a very bad rack." An excellent
reply to a silly question. But those familiar with Jowett's commen-

battlefields, as today they are realizing it on submarine-chasers and mine-sweepers. A London newspaper recently printed a letter from a young aviator to his mother, which was opened and read by his superior officer after the lad had been killed. This boy of nineteen or twenty begged his mother not to grieve if he should be lost, because he had come clearly to realize that in doing his duty to his country he was fulfilling the true end of his existence.

In like manner, Scott, the Antarctic explorer, in the last moments before his death of cold and starvation, wrote in his journal that he did not regret the journey which was thus ending, because its disastrous close had shown him the heroism and self-renunciation of which his comrades were capable.

Now let us—again for the sake of argument—assume the materialist's position. Let us suppose that when Scott died that was the end of him; that when the martyrs perished in the flames, they went only to eternal oblivion. I contend that in and of themselves, and apart even from their exemplary influence upon other men, those lives, so ending, were abundantly worth living. They who lived them triumphantly declared them so; and on this point their consciousness is the final court of appeal. Nor did their verdict depend upon anything in their personal beliefs which we may hold to have been illusory. It depended upon the inherent, self-attesting

taries on his magnificent translation of Plato will have no doubt of his agreement with our contention that (even on a very efficient rack) a good man might realize the absolute worth of life.

worth of the personal qualities they had realized in themselves and discerned in others. They found the worth of life in their own consciousness of loyalty to the inner light, to ideals of right and of manhood which ought to be realized even if they are not, and in their sense of playing the game according to the standards of character and honor they revered. They found it in the triumphant zest of their own realized power to encounter, undaunted and undefeated, the utmost hostility of man and of fate.

Thus Socrates, although the labors and sorrows of his career were lightened by his hope of a nobler after-life, deliberately set this consideration aside when he defined for himself and his friends the spirit in which a good man should encounter death. For he remembered that his hope of immortality was but a hope, and could not become a matter of knowledge; and he realized that the final verdict upon life should be based only upon verifiable certainties. Accordingly, his farewell utterance formulates the ethical discipline which he had so worthily practiced: "Let a man be of good cheer about his soul, who has cast away the pleasures and ornaments of the body as alien to him, and has followed after the pleasures of knowledge in this life; who has adorned the soul in her own proper jewels, which are temperance and justice, and courage, and nobility and truth."

Now if, as is the abundantly proven fact, men have found life worth living under the extremest circumstances of pain and misery—nay, never more intensely

worth living than under those circumstances—it follows that those who find it so under conditions less
tragic and terrible, have still clearer justification for
their attitude. And the average life, inheriting the
great common treasure of civilization, upon which each
in his measure may draw, embraces not only its demands for the high courage and loyalty to principle
which the martyrs displayed, but also, fortunately,
plenty of occasions of love and friendship, happiness
and joy. Heroes innumerable have shown that life is
still worth living when some or all of these things fail
us. But only a churlish cynicism or a mad asceticism
would deny that they are a precious surplus added to
those bedrock realities from which life derives its un-
failing worth.

I personally hold, with that great school for which
the thought of Plato was the fountainhead, not merely
that there is a spiritual universe, but that this is the
real universe; that "what is excellent is permanent,"
since Wisdom and Goodness, Truth and Beauty, are in
their very nature eternal. By this I mean that it is
impossible to think of them as having originated in
time, or as being the products or effects of any conceivable interplay of force and matter; and it is impossible to imagine any personal mind to which they are
not prior and authoritative. But if this be so, then in
so far as we lay hold upon these realities, we enter here
and now into eternal life and incorporate in ourselves
the absolute values.

The point, however, which was overlooked by sophistical writers like Mallock, and, more surprisingly, by William James, is that these eternal realities can be experienced by all men, irrespective of any recognition of their metaphysical nature. Most fortunately it is not necessary to grasp their eternality in order to appropriate that good in them which nevertheless depends upon it; any more than a happy child, playing in the country on a summer's day, needs to understand the physics of light in order to appropriate to itself the benefits of sunshine.

Thus the argument brings me at last to what is, in truth, my own philosophic conviction and religious attitude. The worth of life does indeed depend upon our certainty of the reality of something other than matter and its combinations. But—in opposition to the thinkers I have criticized—I affirm that this intrinsically real and precious thing is met with in present experience; and that its worth, being self-evident and self-attesting, can be, and is, realized independently of any theory respecting its origin or destiny.

It is what I here and now encounter in my neighbor that makes life worth living; not what I may hope for him in another world or a future life. For though there be such a world and such a life, these too will depend for their worth upon the very same spiritual qualities that make this one precious. The reality of the universe of spiritual values lies forever beyond doubt to him who, in the eye and heart of friend and neighbor, has *found* these values, and thus verified experimentally the grand saying, "The Kingdom of God is within you."

Chapter XIII

THE BIRTH OF THE RELIGION OF CONSCIENCE

IN A PERIOD when war is raging abroad, and our own land presents a chaotic spectacle of formidable problems and divided counsels, it may seem eccentric to turn one's mind to a period twenty-seven hundred years remote in time, and to a scene so far distant as Palestine and the adjacent territories. Yet I shall now do this deliberately. For the study of history, whether that of the fortunes of nations and empires, or of political and economic developments, or of those religious and moral ideas which constitute the real foundations of society and prompt the major decisions of the human will, is never more profitable than in periods of such disturbance. And it is far too generally neglected; with dire effects not only upon our culture, but upon our personal and collective actions.

We commonly designate as "provincial" the man who knows nothing but his own street or fields; who has not traveled the world, or troubled to learn what maps and treatises of geography could teach him about it. I suggest, however, that there is another kind of provinciality; one that relates to time rather than to space. Many a man has roamed the world, but has seen it only as it momentarily appeared; and, knowing nothing of its past, has failed entirely to understand its present. For this provinciality a study of history is the remedy.

It is often complained, especially by spokesmen of the churches, that the present generation neglects and ignores the Bible. This is unhappily true. But the responsibility for it lies largely with the churches themselves. Their spokesmen in general have deliberately withheld from the laity the fascinating truth about the Bible which has been revealed by historical and literary criticism, and by the progress of archaeological research. We are also told that the present generation cannot read with understanding and pleasure the glorious Elizabethan English in which our King James and Revised Versions are written. So far as this is true, the fact constitutes a grave reflection upon our schools and colleges. We have, indeed, admirable modern versions. They became necessary because of the greater accuracy attained through the study of recently discovered manuscripts, and the use of various sources of information that were not available to the King James men. But if modern methods of education had not resulted in leaving pupils incompetent to appreciate our language as it was written in the heyday of its greatest power and beauty, these results of modern scholarship might well have been incorporated in revisions or footnotes to the older versions.

My own experience has proved to me that the Bible becomes absorbingly interesting to the present generation when it is exhibited to them in the light of the

results achieved by the studies embraced under the
term "higher criticism." I have held many a class of
this description; but never without having one or more
of the members say, "Why, I never heard a word of all
this in the orthodox church in which I was brought
up!"

There are those who speak with contempt of any
turning to distant times or remote lands as a mere
seeking of "escape" from the problems of the present.
But, as we saw when discussing "Utopias," the charge
is foolish. And certainly in none of its forms does history offer such an "escape." What it does is to show
that the problems which trouble us now are by no means
new. It teaches us how men in the past struggled with
the same enemies we face today, and what have been
the various fortunes of the struggle. So often does it
show how these present enemies in their former guises
were overthrown that it brings us back to our own tasks
with new serenity, and with the strength we need to
accomplish them.—But now to our special theme.

The saga of the Prophet Elijah is one of the most
dramatic and vivid things in all literature. So familiar
was it to our fathers that many phrases quoted from
it became "household words" in our language, and, like
many of the expressions of Shakespeare, were currently used by persons who had no idea whence they
were derived. This saga haunted the popular imagination of the Hebrew people down to the beginning of
the Christian Era,—a fact certified to us by the influence it exercised upon the writers of the Gospels.

We read in them that at the Transfiguration of Jesus, Moses and Elijah appeared in visible form upon the mountain to testify to him. Now, according to the Hebrew tradition, Moses was the founder of the Law, and Elijah the originator of prophecy in its true and distinctive Biblical sense. When we remember the immense reverence of the Jews for Moses, the presentation of Elijah as his peer in the Transfiguration story shows how high a place the latter held in the popular esteem.

We also learn from the Gospels that when John the Baptist appeared upon the scene, combining the long-intermitted function of the prophet with the life of the desert nomad, the popular fancy immediately supposed him to be a reincarnation of Elijah; and his appearance is described in words quoted from the first chapter of the Second Book of Kings.

According to the Jewish tradition, though there had been prophets of a sort before Elijah, yet he was the first of the true prophetic dynasty. This tradition is certainly right in essentials; for the earlier prophets, such as Saul and Samuel, had been mere soothsayers, diviners, or necromancers. They were not champions either of the national religion against foreign idolatry, or of its central ethical substance against the externalism and ritual with which this substance became so dangerously overlaid in the Temple service. But Elijah was a pioneer in both these departments. Hence it was that "the mantle of Elijah" became the symbol of the spirit of prophecy. According to the old story, the great prophet's mantle descended literally upon his successor Elisha. But all subsequent prophets were understood to be the spiritual inheritors of that mantle; *i.e.*, to speak "in the spirit and power of Elijah."

Despite this lofty position of Elijah in popular esteem, one might be tempted, upon first reading his story, to doubt whether there was any fragment of historical basis for it. With one solitary exception, all the episodes told of him are bizarre, spectacular, preternatural, and incredible. He is the rain-maker and the bringer of fire from heaven. He multiplies and perpetuates stores of food and oil; he raises the dead. How, then, can we suppose him to have been historical, any more than Samson the Sun-God? Sir James Frazer's demonstration of the mythical character of Samson, and of the saga that narrates his adventures,* has now been accepted by orthodox scholars; and it has been maintained by some critics that Elijah himself is but another variant of that ubiquitous solar myth which pervades the records of all primitive peoples.

To this school of critics even the name of the hero looks suspicious; for it means "Yahweh is God." The bearer of this name is represented as acting like the god of rain and drought. At our first glimpse of him, as he strides abruptly into a narrative of which the original beginning has apparently been lost, we find him declaring that there was to be a drought which would last for several years, and not be broken until

* In his "Folklore in the Old Testament."

he gave the word. The fulfillment of this prophecy having begun, the Lord sends Elijah into hiding by the Brook Cherith, where he is miraculously fed morning and evening with bread and flesh by the ravens. Some of my readers will recall the beautiful passage in Milton's "Paradise Regained," where it is represented as part of the temptation of Jesus, starving in the wilderness, that this old miracle came before his fancy in a dream:

"Him thought he by the Brook of Cherith stood,
    And saw the ravens with their horny beaks
    Food to Elijah bringing even and morn,
    Though ravenous, taught to abstain from what they
        brought."

Elijah in the legend is represented as being miraculously transported from place to place; so that Obadiah, for example, is afraid to take a message from him to Ahab, lest the elusive prophet should have vanished by the time he returned. In such fashion he passes from the scene by the Brook Cherith out of Israelite territory into the land of Zidon. Here he performs the miracle of perpetuating the meal and oil of the Tyrian widow, whose son he also raises from the dead. In our older speech, at least, this "widow's cruse" became a proverbial designation for anything of which the supply seemed unexpectedly enduring.

The next scene of Elijah's drama is the famous one on Mount Carmel, wherein he challenges the prophets of Baal to bring down fire from heaven by prayer to kindle their sacrifice. There are four hundred of them confronting his solitary figure. For hours they invoke their deity, interlarding their ejaculations with ritual dances, and gashing their bodies with knives. Then Elijah mocks their failure: "Cry aloud! For he is a god; either he is musing, or he is gone aside, or he is in a journey, or peradventure he sleepeth and must be awaked." But "there was no voice, nor any that answered." Then Elijah in turn offers his prayer; and, to magnify the miracle, he causes the sacrifice to be repeatedly flooded with water. Despite this, his invocation of Yahweh is followed by the fire from heaven, which utterly consumes the offering. Hereupon the multitude, startled into conviction, sides with Elijah, who proceeds to exterminate the prophets of Baal.

This done, he announces to Ahab the approaching end of the drought. But there is some delay in the fulfillment of this prophecy; a delay which proves a strain even to the prophet's own faith:—

"Elijah went up to the top of Carmel; and he bowed himself down upon the earth, and put his face between his knees. And he said to his servant, 'Go up now, look toward the sea.' And he went up, and looked, and said, 'There is nothing.' And he said, 'Go again seven times.' And it came to pass at the seventh time, that he said, 'Behold, there ariseth a cloud out of the sea, as small as a man's hand.' And he said, 'Go up, say unto Ahab, Make ready thy chariot, and get thee down, that the rain stop thee not.' And it came to pass in a little while, that the heaven grew black with clouds and wind, and there was a great rain."

No sooner has this happened than a message is brought to Elijah from the enraged Queen Jezebel that she will, by next day, treat him as he has treated the prophets of her faith. At this his courage fails him and he flees in terror. Such a reaction after his great triumph is very human, and shows good dramatic insight in the writer. But having gained the security of the desert, Elijah becomes ashamed of his flight from the scene of his duty; he is overcome with the sense that his cause is hopeless, and he longs to die. But again he is assured that the Lord is on his side, by finding himself miraculously supplied once more with food and water in the desert; and so, following an inner prompting which seems to him to come from without, he journeys on to the traditional place of Yahweh's manifestation at Mount Horeb. To the Hebrew imagination this was classic ground, as having been the scene of the first theophany to Moses. Thus we read in Exodus, "Now Moses was keeping the flock of Jethro his father-in-law. . . . And he led the flock to the farthest end of the wilderness, and came to the mountain of God, unto Horeb."

With what there happened we shall deal later. After this episode, Elijah appoints Elisha as his deputy and drops out of sight for a time. He reappears in connection with the story of Naboth the Jezreelite, who was treacherously slain by Jezebel in order that she might steal his vineyard and give it to her husband. The famous denunciation of Ahab and Jezebel by

Elijah for this crime is the only non-miraculous episode in the story of the prophet.

Subsequently to this, we hear only of his fiery protests against the idolatry of King Ahaziah, and of his miraculous slaughter of certain companies of Ahaziah's soldiers. The story then closes with the mythical scene of Elijah's ascent to heaven in a "chariot of fire," from which, as it rises, his mantle falls upon Elisha.

Now in view of the nature of all these episodes, one might well dismiss the entire story as mythical. Much of it palpably is so. But we are stayed by certain weighty considerations from regarding Elijah as an imaginary personage. The first of these is that the characters with whom he is depicted as holding inter-course are certainly historical. Ahab is the son of Omri; and Omri was a monarch whose actuality is attested by contemporary documents, including the famous Moabite Stone. Nor can there be any reasonable doubt about the actual life and reign of his son Ahab, or about Ahab's Tyrian wife Jezebel, however much the character of the latter may have been blackwashed for didactic purposes by the author of the narrative.

Another reason for pausing is the obviously early date of some of the documents on which the Books of Kings are founded. There are several touches which lead scholars to hold that the Elijah story was put into writing prior to the year 722 B.C. In that year Samaria was conquered; but that event is clearly not present to the consciousness of the writer. This line of criticism also shows the story to have been written by a subject of the northern Israelite Kingdom; for only to such a writer would it seem natural to use the expression "Beer-sheba, which belongeth to Judah."

What is more, the main theme of the story is that of a struggle to preserve the distinctness of Israel's nationality (and therefore of its religion) from fusion and confusion with the surrounding peoples and their cults. Now this struggle is beyond question historical. Whether or not it was accompanied by any such drama as the contest on Mount Carmel, it really did take place. Regarding its nature we cannot do better than to quote the words in which it is summed up by the great German critic, Wellhausen: "To him" (Elijah) "Baal and Yahweh represented, so to speak, a contrast of principles, of profound and ultimate practical convictions; both could not be right, nor could they exist side by side. For him there existed no plurality of divine powers, operating with equal authority in different spheres, but everywhere one holy and mighty Being, who revealed Himself not in the life of nature, but in those laws by which alone human society is held together, in the ethical demands of the spirit."

It is also evident that the great eighth-century school of prophets, which included Amos, Hosea, and the original Isaiah, cannot have sprung up *in vacuo*. Every one of these men appeals to the past, and to a national ethical ideal associated in the past with their God. They are thus clearly the products of a long course of development. After the compliances of David and Solomon with foreign worships (especially the far-

spread matrimonial alliances of Solomon, and his commercial transactions with Tyre), it is obvious that there
must have been a struggle to maintain the identity of
the Hebrew people and their religion. In those days,
religion and nationality were inseparably blended. Nobody thought of questioning the rule, which continued
to prevail down to the time of the Reformation in
Europe, "*Cuius regio, eius religio*": every man must
hold the religion of the State to which he belongs.

Elijah, to be sure, is depicted as meeting the ruthlessness of his enemies with an equal ruthlessness of his
own. But our judgement of the ferocity of such
episodes as the slaughter of the Baal prophets must be
tempered not only by the certainty that it is at least
greatly exaggerated, if not entirely fictitious, but also
by our knowledge of what the Tyrian religion was
really like. In common with most of the cults of the
peoples surrounding the Hebrews, it was full of sensu-
ality and orgiastic observances; and, even beyond many
of them, it was befouled by abominations of human
sacrifice.

To us, "the fire of Moloch" has become a mere figure
of speech. We find it hard to imagine what it would be
like if such a fire were a reality among our immediate
neighbors. Now in recent years excavations at Carthage
(a Tyrian colony) have resulted in the discovery of the
furnace that was actually used for the purpose of con-
suming the little children who were offered to this
bestial deity; and about it were piles of the children's
bones. Chesterton, I suspect, was right when he at-

tributed the extreme and unparalleled ferocity of the Punic Wars, and the stern thoroughness with which the Romans destroyed Carthage, to the horrified recoil of even their pagan hearts against this most demoniacal of cults.*

The slaughter of the prophets of Baal by Elijah, as we have admitted, is probably unhistorical. But only by realizing the abominations of devil-worship with which they were threatened can we do justice to the seemingly fanatical hostility of the Bible-writers to what they termed "idolatry." The violent language they used in condemning apostasy from the worship of Yahweh finds its explanation here.

Their nation, with its unity based upon an unique religious tradition, and the already comparatively high ethical level of that religion, were in real and present danger. Foreign intercourse was crowding their royal court and their cities with resident aliens, and the Israelite kings were compromising with the "abominations," as the prophets rightly called them, of the foreign cults. Both Omri and Ahab, like Solomon before them, had entered into marital alliances and commercial intercourse with Tyre. The Baal-worship was set up on Israelite soil, for the pleasure of a Tyrian queen who seems to have been zealously bent on proselytizing. After

---

* "At Carthage children were sacrificed to him, and in his temple there was a colossal bronze statue, in the arms of which were placed the children who were to be sacrificed. The children slipped one by one from the arms into a furnace amid the plaudits of fanatical worshippers. These sacrifices persisted even under Roman rule; Tertullian states that even in his time they took place in secret."—Prof. Babelon, in "Encyclopaedia Britannica."

the manner of politicians, the kings and their advisers saw no difficulty about "compromising" the rival claims of Baal and Yahweh, and blending the worship of the two. Had this precious scheme been successful, the Yahweh worship, which alone contained any ethical elements, would certainly have been swamped. Ethical standards were not reconcilable with the fire of Moloch; and the idea of compromising with it was as insane as the delusion of European statesmen in recent years, that they could compromise with neo-pagan political systems which were created for no other purpose than to destroy European civilization and its ethical foundations.

Now in every nation, and especially in the old days before there was popular education, the mass of people has been blind to the nation's long-run interests. The consciousness of a people's destiny has always resided with a small minority; a "remnant," as the Bible calls it. Apparently this "remnant" in the days of Elijah was small. There were but a few thousand in all Israel who had not "bowed the knee in the House of Baal."

Elijah is the spokesman of this "remnant," this little party which understood the traditional Hebrew policy, and kept its ideal alive in their souls, and was aware of its permanent meaning and purpose. Even if the man Elijah were completely unhistorical (which is not the case), yet there was such a party in the ninth century B.C., and it did make the struggle attributed to him. It gave rise to the great prophetic outburst of the next century, thereby becoming a point of departure for the spiritual development of humanity in all subse-

quent times. It is noteworthy that Elijah's main enemy
was not the vacillating and compromising king Ahab,
but his determined, Lady Macbeth-like queen, Jezebel.
And she was a Tyrian. Under her influence the Baal-
worship had been established in Samaria, and the sacred
asherah—the idol-image—set up. Like a modern dicta-
tor, she was out not for compromise, but for conquest;
and she saw in Elijah the embodiment of the religion
that she was bent on destroying.

Some students have deplored the fact that the Second
Commandment entirely prevented artistic expression
among the Jews. This is doubtless regrettable; but we
become reconciled to the loss when we remember from
what unimaginable and unfathomable degradation that
Commandment helped to save the Hebrews and, through
them, all future civilization. Opposition to "idolatry"
often seems to us fanatical, because we fail to realize
what evils were summed up in that word. At its best,
image-worship has been a barrier to religious development and the spiritualization of the idea of God (or
the gods). At worst—as in the devil-cults of Tyre and
Carthage—it was the very nadir of superstition.

We find in the second Book of Chronicles an expression of the reason for prohibiting images which must
have been written in a later age, when Hebrew thought
was maturely developed: "Lo, the Heaven of Heavens
cannot contain Thee: how much less this house that I
have builded." * These words are placed upon the lips
of Solomon when dedicating his new temple; but never

* II Chron. vi 18.

can they have been uttered by the historical Solomon. They represent the highest development of prophetic insight, a stage which certainly had not been reached in the age of Elijah, but toward which that age was ascending. The prophetic Hebrew contribution to religion is the sublime conception of a universal and eternal spiritual power, which on earth is manifested only in the conscience of man.

The scene on Mount Horeb is a mythical embodiment of the stages through which this Hebrew conception of God evolved. Its profound significance, to say nothing of its rare literary beauty, should win for it our close attention:—

"He came thither unto a cave, and lodged there; and behold, the word of the Lord came to him, and he said unto him, 'What doest thou here, Elijah?' And he said, 'I have been very jealous for the Lord, the God of hosts; for the children of Israel have forsaken thy covenant, thrown down thine altars, and slain thy prophets with the sword: and I, even I only, am left; and they seek my life to take it away.' And he said, 'Go forth, and stand upon the mount before the Lord.' And, behold, the Lord passed by, and a great and strong wind rent the mountains, and brake in pieces the rocks before the Lord; but the Lord was not in the wind: and after the wind an earthquake; but the Lord was not in the earthquake: and after the earthquake a fire; but the Lord was not in the fire: and after the fire a still small voice. And it was so, when Elijah heard it, that he wrapped his face in his mantle, and went out, and stood in the entering in of the cave. And, behold there came a voice unto him, and said, 'What doest thou here, Elijah?' "

THE BIRTH OF THE RELIGION OF CONSCIENCE

Note well the series of episodes: the wind, the earth-quake, and the fire. Contemporary paganism would have treated each of these as the expression of a personal will; that is, in each of them it would have found "a god,"—a separate god. So too would the Hebrews have done in their tribal infancy. It meant inexpressibly much to the whole future of the world that already in the eighth century before the Christian era a Hebrew writer could declare emphatically that Yahweh was not in the wind, or the earthquake, or the fire. And it meant still more that he *did* find Yahweh in the "still small voice"; for *that* was quite obviously the voice of Elijah's own conscience rebuking him for his fear and his flight. "What doest thou here, Elijah?"—"Is *this* your post of duty? If you really are, as you suppose, the only champion of the truth left in Israel, is not your desertion of the scene of the struggle all the graver crime?"

No more important turning-point in human development has ever occurred than that in which this conviction first came home to a prophetic thinker: "The only divine voice to be heard on earth is the voice which speaks in the conscience of man." And the Elijah saga is a dramatic, imaginative record of the attainment of this insight among the Hebrews. I cannot understand how any man who has studied the nature and practices of the cults of Babylon and Assyria, of India, and even of Egypt, can be oblivious to the incomparable worth of the service to civilization done by the Hebrew people in denouncing and banning idolatry, and substituting ethical ideas in religion for the completely non-moral worship of natural forces which the rival cults embodied.

The psychology of Elijah's flight and collapse are imagined with true dramatic insight. Nothing more skillful was ever written than this picture of abrupt transition from the height of triumphant exaltation to the depth of depression and despair. Since we are living in times when the temptation to despair is prevalent and powerful, we may do well to pause for a moment on this feature of the story, in order to recall that such incidents have occurred in every life which has accomplished anything of worth to mankind.

For my part, I was reminded of this passage in the Elijah story when I first read of Washington's despair at Trenton, after his brave men had long been starving in rags because of the neglect of the Continental Congress. Nor does it seem far-fetched to find a like connection in Washington's outburst, many years later, that he "would sooner be in his grave than in the Presidency," so weary had he grown of the foul and scurrilous attacks which he had for years endured.

But into all lives, and not only those of men of outstanding eminence, do such moods and such temptations come. How can we guard against them? First, by remembering that they are natural and psychologically normal. After any period of intense and protracted exertion, especially if it has produced some measure of triumph, there is liable to be a correspondingly deep reaction, just as the ebb seems lowest after the height of a spring tide. If we remember this when the black mood is upon us, we shall be helped and sustained in living through it; as we also shall if we remember likewise that the mood of depression, like all others, is a transient thing, through which rest and refreshment, and diversion and change of occupation, will carry us. This is a most important matter, because the illusion of the finality and incurableness of the mood of despair has caused many a suicide which would not have occurred had the victim remembered that his state of misery was no more permanent than a headache or a cold.

Above all, we must brace ourselves to hold fast, even in the blackest depths of the darkness, to the conviction of the worth of the task we have been pursuing. In moments of utter weariness we find ourselves impelled to doubt this; and that impulse is the worst symptom of the malady. It is the very temptation of the devil, taking advantage of our weakest moment. Before the hour of trial comes, set your mind and will, in all clearness, not to let the biased and beclouded judgment of an abnormal period overbear the deliberate conviction of your best hours. Above all in time of war, when the ideals for which we have labored seem to have faded like dreams, and been replaced by a grim and ghastly reality, must we hold fast to our faith in that fraternal order of peaceful intercourse among men which ought to be and must be, and against which warfare is blasphemy.

To these counsels may be added a fourth available resource; one which I should venture to call "the reflection of rational humility." This is the conviction that

a cause intrinsically worthful cannot depend exclusively
on any one individual.

> It fortifies my soul to know
> That though I perish, Truth is so.

Elijah may believe himself to be the last living witness
to Yahweh; but if Yahweh is a real God he can and
will raise up new witnesses to himself. Or (to translate
this poetry into a prose that will now be more intel-
ligible), Elijah should say, "The resources of the universe were not exhausted in producing *me*. I shall die;
but the ideals for which I have labored are eternal and
imperishable. Though today they seem by most people
to be forgotten, their reality and necessity will surely
dawn again on better minds than mine; and they will
become the motives of action for men more able than I
to bring them into general realization and adoption as
the norms of conduct."

The difference, then, between the religion for which
Elijah and his party stood, and that which was championed by Jezebel and the prophets of Baal, was the
difference between the worship of conscience and the
worship of the non-moral forces of nature. Our insight
into the religion of conscience we owe primarily to the
Hebrew prophets, but in some measure also to those
Greek philosophers who incurred the reproach of being
non-religious or anti-religious, because they rejected
the gods of force and fertility. In the evolution of religion there must have been, as George Tyrrell surmises,
a breach of continuity. The ethical religions have grown

from an originally non-religious morality, not from an originally non-ethical religion. For out of such a system, developing on its own lines, a doctrine and worship diametrically contrary and fundamentally alien to it could never have emerged.

It is well for us to remember, moreover, that amid all the differences which have arisen to separate the spiritual descendants of the Hebrew prophets and the Founder of Christianity, the central divinization of conscience remains as a uniting factor. This might be illustrated from innumerable sources. I select at random the following eloquent passage from a letter written by Cardinal John Henry Newman to the Duke of Norfolk in the year 1875:—

"The Divine Law ... is the rule of ethical truth, the standard of right and wrong, a sovereign, irreversible, absolute authority in the persons of men and angels. . . . This Law, as apprehended in the minds of individual men, is called 'Conscience'; and, though it may suffer refraction in passing into the intellectual medium of each, it is not thereby so affected as to lose its character of being the Divine Law, but still has, as such, the prerogative of commanding obedience. . . . The rule and measure of duty is not utility, nor expedience, nor the happiness of the greatest number, nor State convenience, nor fitness, order, and the *pulchrum*. Conscience is not a long-sighted selfishness, nor a desire to be consistent with oneself ... but it is a prophet in its informations, a monarch in its peremptoriness. . . . If I am obliged to bring religion into after-dinner toasts, . . . I shall drink—to the Pope if you please; still, to Conscience first, and to the Pope afterwards."

In stressing the opposition between nature-cults and the worship of conscience, we must carefully avoid the puritanical and ascetic error of regarding nature as our enemy. This error arose from a just revolt against the worship of natural forces which are themselves non-moral, but the imitation of which by men involves immorality. A complete religion will certainly include all the artist's and poet's aesthetic appreciation of the beauty of the world, and all the scientist's intellectual insight into its majestic order. But in a mature and soundly-balanced religion, the object of supreme loyalty will ever be found in the "still small voice," and not in the earthquake or fire, either as the artist depicts or as the scientist understands them.

The recent death of Dr. Freud calls to mind the interesting fact that in him we find a quite unexpected corroborator of the doctrine of the supremacy of conscience. This becomes plain to the student (though apparently it was not so to Freud himself) upon analyzing his theory of the "censor" of the unconscious,—that mysterious factor which will not permit the real motivations of the hidden self to appear in their stark reality even in dreams, and therefore transforms them into the "symbolisms" which Freud undertook to interpret. This theory may be quite unsound; it probably is so; but if there were any such "censor" of our dreams, what could it be but that very conscience which judges all human motivations, not according to their felt strength and importunity, but according to their discerned worth and legitimacy?

This conscience, moreover, is not to be imagined or thought of as some occult entity mysteriously super-added to human nature, any more than reason is. We mean by it simply the man himself, the unitary subject of experience, the super-temporal being who continues self-identical while his body is in constant change. "Conscience" indicates this man when engaged in appraising himself and the world from the standpoint of what they ought to be; just as "Reason" means the same man when engaged in appraising himself and the world through scientific investigation of their phenomena and laws.

It is for the very reason that conscience is man's inmost selfhood that it is authoritative over us. It could not be so if it came from any alien source; not even from a source regarded as divine. Elijah is recalled to his duty by the only power that has a right to command him; namely, that universal will, or law of right, which is also his own real will, his deepest self, and therefore sovereignly authoritative over the shrinking timidity of his lower nature.

It is manifest enough that in this sense of "reverencing our Conscience as our King," our age needs, as Elisha did, "a double portion of the spirit" of Elijah. Never was "the mantle" of the brave prophet more sorely needed than today.

And the relevance of this study of an ancient story comes vividly home to us when we realize that it is the same old enemy—power-worship, the doctrine that might is right—against which we have to wage our warfare.

Our nation may escape the actual military clashes which are occurring in Europe; but in a hundred less extreme and more subtle forms this enemy is at work among us. It prompts the sacrifice of spiritual values to material gains; it lowers and corrupts the standards of public life; it poisons and embitters the relations of class with class; and it vitiates the private heart. That which was the very essence of ancient Paganism still marches militantly, with rapid strides, in pursuit of its unchanging purpose of destroying civilization. The struggle between Elijah and the prophets of Baal,—between the conviction that conscience is divine and the pretence that conscience has no rights against forceful self-assertion,—is not this the very struggle of our time?

This is the fundamental truth that we need to keep clearly before our minds amid the rush of contemporary events. If conscience is an expression of the higher nature of man, no less true is it that all the non-moral forces of nature find their reflex in immoral tendencies which are the expression of man's lower nature. When we look beneath masks and disguises, we discover that the parties at strife in the ninth century before the Christian era were completely identical with those now warring; so that after telling the ancient story of Elijah to our own age, we might well add, in the words of the Roman poet, *"Mutato nomine, de te fabula narratur"*—"Change but the name, of you is the story told."

The late Pope, in several weighty utterances, quite rightly defined the issue as a contest between atheistic

materialism and those ethical foundations of civilization which he summed up in the word Christianity. The
war in Europe may not be our war in the sense that we
should feel called upon to enter it physically. But
spiritually it is our war, and that of civilization everywhere; because in other forms it is being waged everywhere, and the future of the whole world depends upon
its outcome.

In this sense, Elijah is still at strife with the prophets
of Baal; and now, as of yore, Elijah is a very faulty
champion of a very lofty cause. But when we remember
how urgently that cause needs to be championed in
every land, albeit with other than military weapons, we
shall feel the obligation to redouble our vigilance and
our faithful persistence in maintaining the contest; lest
at some moment of untimely self-indulgence and abstention from the conflict we too should hear, as of old,
the stern, authoritative voice demanding of us, "What
doest thou here, Elijah?"

CHAPTER XIV

THE LIFE ETERNAL:

(WRITTEN IN COMMEMORATION OF FELIX ADLER.)

THANKS TO the radio and kindred inventions designed
for the destruction of peace of mind and self-
possession, the present generation lives in the passing
moment, oblivious of past and future, as men never did
before. This is bringing about the extinction of an
ancient custom of human piety, that of commemorating
the deeds of distinguished servants of mankind. "Let
us now praise famous men," says an eloquent Jewish
writer of the period shortly before the Christian era;
and he proceeds to give a complete catalogue of the
heroes of Israel from earliest times down to his own
date, with a concise account of the achievement of each.
How many of us could do so much in the way of listing
and characterizing the great Americans, even of the
short period since 1776? Our habit of annually commemorating the two most eminent of our national
figures, and those two only, seems to make the younger
generation tired of their very names; and the fact that
we thus honor them alone produces a kind of obliviousness of the immense galaxy of men and women eminently
worthy of such recognition. Apparently we no longer

agree with George Eliot's statement that "a just life should be justly honoured."

It is we who are the losers by this. Great lives should be greatly commemorated, not, indeed, for their own sake alone, but for the sake of humanity and the future; in order to impress upon the living generation their character, spirit, and achievements, as incentives to emulation.

The greater men are, of course, the less are they ambitious of such posthumous renown for themselves. Felix Adler, whom I here honor, spoke of it in these words:

The idea of living in the *life* of future generations is one thing; that of living in the *memory* of future generations is quite another thing. The latter has never appealed to me. Some of the greatest benefactors of the race in the past have been forgotten—not even their names have come down to us. Those that are remembered are few in number, and their memory is often disfigured, and their teachings, as in the case of Jesus, distorted. Not to be quite forgotten by those whom we have loved and who love us is a pleasing thought; but they who remember us will in turn soon pass from the scene, and our so-called earthly immortality will die with them.

Yet my colleagues and I owe it to him, and still more to ourselves, to see that his "earthly immortality" does not thus die. For his life was that of the Ethical Movement to which we are devoted. His highest interest on earth was in the task of transforming life by the light of that Movement's ideals, and of clarifying and verify-

ing those ideals under the testing of life. This fellowship, therefore, which has meant and means so much to
every one who has belonged to it, and has contributed
so enormously to the liberalization of the churches of
America and the improvement of their ethical teaching,
we owe to him. Though he be dead, we must hear him
yet speaking to us, because the continued life and
growth of our fellowship will only be possible so long
as it continues to be animated by that spirit of free
rationality and severe scientific truthfulness, combined
with religiously passionate energy for self-betterment
and the betterment of society, which animated him.

The common idea of a philosopher is that of a
cloistered recluse living in his ivory tower. Like many
common ideas, it is completely false as applied to all
really great philosophers. Aristotle and Plato of old
were immersed in the public life of their time, busied
throughout their days with its political and civic problems. The great philosophical tradition of our own
language was built up by men of action, who learned
of the problems of life by actual grappling with them,
and whose attempt to interpret them philosophically
was the leisure-time hobby of gentlemen amateurs. Such
was the case with Bacon, with Locke, with Berkeley and
with Hume.

Prior to my own meeting with Adler, I found my
inspirer in this department in Thomas Hill Green, the
profoundest English metaphysician and ethical philosopher of the nineteenth century, who lived up so intensely to this old tradition of learning his philosophy

as much from active life as from books that he died of
overwork in his early forties, to the permanent impoverishment of human thought. He labored indefati-
gably on temperance committees, because in his day
drunkenness was the great disgrace and problem of
England. He sat as a member of the Oxford Town
Council. He spoke frequently from political platforms,
advocating State education and workers' enfranchise-
ment,—the next steps then necessary in social and political reform. One cannot read his master work, "Prolegomena to Ethics," or his invaluable lectures on "The
Principles of Political Obligation," without finding
them replete with the practical wisdom thus "hewn from
life." They abundantly justify his own saying, that
"There is no other genuine 'enthusiasm of humanity'
than one which has traveled the common highway of
reason—the life of the good neighbour and honest citizen—and can never forget that it is still only on a
further stage of the same journey."

The life of Felix Adler,* fortunately far longer than
Green's, was expended in the same fashion and enriched
by the like discipline. When one went to call upon him,
it was an open question whether one would find him
teaching a class of children, or arbitrating a labor dispute, or presiding over a committee of the National
Child Labour Association, or writing one of the more
difficult metaphysical chapters in his "Ethical Philosophy of Life." At my last meeting with him, after his
eightieth birthday, and within a month or two of his

* 1851-1933.

death, I asked him whether he had any writing in hand. He told me that he had; he was trying to work out the philosophy of the State, as illuminated and transformed by his fundamental ethical ideas. When I asked whether we might expect a speedy publication of his results, he laughed and answered, "My dear fellow, what I have in mind is a task for a decade."

The popular fallacy is still current that "religion is a matter of the heart, and theology a matter of the head." This is generally construed as a disparagement of theology (by those who have never troubled to study it). In like manner, common speech abounds in contrasts between theory and practice, the purport of which is the discrediting of theory. How often in recent years have we heard critics of Mr. Roosevelt's "New Deal" ascribe its blunders and follies to the Washington "theorists,"—the critics boasting, by implication, that they were "practical men." The answer, of course, is that the faults of the "New Deal" were due not to theory as such, but to false and contradictory theories; and that where "practical men" are successfully holding their own in any department of the nation's economic life, this is possible only because they have had the good fortune to inherit organizations created and directed by the sound theories of their predecessors.

Even an automobile needs both motive power and steering gear; and human life in every department needs "the heart" to inspire "the head" and "the head" to guide "the heart." In other words, thought must be quickened by feeling, but feeling must be guided and regulated by thought. Whoever neglects either imperils the human balance, and at least retards advance if he does not fatally misdirect it. Theory must constantly be tested by practice; but practice must always be guided by theory. And in fact it always is, even when the "practical men" don't know it.

Though not an expert in any physical science, Adler had that supreme and passionate interest in truth for its own sake which is the hallmark of the genuine scientist, as well as of the true philosopher. But the only available and valid test of philosophical and moral truth is its application to human life. Adler was as far from being a Pragmatist as it is possible for a philosopher to be. But he fully admitted—nay, he insisted on—the validity of the pragmatic test of ethical theories. Ethics is the science and art of right conduct. Whether, therefore, any doctrine in this sphere be really true, can only be judged by studying the kind of character it inspires, the quality of conduct to which it leads, the sort of social and personal life it promotes.

Any memorial tribute to Adler, accordingly, should partake of the severely practical character of his own philosophy and his own life. Such a memorial might properly be a children's festival, a "round-table" of employers and workers aiming at economic justice and mutual friendship, a conference for better housing, the abolition of child labor, or international peace, a rally of workers in social settlements, or (as in the case of this present writing) an attempt to interpret or de-

velop some phase of his philosophy. Religion is the
quest of "more life and fuller." Ethics, aiming directly
and disinterestedly at making life better, is yet inspired
by the conviction that in becoming better it could not
fail to become richer and happier. Never was the quest
inspired by this conviction more needed than now, when
the peace of the world has been destroyed and liberty
and justice are in mortal danger; when corruption of
various horrible types is rampant throughout our own
and other nations, and the economic crisis (itself ultimately due to lack of character and moral insight) has
disclosed all sorts of spiritual rottenness in quarters
where it was least suspected.

Now the first thing clearly indispensable, if mankind is to triumph over these tendencies, is that men
should become convinced of their *power* to do so. The
belief that these evils are inevitable and irresistible,
because we human beings have no resources in our
mental and moral nature which would enable us to conquer them, even though it be totally false, yet cannot
fail to crush our energies and lame our arms.

Once, when listening to the late M. Coué, the French
exponent of auto-suggestion, I witnessed the following
incident: A paralyzed man, wholly unable to walk, was
carried up to the platform. M. Coué, who had a peculiar
gift of psychological insight, as well as considerable
manipulative skill, in two minutes had this patient not
only walking, but dancing around the stage. He then
explained to the audience that the patient undoubtedly
had been paralyzed some time previously; a blood-clot

had prevented the use of his legs. The clot, however, had been completely dispersed and absorbed. But since the patient did not know this, he had been inhibited from the use of his limbs solely by the power of a false idea.

In like manner, there are beliefs which paralyze the spiritual energies of men. Such is the conviction that life is a scene not only of inevitable frustration (as indeed it is), but of a frustration which is complete, and uncompensated by any ulterior achievement or insight. Such too is the belief that man possesses no liberty of will and no originative power in his intellect. And such again is the doctrine that the difference between right and wrong is not really objective, but only a matter of tradition, convention, or superstitious delusion.

My work as the leader of an Ethical Society attests my conviction that these paralyzing beliefs are false. If they were true, an ethical movement, or any other form of spiritual religion, would be an absurdity. And if I or any other preacher thought them true, our profession would be a proof either of imbecility or of hypocrisy. The point to be stressed, however, is that if these beliefs be *accepted* as true, they will be as powerful, despite their falsity, as though they were really true. History is full of discouraging demonstrations of what Johan Bojer called "The Power of a Lie." A false idea, so long as it is believed, produces effects as real as those of a true one.

A contemporary proof of this is the cluster of lies disseminated these many years in Germany by the

Hitler party. Like the dragons' teeth in the old fable, these have sprung up armed men, to destroy liberty, to recreate the materialistic Pagan State, and to plunge the world anew into war.

It is immensely important, therefore, that our ideas about the make-up and resources of human nature, and its relation to the whole of reality, should be true ideas. We must not accept, upon anything short of completely demonstrative and compulsive evidence, any view which will act upon human life as the belief of M. Coué's patient in his paralysis acted upon him.

My present purpose, though it will involve some indication of the most fundamental and difficult ideas in Adler's philosophy, is in essence a very simple one. It is to honor Adler by contributing towards the vindication of certain beliefs which he held, which are natural to us and spontaneous in us, and which nobody except a few sophisticated philosophers or misguided scientists has ever really doubted. What is more, even those sophisticated and misguided people themselves can no more avoid acting upon these beliefs "as if" they were true, than can the man in the street.

To make this clear, let us consider an elementary case of moral experience. Suppose that a small boy has confessed to being concerned with others in some game or practical joke by which another child has been injured. Having confessed, the truthful lad is subjected (as he foresaw that he would be) to some punishment or painful discipline. But suppose another member of the gang, equally responsible, lies, or holds his tongue, and thereby escapes the punishment.

The truthful boy will feel indignant with his dishonest comrade. Being only a small boy, he will not be able to analyze either the motive of his own action, or the causes and justifications of his indignation. He will have no notion of the vast corollaries these imply. Maturer onlookers, however, can make this analysis and establish these corollaries. And they can rightly do so, I contend, only in one way, and to one result.

Why does the honest boy confess? He would prefer not to, in so far as by keeping silence he could escape the foreseen penalty. He feels the strength of the temptation to act thus, exactly as does the sneak. But as between his desire for immunity, which is prompted by one spring of action, and his reverence for truth and fair play, which arises from another, he intuitively feels the superior authority of the latter. His indignation against the sneak implies two things: (1), that the impulse to action which he has obeyed at his own cost *ought* to have been equally authoritative for the other boy; and (2), that the sneak was no more under compulsion than himself, but had the same liberty as he to choose whether he should do the right or the wrong thing. For only on this supposition could his wrongdoing be held culpable.

Now the whole vast problem of the psychology of conscience, together with its implications regarding the reality of an eternal supersensible world, is contained in miniature in such a case as this; just as, ac-

cording to the popular story, Sir Isaac Newton discerned in the fall of a single apple the law of the force
that restrains the planets to their orbits and plots the
pathways of stars millions of light-years distant.
Whether we really do, by reason of our distinctive nature, perceive in the impulsions to action that arise
within us a difference not only as regards their felt
strength, but also as regards their discerned worth and
authority,—this is one great question. And whether we
truly possess a power of election and self-direction,
which enables us to choose among these solicitations by
reference to their authority and not their strength, is
the other.

The plain sense of unreflective mankind has always
answered both these questions in the affirmative. In
recent times, however, a minority of sophisticates, scientific and philosophical, has answered them in the negative. The case of those who thus repudiate the all but
unanimous testimony of mankind is that the common
judgment in this matter reflects an illusion; just as
does our language about sunrise and sunset, which survives from a time when the motion of the earth was un-
suspected.

To a student of philosophy it is a refreshing experience to find himself obviously and unmistakably engaged in vindicating that "common sense" which metaphysicians are supposed to disdain. Of course, they do
not really disdain it. Or if any of them do, the worse
metaphysicians they. For the task of the true worker
in this sphere has always been, not (as Bradley iron-

ically put it) "the finding of bad reasons for what we believe upon instinct," but rather (as he really meant) the seeking of *sound* reasons for what we believe upon instinct. Most especially is this the imperative task now confronting moral philosophy. As a worker in this field I would say that the man in the street is right as to his immediate intuitions here. It is, however, the task of the philosopher to prove this for him, as well as to refute his gainsayers, and to think out fully and fearlessly—as Adler did—all that these immediate intuitions imply.

The ethical philosopher must do this by a process of psychological analysis, and of reflection upon the nature of knowledge and of moral experience, which the plain man, busy with other affairs, cannot undertake for himself; just as, in an analogous field, it is the business of the physician to find the cause, and if possible the cure, of aches and maladies to which the plain man's consciousness infallibly testifies.

We say that the plain man is right—*i.e.*, is bearing witness to real facts of experience—when he judges, for example, that lying, whether by speech or silence, is wrong; that taking the life of another man is an act altogether different in character from killing an ox or sheep; that among the wide range of impulses to action which are awakened in him by the challenges of other men and of the outer world, there is an order of recognized authority which is not identical with the order of their felt strength or enticingness.

We further affirm that the sophisticated, when in the name of science or philosophy they deny this or reduce it to illusion, should be called upon in the name of logic to show cause why they reject the direct and immediate testimony of consciousness in this department, whereas they never dream of rejecting it in regard to the ultimate or self-evident principles and postulates of mathematics and physical science, *which have no other basis and no better justification.*

What is more, we undertake to show *how* their objections to the reality of conscience and the authority of its promptings arose. These objections, we maintain, are traceable to a strictly illogical intrusion, into the realm of human self-consciousness, of conceptions which everybody accepts as true in the realm of matter and motion. The whole question at issue is this: whether the laws which are found valid in the time-and-space order can determine an essential human nature which clearly proves upon rational analysis to be *not* a phenomenon of space or time, but to belong, as Adler urged, to an eternal spiritual universe, and therefore to verify the reality of that universe.

Thus the self-determination of the human will (popularly but misleadingly called "free will") is denied on the strength of the law of cause and effect. To avoid unnecessary argument, we will provisionally concede that in the physical world the antecedent does determine the consequent. We will not take shelter behind the skepticism of David Hume on this point, even though we hold that that skepticism has never been effectively refuted. We accept the contention of the scientist that the stone or apple *must* fall when its support is withdrawn; that a material object can no more have "choice" in such a matter than an idea, for example, can have color. The golf-ball *must* take a course the length and direction of which are determined by the force and incidence of the club's impact, the frictional resistance of the air, the pull of gravity, and the like.

Now, says the objector, man is a physical object, and as such is "governed" by this law.

Neither shall we trouble to dispute the contention of the scientific mechanist that animals are dominated by what is called the pleasure-pain motivation; that the factor vaguely termed "instinct" is only a device of nature to preserve each animal species through the automatic operation of its machinery. For the purposes of the present argument we will accept the quite un-provable contention that in the sub-human realm each creature is irresistibly moved to seek what gives it pleasure and escape what gives it pain; and that these two classes of objects always turn out to be synonymous with what sustains or threatens its life.

But this, says the objector, is true of all animals; and man is an animal.

These positions, then, we shall not here and now dispute. We point out, however, that in all this argu-mentation two unwarranted assumptions are made; two crucial questions are begged. One of these assump-tions is that the distinctive nature of man, as well as his body, lies within and forms part of the causally-determined order. This involves, among other consequences, the astounding supposition that the reason of the scientist is itself a derivative part of the order which he explores. It imposes upon our opponents the responsibility of pointing out a stage at which atoms of matter became capable of thinking, and showing how the conscious subject of experience was juggled out of the object. For this is what Schopenhauer rightly called "the absurd undertaking of materialism."

The second unwarranted assumption alluded to is this: That it is not possible for a higher stage of reality, previously latent and unmanifested, to have laid hold upon a sufficiently evolved animal organism in such wise that man, while remaining physically an animal, became spiritually something else.

Let us illustrate this argument by a crude analogy. Suppose that on a table before us lie a sheet of paper, a pen and a bottle of ink, and that we obtain from a chemist a complete and exhaustive analysis of their physico-chemical constitution. But then suppose that a man called Shakespeare transfers to the paper certain drops of the ink, in such an order that when he has finished we read there, say, a sonnet beginning

"When in disgrace with fortune and men's eyes,"

or another beginning

"Full many a glorious morning have I seen."

Our chemist, upon re-analysing paper, pen and ink, will find in them no trace of any element in any wise different from what he found before the ink was conveyed to the paper. In like manner, we admit that from the standpoint of the biologist man is just as truly, just as through and through, an animal after he has become man—*i.e.*, after his brain has become organic to that spiritual nature which makes him truly man— as his forebears were before this completely mysterious transformation had occurred.

Suppose, then, that we find ourselves driven (as in fact we do) to affirm that the consciousness of man is not in time or space. How, then, can we be forced to think of it as determined *in the same way* as things in space or events in time are determined?

This second assumption, then, needs only clear statement to show its unwarrantableness. It is the notion that because man is unquestionably an animal, he therefore cannot possess a distinctive nature which is anything other than a development of what is found in rudiment in his animal ancestors. This plainly gratuitous dogma is the one sole argument used to prove that conscience creates an illusion when it seems to tell us of a scale of authority in our springs of action distinct from the scale of their strength.

It is here only possible to indicate these questions. They are too large and too deep for adequate treatment in such a work as this, which is not addressed to specialists. We must therefore restrict ourselves to pointing out that this argument against conscience, if admitted at all, destroys the authority of man's consciousness in regard to the bases of art and science to exactly the same extent as it destroys it in regard to morals.*

If my immediate and irresistible feeling that honesty is nobler than theft, or that I ought to keep my pledged word no matter how strong the temptation to break it, is to be discredited as illusory because it is part of the consciousness of an ape's descendant; then on the same ground my invincible conviction that two and two are four, or that a sunset is beautiful and a slum ugly, must be discredited. For these, too, are parts of the consciousness of an ape's descendant. They have the same origin and the same weakness (if it be a weakness) as conscience.

The fact is that as we cannot jump out of our skins, so neither can we really doubt the permanent and irreversible testimony of our normal consciousness. All knowledge, including the highest flights of science, is developed from elements which are self-evident and intuitive. Quite obviously they cannot be proved, for the plain reason that we cannot begin to think without assuming them. What we call "proof," in any direction, is simply the application of these self-evident and intuitive thought-processes to problems which are only perceived *as* problems by virtue of them. If, then, our consciousness can be trusted in respect to *any* of these self-evident ultimates of thought, it can with *all* of them. But if in regard to any one of them it is untrustworthy, it is so in all; in which case every denial becomes as meaningless as every assertion.

* This consideration was partly developed in Chapter III.

This point was excellently stated long ago by James Martineau, in his great work on "Types of Ethical Theory":—

"The only resource for the utilitarian who has admitted our statement of psychological experience is to say that, though such may be the contents of the facts, their evidence is false, and there is nothing in the objective universe corresponding to these subjective representations. To this scepticism respecting the veracity of any one human faculty no answer can be given, except by pointing to the absurd consequences of its equally legitimate application to another. There is as much ground, or as little, for trusting to the report of the moral faculty, as for believing our perceptions, in regard to an external world, or our intellect, respecting the relations of number and dimension. Whatever be the 'authority' of Reason respecting the true, the same is the 'authority' of Conscience for the right and good."

In short, it was Adler's conviction (as it is my own) that by accurately construing the data of psychology, we learn how man can know the principles of *right: i.e.*, by properly interrogating his own nature. Adler, however, would of course have admitted—or rather strongly insisted—that man cannot know what is *wise* or *prudent* without consulting his experience and that of other men. Ethics, he would have said, comprises two departments: a canon of right and a canon of prudence; the sphere of motives and the sphere of consequences; "the springs of action within us, and the effects of actions upon us." Both are of equal practical importance;

but it is the former which ascertains the values applicable in the latter.

We also maintain that a sound psychology reveals in man a power to *do* the right he perceives to be such, even though this often involves taking the line of greatest resistance.

Given, then, the trustworthiness of these two foundations in human nature, ethics and religion become realities, and the glorious transformation of human society in accordance with their dictates becomes a possibility. Cancel both or either of them, and morals and religion automatically become, as some modern sceptics have declared them to be, mere superstitious delusions; in which case we should be doomed to absolute pessimism.

Now upon the insight we have here endeavored to formulate, Adler's entire religion and philosophy are founded. Just as to the physical scientist the actions and reactions of drops of water, or of magnets and iron-filings, or of the electric battery, disclose laws and forces which determine suns and nebulae millions of light-years distant, so to Adler did concrete, everyday moral judgments,—even such as those of small boys ashamed of lying or acting unfairly—disclose the reality of a spiritual universe immensely more majestic and inspiring than the cosmos explored by the astronomer.

"But in that case," it may be asked, "why was he not an adherent of one of the systems of orthodox theology, Jewish or Christian?" There is a whole series of reasons why he was not. But to him the chief and decisive ones were that these theologies lay claim to a kind of knowledge and explanation which are, in truth, beyond the powers of the human mind. What they offer, therefore, is actually pseudo-knowledge, or illusion; and their so-called explanations of the inexplicable mysteries of existence invariably prove, in consequence, to be always misleading and sometimes unethical.

We can know (said Adler) that an eternally perfect spiritual universe is real. We can know this because our moral experience implies it, and is inexplicable without it, as the fall of the apple is inexplicable without gravitation. We can likewise know that in our inmost nature we belong to, we are members of, that spiritual universe. For if we were through and through children of the time-and-space world, we should be incapable of that moral experience. Concerning these transcendent matters, however, this is *all* we can know.

How and why the imperfect subsists alongside the perfect, the finite alongside the infinite; still more, how the infinite nature can be intertwined, as it is in us, with the finite animal nature: this we cannot possibly know. For to *know*, to *explain*, is to think in terms of cause and effect, and to assign causes; and there can be no such relations except within the world of time and space. Theologies, or what our fathers called theodicies (meaning doctrines devised "to justify the ways of God to man"), are attempts to build bridges over the unspannable gulf which divides the infinite from the finite, time from eternity, the perfect from the imperfect. Creation, as Adler was wont to say, is the bridge at the one end, and Immortality is the bridge at the other. Between them comes Redemption, which, whether conceived in terms of Buddhist, Jewish, or Christian doctrine, is an attempted solution of the insoluble problem of evil. Under thorough scrutiny they all break down, and prove both logically and morally untenable.

Let us consider the last words published by Adler concerning the popular doctrine of Immortality:—

"The doctrine of immortality as commonly understood means that the psycho-physical organism will continue to exist in some attenuated fashion in another sphere. The departed will be recognizable, their arms will be outstretched to welcome us, and the like. Or again, the psychic is supposed to be clothed with, to assume (a vague form of speech to which no definable meaning whatever can be attached) new organs unlike the bodily. These evidently are projections of temporal conditions into the admittedly non-temporal; the last outreachings of human tenderness striving to keep hold of the beloved as a concrete object.

"With the doctrine in this version of it I am not concerned. What is required of me is the valiancy of truth. I must train myself to relinquish tranquilly and *in toto* the psycho-physical self. What I retain is the conviction that the spiritual self is the eternal self and cannot perish. And secondly, that this spiritual self of mine, being social or suprasocial, is inseparably bound up with other spiritual selves, and in this sense that those I have loved and I cannot be parted in eternity."

"The spiritual self is the eternal self and cannot perish." In these weighty words does the veteran explorer, at the end of a life devoted to "voyaging through strange seas of thought alone," express his final and deepest conviction. Those of us who share it with him share also his cautionary doctrine that the "spiritual self" is strictly incognizable. We cannot know it as it is in itself. We know it only in and through its effects. Every man, strictly speaking, is an Invisible Man.

But the kind of living which leads a man to these insights is the Life Eternal. To live at that level is to live the Eternal Life here and now; but also to recognize that there is really no question of *here* and *there*, of *now* and *then*, "before death" or "after death." For eternity is the negation of time, as spirit is the negation of body. And both, despite the most complete conviction of their reality, can be known by us only thus negatively, and not positively.

All attempts to know more involve the essentially fallacious extension of time-ideas into the supertemporal, and of space-ideas into the supersensible. The true intellectual humility incumbent upon man commands his abandonment of all such attempts, his acquiescence in the impassable limits of his own intellect, and his consequent resignation to that kind of agnosticism which is inevitable.

This, however, is not an agnosticism as to whether the spiritual universe exists. It relates only to the insoluble problem of the *nexus* between the spiritual and the material, the infinite and the finite, the eternal and the temporal. Its very basis is the utter certainty that the spiritual universe, precisely because it is not in time or space, is the *only* true reality. For everything temporal and spatial, from the flower of a summer's day to the vast nebula whose duration is expressed in billions of our years, begins and ends, and is therefore only partially, not ultimately real. "Alles Vergängliche ist nur ein Gleichnis." No matter how vast the time-span of the duration of any spatial object, it is yet still "vergänglich": transitory. That alone is truly real which is eternal. But the eternal realm of true reality embraces the spirit of man.

Such is "the nimbus of gold-colour'd light" which true insight discerns about the head of man; and such are the vast consequences which follow from reflection upon his moral experience. And that experience is the fruit of the attempt to perfect the relations between men and men here and now on earth; the fruit of the ever-defeated yet ever-renewed effort to transform the human world into a society of friends, lovers, and mutual benefactors. Thus do we learn that the highest religious experience results from utter loyalty to Right and Truth as it is given to us to grasp them, and can result from nothing else.

THE END